LEAN
HOSPITALS

Improving Quality, Patient Safety, and Employee Engagement

Second Edition

"Leaders of today's healthcare organizations are on a continuous journey to improve results, requiring a relentless focus on improving the underlying process of care delivery and leadership practices. Mark has written a book that provides compelling ideas to help create better places to work, practice medicine and receive safe, high quality care."

Quint Studer
Founder and CEO of Studer Group, a 2010 recipient of the
Malcolm Baldrige National Quality Award
Author of Hardwiring Excellence: Purpose, Worthwhile Work, Making a
Difference and Results That Last: Hardwiring Behaviors That Will Take Your
Company to the Top

"Mark Graban is the consummate translator of the vernacular of the Toyota Production System into the everyday parlance of health care. With each concept and its application, the reader is challenged to consider what is truly possible in the delivery of health care if only standardized systems borrowed from reliable industries were implemented. Graban provides those trade secrets in an understandable and transparent fashion."

Richard P. Shannon, MD
Frank Wister Thomas Professor of Medicine
Chairman, Department of Medicine
University of Pennsylvania School of Medicine

"There is an enormous shortfall between the health care we receive and what we actually get. Mark Graban explains how those in the system can make care delivery better for everyone –patients, providers, and payors."

Steven J. Spear
Senior Lecturer at MIT Sloan School of Management and Senior Fellow at IHI
Author of The High Velocity Edge

"Mark Graban has been tirelessly studying the application of LEAN to health care, with an emphasis on respect for the people served by the system as well as the people who provide excellent care. He has an accurate sense of how things work in health systems, which makes his work more meaningful for people who want to make health care better."

Ted Eytan, MD

"The concepts outlined in this book are the most powerful tools that I have ever encountered to foster innovation, ownership, and accountability at the front line staff level. This is a must-read for any leader in today's increasingly complex healthcare industry."

Brett Lee, PhD, FACHE
SVP of Health System Operations, Children's Healthcare of Atlanta

"The Lean approach to healthcare, including a strong emphasis on culture, is the best way to ensure the optimal patient experience. The multiple examples of the application of Lean given in this book provide a wealth of information to draw from for a hospital that is venturing into Lean principles for the first time. In addition, this book emphasizes not only methodology, but also the cultural changes that must occur for sustainability—something often forgotten in change management."

Beverly B. Rogers, MD
Chief of Pathology, Children's Healthcare of Atlanta
Clinical Professor of Pathology, Emory University School of Medicine

"Finally! The healthcare industry has needed this book for many years. Informative, understandable, and timely, Mark Graban's book will leave you with an appreciation for what Lean is and what it can do for your hospital. After you read this book, I'll be surprised if you don't make implementing Lean your highest strategic priority."

Jim Adams
Senior Director, Laboratory Operations, Children's Medical Center, Dallas

"It's obvious that Mark Graban has spent time in the trenches of healthcare and understands the complexities of applying the Lean philosophy and tools to that environment. If you want to improve your chances of surviving in today's healthcare system (both literally and figuratively), read this book."

Dean Bliss
Improvement Advisor, Iowa Healthcare Collaborative

"Graban provides a helpful translation of the terms, practices, and tools of Lean thinking into hospitals' everyday situations and challenges. His book illustrates Lean's elements with many actual examples of Lean applications in typical hospital practices and procedures. Graban's book should definitely be on the reading list for those who want to bring the benefits of Lean thinking to healthcare."

David Mann
Principal, David Mann Lean Consulting

"Lean health care is becoming a global movement. The reasons given are overrun costs, errors that compromise patient safety, time of patients wasted, and general bureaucratic inefficiency. In Lean terms the problem is how to eliminate waste. Health care is different than car making. This is true but many, many hospitals are finding the principles of the Toyota Production System apply well and are making remarkable improvements. Unfortunately the remarkable improvements are in specific areas and challenging to sustain because of a mysterious ingredient that the folks at Toyota seem to understand quite well—humans. The humans that health care exist to help also operate the system and are far from perfect. Toyota's system is actually designed to support the development of people, not to provide a quick fix set of technical solutions, and this takes time and patience. Many health care consultants have rebadged themselves as Lean consultants and do not understand the real thinking behind the Toyota Production System. Mark Graban is an exception. He has worked hard to study the philosophy and stay true to the thinking of Toyota. His book is a welcome translation of the Toyota Production System into language any health care professional can understand."

Jeffrey K. Liker
Professor, University of Michigan
Author of The Toyota Way

LEAN HOSPITALS

Improving Quality, Patient Safety, and Employee Engagement

Second Edition

MARK GRABAN

Foreword by John Toussaint, MD

CRC Press
Taylor & Francis Group
Boca Raton   London   New York

CRC Press is an imprint of the
Taylor & Francis Group, an **informa** business

A PRODUCTIVITY PRESS BOOK

CRC Press
Taylor & Francis Group
6000 Broken Sound Parkway NW, Suite 300
Boca Raton, FL 33487-2742

Printed in the United States of America on acid-free paper
Version Date: 20110707

International Standard Book Number: 978-1-4398-7043-3 (Paperback)

Library of Congress Cataloging-in-Publication Data

Graban, Mark.
  Lean hospitals : improving quality, patient safety, and employee engagement / Mark Graban. -- 2nd ed.
    p. ; cm.
  Includes bibliographical references and index.
  ISBN 978-1-4398-7043-3 (pbk. : alk. paper)
  1. Hospitals--United States--Administration. 2. Hospital care--United States--Quality control. 3. Hospital care--United States--Cost effectiveness. 4. Patients--United States--Safety measures. 5. Just-in-time systems. 6. Total quality management. I. Title.
  [DNLM: 1. Hospital Administration--economics. 2. Hospital Administration--methods. 3. Efficiency, Organizational. 4. Total Quality Management--methods. 5. Total Quality Management--organization & administration. WX 157.1]

RA971.G647 2012
362.11068--dc23

2011020421

Visit the Taylor & Francis Web site at
http://www.taylorandfrancis.com

and the CRC Press Web site at
http://www.crcpress.com

Contents

Foreword

America is broke. I believe leaders in healthcare organizations caused this or at least contributed to it by not focusing on delivering high-value healthcare. Value can be simply expressed as an equation in which value equals quality over cost. Poor quality and high cost offer poor value in healthcare, and this is what we have been delivering, before Lean.

Like all processes, however, our healthcare processes and systems are perfectly designed to deliver the results we have been getting. Interestingly, Dr. W. Edwards Deming's words still ring so true even today and very pointedly in healthcare. As we surge toward 20% of the U.S. gross domestic product (GDP) being spent on healthcare, we now have a big problem that probably could have been avoided by Lean thinking but now must be solved by it or our status in the world economy will continue to slide. Other countries are faced with similar financial burdens caused by increasing healthcare costs. While the U.S. costs are significantly higher, no country is happy with its current cost curve.

Since 2003, we have proven Lean works in healthcare, so let's stop arguing about it. Whether it is the ThedaCare story as published in myriad peer-reviewed journals, Seattle Children's results, or Virginia Mason, the answer is in: Lean works. The question now for all of you is, How are you going to do it? What is the leadership model required? What resources are needed? How do you learn what you do not know and from whom? There will be many questions, and I believe starting with Mark Graban's updated book *Lean Hospitals* is a good first step.

Mark Graban knows what he is talking about with Lean. Mark has dedicated his career to learning and teaching the Lean methodology to healthcare professionals, and this book is a testament to that. He includes new learnings and examples that give the book more depth, with the intent to try to help us all deliver lower-cost and higher-quality patient care—better value.

But, you must know also that you cannot learn Lean from books alone. Books are for creating a different framework for thinking about problems and, like this one, can build confidence that an idea might work. The only way to know, however, is to go the *gemba,* which means the place where the work is done and observe, learn, and experiment. If a leader is not spending at a minimum of at least 20% of the day at the *gemba,* the leader will never learn or be able to apply Lean. At ThedaCare, "meeting free zones" had to be established during which all executives go to the *gemba.* This occurs between and 8 and 10 a.m. every morning and has led to remarkable improvements in quality, safety, and cost for our patients. The more often executives go to the *gemba,* the less time they are firefighting because they are getting upstream of patient complaints and problems, which leads to defect avoidance and more time for improvement.

This is not an easy journey, however. It is difficult to break down the traditional healthcare notions that everything is done by committee and the most powerful win, squelching the ideas of the frontline workers (nurses, doctors, technicians, etc.), who actually understand the problems and can craft the best solutions.

This book lays out the nuts and bolts of the Lean methodology and describes the more difficult challenges, which have to do with managing change. *Lean Hospitals* is full of wins—these are the same type of wins that are happening at ThedaCare every day. I wish I could have read this in 2004, as it might have prevented some of the mistakes we made in our Lean transformation journey.

Lean thinking changes all "conventional healthcare thinking," and that is good because we need a complete transformation in our industry if we have any hope of improving patient value. In this book, Mark has written about some of the new thinking that is the core of Lean, such as focusing on the process and getting away from blaming individuals. These new mindsets, along with the Lean techniques described here, are the keys to reducing errors, improving quality, freeing up more time for patient care, and improving patient flow. These improvements all lead to better quality and lower cost—in other words, better value.

John Toussaint, MD, CEO
ThedaCare Center for Healthcare Value

Preface

This is a book I feel privileged and honored to write, as it would have been hard to imagine my career would bring me into healthcare after a decade of working in the manufacturing world. My undergraduate education was in industrial engineering, which was always focused on factory production and business issues. In some eerie foreshadowing, my senior group project at Northwestern University was done at a local blood banking and distribution operation, something that seemed like a poor fit for a "manufacturing guy" at the time. Little did I know I would run across blood banks again about 10 years down the road.

After growing up near Detroit, Michigan, I was somewhat skeptical of career paths in the automotive industry, but I took a job with a General Motors (GM) plant that said (during college recruiting) it managed under the Deming philosophy. That was a real attraction for me, as I had been exposed to Dr. W. Edwards Deming by my father, and I might have been the only college kid to read Deming's *Out of the Crisis* over a winter vacation for fun. Unfortunately (and ironically), the Deming philosophy was really just a sign hanging on the wall, as the plant management operated under the very traditional auto industry management approach—far from Toyota ideals (which were influenced heavily by Deming).

So there I was, a 21-year-old engineer, working in an environment in which managers yelled and intimidated; employees were not listened to, being the source of the problems (being lazy or careless) in the eyes of management. I was first introduced to the phrase "check your brain at the door," as many workers claimed to have been literally told this. Most employees cared about quality and had pride in their work building premium Cadillac engines, but management wanted them to keep the line running at all costs. Production trumped quality, and both suffered under that system.

From this experience, I learned that the problems at the plant were not the fault of the workers; it was a management system problem. It was not even that the individual managers were bad people; it was the system they were taught and the expectations they were given. Seeing so many disgruntled employees created a deep empathy in me for those who are mistreated in the workplace, any workplace. Our results in quality, cost, and productivity were lousy, and nobody was sure if our plant had much more than a few years left to live. This old way of managing was not doing much good.

While I had learned about Toyota and Deming in college, I learned firsthand from some incredible mentors I had at GM. These experts took me under their wing and used the plant, full of its problems and waste, as a teaching opportunity. We observed the process and talked to the people. My mentors talked about how things should be, and we tried implementing small improvements, but the overall environment was still pretty unwelcoming to any major change.

While the prevailing management method and results left a lot to be desired, our plant manager was finally replaced by corporate—it was more likely the results, not the method that did him in. Our new plant manager, Larry Spiegel, was an outstanding leader who had been trained in the Toyota Production System at NUMMI (New United Motor Manufacturing Inc.), the GM-Toyota joint venture plant in California. He spent much of the time over the first few months just walking and looking through the factory, often alone, stopping to talk with employees. He wanted to see problems firsthand and make sure the employees knew he knew what the problems were. Spiegel stood in front of the entire plant, all eight hundred employees, and told them the problems were not their fault—it was the management system. The management system was going to change, and everyone, if they participated, would see better results. The old blaming and finger-pointing were slowly ending.

With the new leadership and the rejuvenated Lean coaches, we conducted a lot of training and started implementing many improvements with the production workers. The plant, over the course of a few years, went from being the worst auto plant in the United States (or so the plant manager argued, having data to back his claims) to being in the top quartile of its peer group.

Thanks to the urging of one of my GM mentors, Steve Chong, I left to attend the Leaders for Manufacturing Program at the Massachusetts Institute of Technology, where I took some courses on Lean and had a chance to first meet Jim Womack, one of the world's leading Lean gurus. Later, after finishing graduate school, I was working in Phoenix, Arizona, and was part of an informal network called the Valley Lean Council, a group of Lean zealots from different companies who met quarterly to compare notes and tour a facility. One of those tours was a hospital in Scottsdale, Arizona, that was using Lean methods to improve its emergency department. That was my first exposure regarding the applications of engineering to healthcare since my senior project, and it really piqued my interest. Shortly thereafter, my wife had a new job offer in Texas, which put me in the job market.

I was very lucky to receive a phone call from a Johnson & Johnson recruiter, who was looking to fill a consulting position in the ValuMetrix Services group, a consulting arm of Ortho-Clinical Diagnostics, which helps hospitals learn and implement Lean and Six Sigma. By far, the Lean work I have done in hospitals has been the most rewarding, most exciting, and most gratifying work I have ever done. It is not always easy, but anything worthwhile has to be a bit of a challenge.

One thing I was surprised to see, and maybe should not have been surprised by, was that the human dynamics in a hospital can be similar to those in a factory. After all, it is just people being people. Medical technologists said things I remembered production associates saying, that their supervisors did not listen to them and never saw what the problems were. Suggestion boxes had locks, and nobody could find the key. I saw people bandaging the process instead of being able to stop to fix the problem so it would not occur again. I saw people who were stressed out and no longer enjoyed their work. The motivation for improving the management system for the sake of the employees was the same, sometimes sadly so.

What is different, however, is the motivation to help patients. I mean no disrespect to the medical community, since our physicians and surgeons do amazing work that saves many lives and improves many more. There are many brilliant people, most of whom are trying their hardest in often-heroic fashion—yet the system is broken. We need to get the medical practitioners on board and collaborate with them in Lean since Lean will support them in being able to spend more time doing what they went to medical school for and less time on the problems and the frustrations. The Lean thinkers and the process types cannot do it all themselves, but there is amazing potential to improve the healthcare system in ways that the clinicians and caregivers generally have not been doing. We cannot blame them, as most doctors received as much process improvement training as I received anatomy training, and pharmacists received as much training on inventory management as I received on formulating intravenous solutions. For this to work, we all have to partner up, put our egos aside (if need be), and be willing to admit what we know and what we do not know, figuring out how to combine our knowledge in a way that works.

This book is intended to help answer the question "What is Lean?" for an audience of hospital or healthcare leaders, managers, physicians, and employees. One assumption is that hospital readers know what their problems are and are looking for new ideas and approaches. So, I have tried not to be encyclopedic in my documentation of the problems facing patients and hospitals. Rather, I have tried to capture some particular issues that can be addressed with Lean (while highlighting a few that are somewhat out of scope for Lean).

I have tried, also, to summarize some of the key problems for readers who are new to healthcare, including those who are following my career path of transitioning from manufacturing to healthcare improvement. To those readers, I hope you will find confidence that your methods and experiences can be helpful to hospitals, provided you are respectful of how this environment is different. Hospitals are much more mission based, and profit is not usually a priority (of course, before Lean, many factories seemed to have been run as if profit were not a priority).

This book is also not meant to be a comprehensive "how to" guide, as far as the details of how to implement specific Lean tools. There are many existing books, including the Productivity Press Shopfloor and Operator series of books on topics like 5S, *kanban*, and other Lean tools that can be adapted to hospital settings. The tools are the same; the key is why you use them and what you are working to improve, so that is the focus of this book. We are now, in 2011, seeing the publication of healthcare-specific books on Lean tools, as well as new books that share the experiences of hospitals like ThedaCare, Seattle Children's Hospital, and Virginia Mason Medical Center.

This book also generally limits its scope to hospital operations instead of the global issues of healthcare. It is not possible to include examples of every possible application of Lean, so the exclusion of a department or patient pathway should not be considered an indication that Lean does not apply. There are many forms of waste to be found throughout healthcare, and Lean methods can be applied to ongoing health maintenance, prevention, and primary care relationships, but those topics are left for somebody else's book, including those now being published about Lean in primary care, emergency medicine, and other more specific settings.

One other comment I will make is that it was a challenge to create a linear structure (a book form) for a set of Lean concepts that are very interconnected. I hope the book inspires you to take action, to learn more, and to share what works (and what does not work) with your colleagues in the industry.

I thank all of those who have mentored me and taught me about Lean throughout my career, including Sid Siddiqi, Glen Elmore, Rich Rachner, Paul Scheel, P. L. Godwre, Blake Headey, Mike Santarelli, Mark Spearman, Stan Gershwin, and Steve Graves.

I owe a debt of gratitude to Dean Bliss for referring Productivity Press to me in the first place. Dean has been a regular reader of my blog (http://www.leanblog.org) and knew of my work in hospitals. This would have never happened without his help and support.

I also thank my former leaders and colleagues at ValuMetrix Services for supporting the initial efforts for this book and lending their assistance. Thanks to Rick Malik, Steve Friedland, Jo Ann Hegarty, Jamie Miles, Audrey Knable, Lewis Lefteroff, Ken LePage, Shana Padgett, Norka Saldana, Chetan Shukla, and Susan South, among others, for your help, insights, and encouragement. I was truly fortunate to be part of such a strong team so dedicated to improving healthcare. Thanks to everyone in our group and those who previously worked for us and taught us, especially

Charlie Protzman and Mike Hogan, for building a foundation for our current and future success. Not all of the examples in this book are from my firsthand experience, so I am not trying to take credit for all of the fine work these other Lean change agents have done before me.

Thanks also go to those who reviewed drafts and gave input, including Jim Adams, Lee Fried, Dr. Ted Eytan, Andrew Castle, David Meier, Jamie Flinchbaugh, Gwendolyn Galsworth, Naida Grunden, and Norman Bodek. Special thanks to Jeff Maling and Bryan Lund for their tireless research efforts about the early uses of Lean and the Training Within Industry methodology in healthcare. Thanks also to Mike Wroblewski for finding a great example of Henry Ford and a "Lean hospital" from 1922. Special thanks go to Dr. Sami Bahri, the "world's first Lean dentist," as the innovative Lean work in his dental practice is quite an inspiration to me. I could not have done this without the efforts and dedication of my wonderful clients, leaders, and project team members, especially Jim Adams, Dr. Beverly Rogers, Stephanie Mitchell, Dr. Mark Pool, Robin Aldredge, and Kim Morris. It is an honor to work with each of you and to support your important missions. There are too many other stimulating people I have worked with to mention them all, but if you have worked with me before, please forgive me for not mentioning you here (and forgive me for the moments I did not live up to the leadership ideals laid out in the book).

I absolutely appreciate the efforts of Cheryl Fenske, who assisted greatly with editing and helped to focus my writing as I went. Thanks also go to my acquisitions editor, Kris Mednansky, for bringing this opportunity to me and for helping to keep me calm as deadlines approached. Thanks also to the original publisher, Maura May, and our editor, Lara Zoble, for their support and assistance.

In much of the three years since the publication of the first edition, I have been fortunate to work with the Lean Enterprise Institute, a nonprofit education and research institute. I have been honored to be part of the team that has helped build our Healthcare Value Network, a collaboration of North American hospitals that are committed to improving healthcare using Lean thinking as well as sharing their lessons learned with other members and the broader healthcare world. Many thanks go to Helen Zak and Dr. John Toussaint for their leadership and inspiration and to the entire team for the learning opportunities that I have been able to use to advantage. My gratitude also goes to the groundbreaking leaders in these network organizations, including but not limited to Dr. Jack Billi, Dr. Michel Tétreault, Dr. Dean Gruner, Dr. Zeev Neuwirth, Barbara Bouche, Paul Levy, Alice Lee, and Amir Rubin.

I thank my parents, Bob and Marlene Graban, for their love and support—in particular, their support of education throughout my life, from preschool to graduate school, and the sacrifices they made to create opportunities for me along the way.

I also thank my in-laws, Charlie and Debbie Gowder, for sharing their daughter and their love with me. To my wife, Amy, thank you for your love and support, which never ends. Beyond our love and friendship, I am always inspired by your drive, intellect, and professional success. I am proud to be your husband and I am very happy you are my wife. Thanks for being my supporting partner in making this book happen.

About the Author

Mark Graban is a consultant, author, keynote speaker, and blogger in the world of Lean healthcare.

Mark is an experienced consultant and change agent, with a background in industrial and mechanical engineering and an MBA from the MIT Sloan Leaders for Global Operations Program. Prior to healthcare, Mark worked in multiple industries, including automotive (General Motors), electronics (Dell), and industrial products (Honeywell). At Honeywell, Mark was certified as a "Lean Expert" (Lean Black Belt).

Since August 2005, Mark has worked exclusively in healthcare, where he has coached Lean teams at client sites in North America and the United Kingdom, including medical laboratories, hospitals, and primary care clinics. Mark's motivation is to apply Lean and Toyota Production System principles to improve quality of care and patient safety, to improve the customer/patient experience, to help the development of medical professionals and employees, and to help build strong organizations for the long term.

From June 2009 to June 2011, Mark was a Senior Fellow with the Lean Enterprise Institute (LEI), a not-for-profit educational organization that is a leading voice in the Lean world. In this role, Mark also served as the Director of Communication & Technology for the Healthcare Value Network, a collaboration of healthcare organizations from across North America, a partnership between LEI and the ThedaCare Center for Healthcare Value. Mark continues as an LEI faculty member.

In June 2011, Mark joined the software company KaiNexus as their Chief Improvement Officer, to help further their mission of "making improvement easier" in healthcare organizations, while continuing his other consulting and speaking activities.

Mark was raised in Livonia, Michigan and currently resides in Keller, Texas with his wife, Amy.

To interact with Mark and the Lean healthcare community, visit www.LeanHospitalsBook.com.

Chapter 1

The Case for Lean Hospitals

Why Do Hospitals Need Lean?

Taiichi Ohno, one of the creators of the Toyota Production System, is often quoted as saying that organizations must "start from need." In today's world, the "need" for Lean in healthcare is very clear in terms of quality and patient safety, cost, waiting times, and staff morale. Hospitals face a growing number of external pressures and challenges as well. Hospitals do many wonderful things, but a senior leader at a prestigious university hospital summarized their internal challenges by lamenting that "we have world-class doctors, world-class treatment, and completely broken processes."

So, how can an approach called Lean help healthcare organizations? On first hearing the word, people might complain that they are already understaffed and do not have enough resources. The everyday use of the term *lean* and countless newspaper headlines reinforce what are often negative connotations. Rest assured, the approach presented here is not about mass layoffs. The idea of "preventable" errors may bring skepticism, as employees and physicians believe they are already being as careful as possible. Hospitals using Lean methods do not improve quality by asking people to be more careful any more than they improve productivity by asking people to run around faster. Lean is very different from traditional "cost-cutting" approaches that have been tried in multiple industries, including healthcare.

Lean is a tool set, a management system, and a philosophy that can change the way hospitals are organized and managed. Lean is a methodology that allows hospitals to improve the quality of care for patients by reducing errors and waiting times. Lean is an approach that can support employees and physicians, eliminating roadblocks and allowing them to focus on providing care. Lean is a system for strengthening hospital organizations for the long term—reducing costs and risks while also facilitating growth and expansion. Lean helps break down barriers between disconnected departmental "silos," allowing different hospital departments to better work together for the benefit of patients.

Someone might ask how Lean methods can help solve the everyday, nagging problems that so many committees and teams have already tried fixing. Lean is different in that people learn how to look at the details of processes, where the people who do the work fix things where the work is actually done, instead of relying on experts to tell them what to do. Lean helps leaders see and understand that it is not the individuals who are broken, but the system itself. This happens in a way in which the system can actually be fixed and improved in small, manageable bites. The Lean approach also requires the continued learning and professional development of employees, for their own sake and the sake of the organization and system.

A Renewed Sense of Purpose

The healthcare profession is driven by an important mission and a strong sense of purpose. The everyday problems, waste, and broken processes interfere with what healthcare providers and employees want to do: provide the best possible care to patients and keep people healthy. These problems can also leave people short on time, interfering with their ability to provide a caring environment for their clinical care.

Dr. Jacob Caron, an orthopedic surgeon and chief of the medical staff at St. Elisabeth Hospital (Tilburg, The Netherlands), is one of their leading advocates for Lean. During a 2009 presentation at a Dutch Lean healthcare symposium, his title slide read, "Lean and Loving … a mission impossible?" To St. Elisabeth, an important motivation for reducing waste is to free up time for clinicians. This newly found time is used not only for better clinical care and improved responsiveness to patient requests, but also for what they describe as "loving care."[1] When nurses are not scrambling to find supplies and medications, they can take time to talk with patients, answering questions and alleviating anxiety they might have about their hospital stay.

Lean Methods Are Not New to Healthcare

Frank and Lillian Gilbreth, sometimes known from the original 1950 version of the film *Cheaper by the Dozen*, were two of the original efficiency experts of the late nineteenth and early twentieth centuries, with many of their methods influencing the later development of Lean. Outside of their primary factory work, the Gilbreths published many studies in medicine, being among the first to demonstrate that industrial engineering methods could be applied to hospitals. One innovation from the Gilbreth studies was having a surgical nurse hand instruments to surgeons as called for, instead of the surgeon taking time away from the patient to retrieve them, a better practice we take for granted today.[2]

Henry Ford, in 1922, wrote about efforts to apply his production methods to a hospital in Dearborn, Michigan. Ford said, "It is not at all certain whether hospitals as they are now managed exist for patients or for doctors. … It has been an aim of our hospital to cut away from all of these practices and to put the interest of the patient first. … In the ordinary hospital the nurses must make useless steps. More of their time is spent in walking than in caring for the patient. This hospital is designed to save steps. Each floor is complete in itself, and just as in the factories we have tried to eliminate the necessity for waste motion, so we have tried to eliminate waste motion in the hospital."[3] Almost a century later, nurses around the world still spend more time dealing with waste in the workplace than they spend at the bedside—until Lean is employed to help. Rather than relying on a few experts, Lean engages everybody in improving their own workplace.

Toyota's Role in Popularizing Lean

Toyota Motor Corporation is sometimes known as "the company that invented Lean production."[4] Toyota developed the Toyota Production System over many decades, starting in 1945.[5]

Inventing and refining a new production system was not an overnight success story, nor will be your hospital's Lean transformation, as changing old mindsets and organizational cultures takes time. Saying that Toyota "invented" Lean is not exactly accurate, as Toyota learned from and was inspired by many others, such as the writings of Henry Ford, the nineteenth-century Scottish self-help author Samuel Smiles, and the restocking practices of American supermarkets.[6] Toyota was also heavily influenced by the visits of Dr. W. Edwards Deming, as the president of Toyota said in 1991, "There is not a day I don't think about what Dr. Deming meant to us. Deming is the core of our management."[7]

Toyota took some aspects of the Ford system, but created its own management system, using and inventing methods that fit its needs and situation. It is critical for hospitals to follow Toyota's model of adapting what you learn from others and developing methods that solve the problems at your hospital. It is important to learn from other hospitals (and other Lean companies outside healthcare) without blindly copying the practices of others. Lean is a thinking process more than a simple to do list of tools to implement. In 1945, Toyota set out to improve quality, while improving productivity and reducing costs, as the company was very cash poor and had a small Japanese market in which to sell cars. Crisis and hardship forced Toyota to be creative and innovative; it did not set out to create a production system per se. It was not until the early 1980s that Toyota started writing down the details of its system. Norman Bodek was one of the first Americans to start taking study tours to Japan, translating to English and publishing the works of Taiichi Ohno and Shigeo Shingo, credited as the founders of the Toyota Production System.[8]

News reports of unintended acceleration with Toyota vehicles in 2010 have many wondering if Lean no longer works or is no longer relevant. It is worth noting that there were never any accusations that any of the runaway vehicles were built incorrectly in their factories. Rather, the accusations centered on product design problems and a slow response from Japan when problems were reported at U.S. dealerships. A 2011 NASA report concluded that the unintended acceleration incidents were the result of floor mats being improperly installed on top of other floor mats or driver error, and that there were no electronic flaws in the cars.[9] That said, Toyota has reflected on the company's path, as chief executive officer (CEO) Akio Toyoda testified in 2010 to the United States Congress that the company had erred by pursuing growth that exceeded "the speed at which we were able to develop our people and our organization," and Toyota would reinvigorate their traditional focus on "quality over quantity."[10]

Origins of the Term *Lean*

While the concepts came to us via Toyota, the term *Lean* is credited to Jon Krafcik, part of the research team at the International Motor Vehicle Program[11] at the Massachusetts Institute of Technology (MIT) and current CEO of the automaker Hyundai. That team, led by James P. Womack, Daniel T. Jones, and Daniel Roos, studied the global auto industry in the late 1980s, looking for practices that led to Japanese success. Through their research, they disproved their hypothesis that all Japanese automakers were doing things differently—it was primarily Toyota. The term *Lean* was coined as a word to describe a system (Toyota's) that managed to get by with half of everything—physical space, labor effort, capital investment, and inventory—and far fewer than half the defects and safety incidents. The term described the results, but the word has also entered the language as a description of the method.

The early spread of Lean started in the auto industry, where it was easy to see the direct applicability of the Toyota method and, more important, there was a strong recognition of the need to improve. Western automakers typically focused on copying tools and practices that could easily be seen with the naked eye, such as *kanban* cards (a method for moving parts to assembly lines). Even though Toyota started sharing its tools through publications and open tours (even allowing competitors to visit its factories), the unseen management system was (and still is) harder to copy.[12] The other automakers did not want to challenge their existing management systems and thought processes; it was easier to adopt a tool like *kanban* and to say "we are doing Lean" than it was to fully adapt the Toyota model. Hospitals that say they are doing Lean should reflect on whether they are using an occasional Lean method or if they are embracing the full management system and culture of Lean.

Lean Is Proven to Work Outside Automotive Factories

Lean eventually spread beyond the automotive industry, as other manufacturing sectors adopted the methods in their factories. Manufacturers also began to understand that Lean was not just a factory system; it was also a business system, incorporating all aspects of bringing a product to market, including design, supplier management, production, and sales. For example, the Toyota Product Development System was renowned for bringing new cars to market twice as fast as their U.S. competitors (half the time, indeed "Lean" by the MIT definition).

Because every type of organization—including hospitals—should be concerned with cash flow, customer satisfaction, and quality, Lean methods and philosophies are being used, at least to some extent, at some banks, software startups, airlines, government agencies, as well as the dominant coffee sellers in the United States (Starbucks) and Canada (Tim Horton's).

Toyota University, in California, has coached some surprising students, including the Los Angeles Police Department (LAPD), in problem-solving methods that come from the factory floor. This has helped the LAPD manage its jails more effectively. A Toyota coach said, after the training classes, "What I saw was a commonality in human behavior, a commonality in some of the issues and challenges that every company faces."[13] This commonality extends to hospitals as well. We all have problems to solve, and we are all looking for better ways to lead and manage employees.

Lean Is Helping Hospitals Improve

It is difficult to pinpoint exactly when hospitals started looking, once again, outside their industry for Lean ideas. Some hospitals started experimenting with Lean methods in the 1990s, in some cases with help from Michigan automakers. Seattle Children's Hospital can trace its Lean journey to early discussions in 1996 with consultant Joan Wellman, who had previously worked with Boeing.[14] In 2001, *USA Today* reported on a study conducted by the Robert Wood Johnson Foundation that looked across hospitals for leaders, those who did things dramatically differently from other hospitals. Foundation Executive Vice President Lewis Sandy said, "We want to see a Toyota in health care. That's been one of the barriers in health care. No one can point to a health system and say 'That's how it ought to be done.'"[15] The motivation was clear that hospitals had to look beyond their peers to find solutions to widespread systemic problems.

There are now many examples of the positive impact Lean is having in hospitals throughout the world. As a sample, Lean methods have resulted in

- Reduced turnaround time for clinical laboratory results by 60% in 2004 without adding head count or new instrumentation; further reduced times by another 33% from 2008 to 2010—*Alegent Health, Nebraska*[16,17]
- Reduced instrument decontamination and sterilization cycle time by 54% while improving productivity by 16%—*Kingston General Hospital, Ontario*[18]
- Reduced central-line-associated bloodstream infections by 76%, reducing patient deaths from such infections by 95% and saving $1 million—*Allegheny Hospital, Pennsylvania*[19]
- Reduced readmission rates for chronic obstructive pulmonary disease (COPD) patients by 48%—*UPMC St. Margaret Hospital, Pennsylvania*[20]
- Reduced patient waiting time for orthopedic surgery from 14 weeks to 31 hours (from first call to surgery); improved inpatient satisfaction scores from 68% "very satisfied" to 90%—*ThedaCare, Wisconsin*[21]
- Increased employee engagement scores by 15%—*St. Boniface Hospital, Manitoba*[22]
- Reduced patient length of stay by 29% and avoided $1.25 million in new emergency department (ED) construction—*Avera McKennan, South Dakota*[23]
- Bottom-line benefit of $54 million, through cost reduction and revenue growth, helping an urban safety net hospital avoid layoffs—*Denver Health, Colorado*[24]
- Avoidance of $180 million in capital spending through Lean improvements—*Seattle Children's Hospital, Washington*[25]

Problems in Healthcare

There are many long-standing problems that hospitals face, a list too long to present here. Lean is not about fixing any one major problem within healthcare; it is about solving the hundreds or thousands of little problems that plague hospitals each day. Rather than just debating far-reaching political solutions, we can take action and improve now, regardless of the payer system. We can do this, together, if we start learning and start taking action today.

Do you have any of these problems in your hospital?

Deliveries of supplies delayed because of improper ordering
Mix-ups in getting supplies
Articles returned by other departments because they were not made correctly
Employee difficulty in handling new-type equipment
Limited storage space (linen and supplies) not properly used
Safety equipment not being used
Minor injuries or illnesses not reported
Correct procedures not followed
Employees leaving to go to other hospitals
Employees passing the buck—let the other person do it

Are these modern hospital problems? Yes, but these were also problems in 1944, as documented by the training materials for hospitals provided by the U.S. Training Within Industry (TWI) Program.[26] TWI was halted after World War II ended, so the methods disappeared from hospitals, as well as factories, but became very influential to Toyota and the development of Lean.[27]

Hospitals everywhere tend to have the same problems because they were often designed from the same template. Physical layouts share similar characteristics, often given to them by architects with a poor understanding of the hospital's work, and processes were developed using the same paradigms and similar educational perspectives. Copying other hospitals and their "best practices" might bring incremental improvements, but we can use Lean concepts to drive more dramatic improvements by looking at our own processes in a new way, engaging our own employees to identify waste and develop their own solutions. In the Lean mindset, we have to be open in our recognition of problems as the first stage of process improvement.

When asked what is needed for improvement, hospital employees might answer, "We need more money, more space, and more people!" Even if adding people were guaranteed to help, we live in a world of finite resources, including shortages of nurses, medical technologists, and other key clinical professionals. If we cannot afford more resources, working harder is not usually an option. Lean thinkers do not blame a lack of hard work for problems at their hospital. We have to improve the system, and sometimes that means that people expend less effort because their work is easier and outcomes are improved for all.

Price Pressures and Cost Challenges

Healthcare costs are increasing rapidly, as U.S. healthcare insurance costs are increasing at a rate higher than inflation. Healthcare spending now consumes 17.3% of the United States' gross domestic product (GDP), reaching levels of over $2.3 trillion per year.[28] Per capita spending in the United States is the highest in the world and is much higher than comparable industrialized countries. The high spending does bring a great deal of innovation and technology, which improves care and saves lives, but the cost increases are likely not sustainable.

In an attempt to control rising costs, payers (the government or private payers) often propose cutting reimbursements. In doing so, they are changing the price paid, but not the underlying costs in the system. Lower prices without corresponding cost reductions will hurt hospital margins, which can slow future investment or jeopardize a hospital's financial future. Price cuts by payers might also, unfortunately, encourage dysfunctional cost cutting by healthcare organizations, in which layoffs and the closure of units and service lines might harm quality or reduce the level of care provided to a community.

Rather than reducing spending by slashing payments or rationing care, Lean methods enable us to reduce the actual cost of providing care, allowing us to provide more service and care for our communities. A hospital that saves tens of millions of dollars by using Lean methods to avoid costly expansion projects is a hospital that costs society less, while providing the same levels of care, if not more.

Cutting prices also drives some physicians out of the market for some patients, as evidenced by the number of American doctors who opt out of the Medicare and Medicaid systems or stop taking on new patients under those programs.[29] Unilaterally slashing prices is more reminiscent of the supplier management practices of the Big Three automakers, who traditionally demanded price reductions annually from their suppliers. Many of these suppliers were squeezed to the point of bankruptcy.

In comparison, the Lean approach, as demonstrated by Toyota, is a partnership between customer and supplier, working together to identify true cost savings. These cost savings are shared, benefitting both parties, as Toyota and its suppliers operate in an atmosphere of trust and long-term relationships. In healthcare, payers and providers should strive to have relationships more like Toyota and its suppliers, rather than squeezing their suppliers—the hospitals or physicians. In some American states and Puerto Rico, the affilliates of a major health insurance company are working directly with hospitals on Lean improvement efforts, sharing the savings.[30]

In the Lean approach, companies are taught that prices are set by the market, and that a primary way to improve one's profit margin is to reduce your own controllable costs. This thinking flies in the face of older "cost-plus" thinking, by which we look first at our own costs and set prices based on a desired profit margin. The reality is that most companies, whether manufacturers or hospitals, do not have market power to set prices as they wish. We have to work to reduce costs, by improving flow and improving quality, or we have to find ways to add value to our services, so that the market might increase or at least maintain what it is willing to pay. No matter how dysfunctional healthcare markets might be, we should focus less on the unfairness of what is paid to us and more on what we have control over—our costs. One study estimated that 13% of a hospital's costs are due to "inefficient practices within control of the hospital,"[31] while other estimates were closer to 20%.[32]

Coping with Employee Shortages

Hospitals suffer from widespread employee shortages, particularly for nurses, pharmacists, and medical technologists. In the United States, nursing vacancy rates averaged 8.1% as of 2008, and 34% of hospitals reported unfilled pharmacist positions.[33,34] Hospitals are often forced to hire costly temporary agency or "traveler" staff, further cutting margins. This is also a problem in the United Kingdom, where the National Health Service (NHS) trusts in London spend $727 million a year on agency nurses.[35] If agency nurses cannot be found (or paid for), hospitals are sometimes forced to shut down units, reducing the amount of care they can provide to their community and reducing the amount of revenue received by the hospital.

Nursing shortages can lead to overworked conditions that harm quality, patient safety, and employee morale. Highlighting the connections among employees, patients, and quality, studies showed that overworked, tired, or stressed employees are more likely to make mistakes that could harm patients.[36] Understaffed pharmacies and laboratories might have slower response times, which could delay care or put patients at risk. Physicians who are unhappy with poor service from staff or ancillary departments might react by moving their patients to a competing hospital, thus exacerbating the revenue problem.

Poor Quality of Care

While there are differences in the healthcare systems across different countries, there are some universal problems that concern patients: preventable errors that lead to injury and death. Instead of focusing solely on the problem of patient access to care, Lean gives us tools for also improving the delivery of care. It is imperative that we examine and understand the details of how healthcare is delivered, implementing processes that support safe, efficient, high-quality care. Lean provides the best way to accomplish this.

Other than focusing on some high-profile incidents, the media often overlook the quality problems with the delivery of care in the United States. More Americans probably know the numbers of the uninsured (approximately 50 million)[37] than the estimates of how many patients die as the result of preventable medical errors each year (estimated in one study at 98,000) and from preventable infections (estimated at about 100,000).[38,39]

Quality and patient safety are not concerns just in the United States. The Canadian Institute for Health Information estimated that as many as 24,000 Canadians die each year due to medical errors, such as surgical errors, medication errors, and hospital-acquired infections. The auditor general estimated that one in nine hospitalized patients will acquire an infection during a stay.[40] In the United Kingdom, the Royal College of Physicians estimated that medical errors contribute to the deaths of almost 70,000 patients per year, and Britain's most senior doctor warned the risk of dying from a preventable hospital error is 1 in 300, a similar risk as in the United States.[41] It is estimated that 850,000 patients are the victims of errors that lead to permanent or moderate injury in 200,000 of those cases. The NHS estimates that half of the errors are preventable, again in line with United States estimates.[42,43]

With advances and systemic improvements in aviation safety, passengers in the general public take it for granted that they will arrive safely at their destination; we should hope for similar advances in healthcare so patients can take it for granted that they will not be harmed in hospitals. In fact, in recent years, hospitals are learning safety and quality lessons from commercial aviation, such as the use of checklists.[44] Some patients blindly trust the healthcare system, assuming they will receive perfect care each time. Lean methods can help us work toward making that goal a reality.

Good Quality Costs Less

As in other industries, many in healthcare have assumed there is an inherent trade-off between cost and quality; better quality must automatically cost more. It is true that some methods for improving the quality of patient outcomes might cost more, such as new technologies, treatments, or medicines. Hospitals do have many opportunities, however, to improve the quality of healthcare delivery methods and processes in a way that also reduces costs. Across all U.S. hospitals, there is a large cost-savings opportunity from preventing errors and improving quality. For example, preventable adverse events from medication errors are estimated to cost hospitals $4 billion per year.[45]

David Fillingham, CEO of Royal Bolton Hospital NHS Foundation Trust in the United Kingdom, has said, quite simply, "Good quality costs less."[46] This was proven to be true as a result of Bolton's Lean improvements; the hospital reduced trauma mortality by 36% and reduced a patient's average length of stay by 33%. ThedaCare documented similar results in cardiac surgery; mortality fell from 4% to nearly zero (11 lives saved per year), with a length-of-stay reduction from 6.3 to 4.9 days, and 22% lower cost.[47] It might sound too good to be true, but many hospitals are proving that you can simultaneously improve quality, access, and cost.

Lean teaches us to see quality improvement as a means to cost reductions, a better approach than focusing directly and solely on costs. Bill Douglas, chief financial officer at Riverside Medical Center (Kankakee, IL), summed it up as the hospital began its first Lean project by saying, "Lean is a quality initiative. It isn't a cost-cutting initiative. But the end result is, if you improve quality your costs will go down. If you focus on patient quality and safety, you just can't go wrong. If you do the right thing with regard to quality, the costs will take care of themselves."[48] Riverside's laboratory, for example, had previously focused primarily on cost, using layoffs and other traditional cost-cutting methods, but the lab's quality of service did not improve. Through their initial Lean efforts, reducing errors and improving flow led to getting test results to physicians 37% to 46% faster, while improving labor productivity.[49] The lab's improved service helped reduce length of stay in the ED, which allowed Riverside to postpone a $2 million expansion.[50] Riverside has since spread Lean to areas including pharmacy, inpatient care, and primary care settings.

A Snapshot of Department Success: Laboratory, Children's Medical Center Dallas

Improvements made in the laboratory at Children's Medical Center (Dallas, TX) help illustrate how Lean can provide benefits to all stakeholders—patients, employees, physicians, and the hospital itself. The lab's leadership team was first exposed to Lean in August 2006 when they saw a presentation by Seattle Children's Hospital, an early adopter of these methods in healthcare. The lab had previously been studying system dynamics through Peter Senge's seminal work *The Fifth Discipline* and had high-level goals of becoming a "learning organization."[51] Lean provided a means for operationalizing this philosophy in a practical way, according to Jim Adams, the senior director for lab operations since May 2005.

Prior to Lean, benchmarking data seemed to confirm the people's view that the lab was good, if not above average. For example, the lab reported 90% of stat test results within industry-accepted time limits. However, an initial assessment by outside Lean consultants in November 2006 helped Adams realize that the lab had actually long been experiencing, in his terms, "delusional excellence" because the benchmarked labs had the same waste built into their own physical layouts and processes. Instead of feeling good about exceeding benchmarks, the lab started looking at their true potential—to be the best lab they could possibly be for its patients.

The early analysis, later repeated by medical technologists as they learned to better understand their own work, showed that 70% to 94% of typical turnaround time performance was time when the specimen was sitting and waiting. The new challenge became minimizing that waiting time. Instead of thinking that benchmarks showed they did not need to improve, the team learned that they had large opportunities to reduce turnaround times by 50% or more, providing better service to patients, ordering physicians, and departments that relied on accurate and timely test results.

A formal Lean project was initiated in March 2007, which the author led. In contrast to the common week-long Lean events that are used in many hospitals (more on this in Chapter 11), a team was formed to work on a 12-week "Lean transformation" project that focused initially on the end-to-end flow of clinical lab testing. This team consisted of four medical technologists and two lab assistants from various parts of the department. This group was dedicated full time to the improvement and redesign efforts, learning deeply about Lean principles, analyzing their current state, and working with the larger group of colleagues to transform both the physical space and their processes in an integrated way.

As another early step, the lab's leadership initiated discussions with internal customers and learned that particular tests were deemed crucial by the ED for the sake of prompt diagnosis and improved patient flow. They were sometimes surprised to learn that tests the lab thought not to be time critical were, in fact, considered to be so by the ED. It became more important to the lab to improve the relationships with those who ordered tests and used test results—an important part of the customer- and patient-focused Lean approach. With this better customer understanding, success would be defined by their customer's needs rather than being defined within the lab.

The full-time team learned and used the analysis methods outlined in Chapter 4 to trace the flow of testing work from specimen collection through the reporting of test results. As in most hospital work, the flow moved across multiple roles in many different departments. The team focused on improving the overall flow rather than looking merely to optimize their own results. which was based on a strictly departmental definition of success.

While there was a longer-term initiative to fully redesign and reconstruct the physical layout of the laboratory (an effort not fully implemented until late 2010), the lab's leadership team, including Dr. Beverly Rogers, the chief pathologist, helped everyone understand that Lean was not a one-time long-term project. Rather, it would become a new management system and a new way of life. Instead of putting all of their hopes on the major redesign, the lab started to take action to make immediate improvements.

Steps were taken to improve specimen flow through small, incremental changes. The blood gas analyzers, used for critically time-sensitive tests, were moved to a point much closer to the tube station, where specimens arrived. This reduced average turnaround times from 20 minutes to about 5 minutes. The "front end" of the process (the nonclinical areas where specimens were received, labeled, and prepped) were reconfigured. Instead of two separate work areas about 25 feet apart (a distance that encouraged batching and time delays), the preanalytical area was set up as four identical, separate "flow benches" where one person could do all of the work on a single specimen without the extra specimen movement and delay. This reduced the average turnaround time for chemistry and hematology tests by 43%.

As the team observed and even videotaped their colleagues in the lab, they helped identify waste (as described more fully in Chapter 3) and took initial countermeasures that could reduce wasted walking and motion in the lab. The lab implemented basic methods including 5S and *kanban* (see Chapter 6) to help ensure that supplies and test reagents were always available at the right locations in the right quantities, reducing the amount of time that highly trained technologists spent hunting and gathering. In the first year of the *kanban* system (a system for planning and restocking inventory and supplies), the lab reduced spending by $80,000. As staff productivity improved, thanks to the waste reduction efforts and new "standardized work," as discussed in Chapter 5, the lab was able to reduce labor costs by $147,000 in the first year, without laying anybody off.

Adams and Dr. Rogers also continued the shift toward a Lean culture, educating all staff members about Lean principles, involving them in the improvement work, and continuing group book discussions on titles like *The Toyota Way*. This talk of Lean culture, such as focusing on processes and systems instead of blaming individuals for problems, was invigorated by a number of management practices, as described more fully in Chapter 10. Daily 10-minute stand-up meetings were held to review performance measures, enabling staff members to talk about their ideas for improving the process. These ideas were tracked on a simple bulletin board, an approach that was far more visual and more interactive than their old suggestion box. As new ideas were implemented, regardless of how small, recognition was given through the documentation and posting of the changes on a "*kaizen* wall of fame," which created positive reinforcement that led to more *kaizen*, or continuous improvement.

As the clinical lab was implementing Lean practices and management methods, leaders and team members introduced these approaches and mindsets to other parts of the lab, such as microbiology, blood bank, and anatomic pathology. Experience in the lab was leveraged to help a team that was subsequently formed within the diagnostic imaging department. Adams reflected on

Table 1.1   Improvement in Employee Engagement Scores at Children's Medical Center Dallas

	Before Lean	12 Months after Starting
3. I have the opportunity to do what I do best every day.	3.11	3.92
8. I feel free to make suggestions for improvement.	2.84	3.48
10. I feel secure in my job.	2.32	3.42
13. Stress at work is manageable.	2.43	3.23
17. I am satisfied with the lab as a place to work.	2.51	3.43
18. I would recommend my work area as a good place to work to others.	2.38	3.46
Grand average of all questions	2.96	3.69

their experience, saying "There was a growing recognition among lab users in the hospital that the lab was focused on understanding and meeting their particular needs. The nurses and physicians started working with the lab staff in a more respectful, collegial way. We felt more a part of the team caring for the patient."

The positive impact of the cultural transformation was illustrated by the results of a staff engagement survey, comparing "pre-Lean" numbers to 12 months after the Lean education and improvement efforts started. As shown in Table 1.1, scores increased in key questions (on a 1-to-5 scale, with 5 being highest). Every single question on the engagement survey showed an improvement, highlighting the benefits of a Lean environment.

As an additional sign of meaningful culture change, two of the lab's Lean team members accepted lab supervisor positions after repeatedly turning down the opportunity in previous years. They each took on the role because the lab's leadership had successfully redefined the role of a supervisor from being a directive "boss" to being a coach and teacher, working with team members to make patient-focused improvements that created a better workplace. Adams commented, "Both have thrived and are effective as supervisors in the Lean culture."[52]

Even as the major reconstruction project has been completed, the lab sees Lean as its culture and a key part of its ongoing improvement efforts. It is not "complete," as this improvement is never ending. Evidence of this mindset and culture shift includes the medical technologists in the clinical "core lab" quickly coming up with ideas for tweaking the newly renovated layout in late 2010, after the years of planning and waiting. Traditional cultures might not look for input, leaving well enough alone with the new design. Instead, the Children's lab let staff members experiment and make changes to the standardized work and layout based on data and their firsthand experiences.

As lab leaders reflected on their first four years of Lean, lessons learned included ensuring that

■ consistent, continuous education about Lean principles and methods takes place, especially in roles with traditionally high turnover;
■ staff members know how core measures, such as turnaround time, are aligned with end patient needs—that this is about improving care, not just hitting numbers; and

■ people do not assume that methods like 5S and standardized work are meant to be controlling and that managers constantly reinforce the importance of staff engagement in continuously improving these standards.

While Children's was named "Medical Lab of the Year 2009" by a major trade publication,[53] it is the culture change and the willingness to never be satisfied and to continue learning that makes it more likely also to be a lab of the year in the future.

From Departmental to Hospital-Wide Success

Lean is not just a methodology that can impact individual departments. Lean can become part of the hospital's core strategy and day-to-day operating approach, as illustrated by examples including ThedaCare, Virginia Mason Medical Center, Seattle Children's Hospital, and Denver Health.

The story of Avera McKennan Hospital and University Health Center (Sioux Falls, South Dakota) is highlighted in Chapter 11, as their initial Lean projects, which started in their laboratory in 2004, eventually became a management system and daily improvement methodology for the entire hospital.

At Avera McKennan, Lean methods are now taught to all employees in all departments and their Excellence in Service and Process program has become a cornerstone of the hospital's strategy and vision. Their goals are not timid, as they state, "Through service and process excellence, Avera McKennan will lead the nation in high quality, affordable health care."

The leadership and passion started with Fred Slunecka, formerly the regional president of Avera McKennan Hospital and now the Chief Operating Officer of Avera Health, and his people throughout the facility. To Slunecka, it is "a moral imperative" to streamline processes and eliminate waste, as "30–40% of all health care is waste—pure and simple." The motivation for improvement came from a realization that government reimbursement was increasing 2–3% a year, while the hospital's costs were increasing 5% a year. "We absolutely have got to do a better job," said Slunecka, and the hospital set out to do just that. Even with the talk of financial motivations, the patient is at the center of their improvements. "The goal is a seamless patient experience, marked by great service, quality care and efficiency," says Kathy Maass, their director of process excellence. "Lean is about examining the patient care process step by step and redesigning it around the patient to eliminate waste. Employees become involved in the solution at the most grass-roots level," Slunecka said.

This is the potential of Lean hospitals, strategically redesigning the physical space and processes that provide patient care, while engaging all healthcare professionals and leaders in never-ending continuous improvement.

Conclusion

Hospitals and their processes are full of waste and inefficiency through no fault of the talented, caring, and hardworking people who work there. The problems that hospitals face could be discouraging—unless we also had a proven methodology for driving sustainable quality and process improvement. That could be overwhelming if we did not have others to learn from and to model our own improvement after—both Toyota and our hospital colleagues who are blazing the Lean trail.

Lean can be described in a simple way: Lean is working. In one way, Lean is about looking at how we do our work and figuring out ways to improve how that work is done. Lean is about improving quality and productivity. Lean is also about learning to fix problems permanently instead of hiding them or working around them.

In another sense, Lean is proving to be an effective methodology for improving patient safety, quality, and cost, while preventing delays and improving employee satisfaction. It can be done. Lean is working; it is effective. Lean helps saves money for hospitals, while creating opportunities for growth and increased revenue. Lean methods can benefit everyone involved in hospitals. Understanding Lean principles is just a starting point. The real challenge is finding the leadership necessary to implement these strategies and to transform the way your hospital provides care.

Those of us who have seen leaders successfully use Lean in many hospitals realize this is not an academic exercise or easy. Lean methods allow us to improve how hospitals are managed today. Lean methods let us improve quality now. But, Lean requires vision, leadership, and persistence. We have scattered instances of Lean success in hospitals throughout the world. As the science fiction author William Gibson wrote, "The future is already here—it's just not very evenly distributed."[54]

Lean Lessons

- Lean methods started in factories but have proven successful in many functions in many industries, including healthcare.
- Quality improvements are a means to cost reductions.
- Productivity improvements and cost savings can be accomplished in ways other than layoffs or head count reductions.
- Lean is focused on patient safety, quality of care, and improved service, not just efficiency, cost, and productivity.
- Improving the system, rather than working harder, is the key to Lean improvements.
- To make major changes, you often have to start with smaller steps.
- Hospitals cannot just copy others; they need to think through their own improvements after learning Lean concepts.

Points for Group Discussion

- Are rising healthcare costs having an impact on your hospital's quality of care?
- How can better quality cost less?
- How does personal satisfaction on the job have an impact on productivity and quality?
- What are the biggest problems our department faces? Our hospital?
- Why does a hospital typically have departmental silos?
- Are there situations in which your departments or processes are not as patient focused as they could be?
- Why have other improvement philosophies not worked before? How can we avoid repeating the same mistakes?
- What percentage of leadership time is spent expediting, firefighting, or working around problems?
- How can our Lean efforts be oriented around the mission and purpose of our organization and our people?

Notes

1. Graban, Mark, "Lean is 'Loving Care'?" January 25, 2010, http://www.leanblog.org/2010/01/lean-is-loving-care/ (accessed April 10, 2011).
2. Weinger, Matthew B., Jason Slagle, Sonia Jain, and Nelda Ordonez, "Retrospective Data Collection and Analytical Techniques for Patient Safety Studies," *Journal of Biomedical Informatics,* 2003, 35: 106–19.
3. Ford, Henry, and Samuel Crowther, *My Life and Work* (Garden City, NY: Doubleday, Page and Company, 1922), 219.
4. Liker, Jeffrey K., *The Toyota Way: 14 Management Principles from the World's Greatest Automaker* (New York: McGraw-Hill, 2004), cover.
5. Ohno, Taiichi, *Toyota Production System: Beyond Large-Scale Production* (New York: Productivity Press, 1988), 3.
6. Ibid., 97.
7. Stratton, Brad, "Gone But Never Forgotten," *Quality Progress,* March 1994, http://deming.org/index.cfm?content=654 (accessed July 1, 2011).
8. Bodek, Norman, "Who Can Shout Louder?" http://www.superfactory.com/articles/Bodek_Shout_Louder.htm (accessed January 7, 2008).
9. Liker, Jeffrey K., *Toyota Under Fire* (New York: McGraw-Hill, 2011), 231.
10. Agence France-Press, "Akio Toyoda's Testimony to U.S. Congress," *Industry Week,* February 23, 2010.
11. Womack, James P., Daniel T. Jones, and Daniel Roos, *The Machine that Changed the World: The Story of Lean Production* (New York: HarperPerennial, 1991), 13.
12. Taylor, Alex, "How Toyota Defies Gravity," *Fortune,* December 8, 1997, http://cnn.com/magazines/fortune/fortune archive/1997/12/08/234926/index.htm (accessed July 1, 2011).
13. Spector, Mike, and Gina Chon, "Toyota University Opens Admissions to Outsiders," *Wall Street Journal,* March 5, 2007, http://www.careerjournal.com/myc/management/20070306-spector.html (accessed December 20, 2007).
14. Wellman, Joan, Howard Jeffries, and Pat Hagan, *Leading the Lean Healthcare Journey* (New York: Productivity Press, 2010), 1.
15. Appleby, Julie, "Care Providers Slam Health System," *USA Today,* May 9 2001, p. A01.
16. ValuMetrix Services, "Clinical Laboratory Improves Turnaround Time by 60%," Case Study, http://www.valumetrixservices.com/sites/default/files/client_results_pdf/CS_Alegent_Lab_OC4029.pdf (accessed April 3, 2011).
17. Ford, Anne, "Thanks to Weak Economy and More, Efficiency Is King," *CAP Today,* April 2010, http://lnbg.us/20T (accessed July 1, 2011).
18. Lefteroff, Lewis, and Mark Graban, "Lean and Process Excellence at Kingston General," *SME Lean Manufacturing 2008,* 53.
19. McCarthy, Douglas, and David Blumenthal, M.D., "Committed to Safety: Ten Case Studies on Reducing Harm to Patients," The Commonwealth Fund, http://www.commonwealthfund.org/Content/Publications/Fund-Reports/2006/Apr/Committed-to-Safety--Ten-Case-Studies-on-Reducing-Harm-to-Patients.aspx (accessed April 3, 2011).
20. California Health Advocates, "Creative Interventions Reduce Hospital Readmissions for Medicare Beneficiaries," October 7, 2010, http://www.cahealthadvocates.org/news/basics/2010/creative.html (accessed April 3, 2011).
21. Toussaint, John, and Roger Gerard, *On the Mend: Revolutionizing Healthcare to Save Lives and Transform the Industry* (Cambridge, MA: Lean Enterprise Institute, 2010), 29.
22. St. Boniface Hospital, "The Health Report with Guest Dr. Michel Tétreault," St. Boniface Hospital, November 7, 2010, http://www.saintboniface.ca/English/template.cfm?tID=291 (accessed April 3, 2011).
23. ValuMetrix Services, "Avera McKennan," Case Study, http://www.valumetrixservices.com/sites/default/files/client_results_pdf/CS_Avera%20McKennan_ED_OC4047.pdf (accessed April 3, 2011).
24. Auge, Karen, "Denver Health Saves Millions Using Toyota Efficiency Principles," *Denver Post,* July 29, 2010, http://www.denverpost.com/ci_15627406 (accessed April 3, 2011).

25. Weed, Julie, "Factory Efficiency Comes to the Hospital," *New York Times*, http://www.nytimes.com/2010/07/11/business/11seattle.html, July 10, 2010 (accessed April 8, 2011).

26. United States, *Hospital Adaptation for the Job Instruction Manual*, August 1944, Subgroup 211.22.3 General Records of the Training Within Industry Service, Records of the War Manpower Commission (WMC), Record Group 211, National Archives Building, Washington, DC, http://chapters.sme.org/204/TWI_Materials/National_Archives_March_2006/Job_Instruction/Hospitals/Materials-Hospitals.pdf (accessed December 20, 2007).

27. Dinero, Donald A., *Training Within Industry: The Foundation of Lean* (New York: Productivity Press, 2005), 48.

28. Truffer, C. J., et al, "Health Spending Projections through 2019: The Recession's Impact Continues," *Health Affairs,* March 2010, 29, (3): 522–9.

29. Hobson, Katherine, "Will There Be Enough Primary-Care Physicians to Treat New Medicaid Patients?" *Wall Street Journal,* March 18, 2001, http://blogs.wsj.com/health/2011/03/18/will-there-be-enough-primary-care-physicians-to-treat-new-medicaid-patients/ (accessed April 3, 2011).

30. Blue Cross Blue Shield of Michigan, "Lean Transformation in Health Care Cuts Waste, Improves Care," press release, April 8, 2010, http://news.bcbsm.com/news/2010/news_2010-04-08-15043.shtml (accessed April 11, 2011).

31. Zuckerman, Stephen, Jack Hadley, and Lisa Iezzoni, "Measuring Hospital Efficiency with Frontier Cost Functions," *Journal of Health Economics*, 1994, 13(3): 255–80.

32. Vitaliano, Donald F., and Mark Toren, "Hospital Cost and Efficiency in a Regime of Stringent Regulation," *Eastern Economic Journal,* 1996, 22(2): 167–75.

33. American Association of Colleges of Nurses, "Fact Sheet: Nursing Shortage," http://www.aacn.nche.edu/media/factsheets/nursingshortage.htm (accessed April 3, 2011).

34. Halvorson, Deanne, "Pharmacy Salary and Staffing Supplement," Pharmacy Purchasing and Products, November, 2010, http://www.pppmag.com/article/796/November_2010/Pharmacy_Salary_Staffing_Supplement/ (accessed April 3, 2011).

35. Marsh, Beezy, "Agency Nursing Costs £450m," *Mail Online*, http://www.dailymail.co.uk/health/article-100135/Agency-nursing-costs-450m.html, (accessed April 3, 2011).

36. Gaba, D. M., and S. K. Howard, "Fatigue among Clinicians and the Safety of Patients," *New England Journal of Medicine,* 2002, 347: 1249–55.

37. Galewitz, Phil, and Andrew Villegas, "Uninsured Rate Soars, 50+ Million Americans Without Coverage," *Kaiser Health News*, http://www.kaiserhealthnews.org/Stories/2010/September/16/census-uninsured-rate-soars.aspx (accessed April 3, 2011).

38. Committee on Quality of Healthcare in America and Institute of Medicine, *To Err Is Human* (Washington, DC: National Academies Press, 2000), 1.

39. Clancy, Carolyn, "Reducing Health Care-Associated Infections," AHRQ, April 1, 2009, http://www.ahrq.gov/news/test040109.htm (accessed April 3, 2011).

40. Morgan, Gwynn, "Private Sector Health Care: Think Quality, Regulation," *Toronto Globe and Mail,* April 16, 2007, http://theconference.ca/private-sector-health-care-think-quality-regulation (accessed June 20, 2011).

41. Hall, Sarah, "Medical Error Death Risk 1 in 300," *The Guardian*, November 7, 2006, http://www.guardian.co.uk/society/2006/nov/07/health.lifeandhealth (accessed April 3, 2011).

42. "Medical Massacre," *Guardian Unlimited*, March 5, 2001, http://www.guardian.co.uk/leaders/story/0,,446385,00.html (accessed June 20, 2011).

43. Committee on Quality, *To Err Is Human*, 26.

44. Gawande, Atul, "The Checklist," *The New Yorker,* December 10, 2007, http://www.newyorker.com/reporting/2007/12/10/071210fa_fact_gawande (accessed April 3, 2011).

45. Zajac, Andrew, "FDA Seeks to Reduce Drug Dosage Errors," *Los Angeles Times*, November 5, 2009, http://articles.latimes.com/2009/nov/05/nation/na-fda-drugs5 (accessed April 3, 2011).

46. Fillingham, David, presentation, First Global Lean Healthcare Summit, June 25, 2007.

47. Toussaint and Gerard, *On the Mend*, 3.

48. Graban, Mark, "Riverside Medical Center Puts Lean in the Laboratory," *SME Lean Manufacturing*, 2007, 56.

49. Ibid., 53.

50. ValuMetrix Services, "For Riverside Medical Center, Lean Is Not Just about Better ROI," Case Study, http://www.valumetrixservices.com/sites/default/files/client_results_pdf/CS_Riverside_Lab_OC 10114.pdf (accessed April 3, 2011).

51. Senge, Peter, *The Fifth Discipline: The Art & Practice of the Learning Organization* (New York: Doubleday Press, 1994) 14.

52. Adams, Jim, and Mark Graban, "CMCD's Lab Draws on Academics, Automakers, and Therapists to Realize Its Own Vision of Excellence," *Global Business and Organizational Excellence*, May/June 2011, 13.

53. Bersch, Carren, "Winning Teams: A Common Vision Yields Uncommon Results," *Medical Lab Observer*, April 2009, http://www.mlo-online.com/features/2009_april/0409_lab_management.pdf (accessed April 3, 2011).

54. Gibson, William, NPR Talk of the Nation, "The Science in Science Fiction," November 30, 1999. http://www.npr.org/templates/story/story.php?storyId=1067220.

Chapter 2

Overview of Lean for Hospitals

What Is Lean?

Countless books have been written on Lean, creating many frameworks and definitions, some of which are shown in Table 2.1. It is difficult to have a single succinct, yet comprehensive, definition, but we can learn something from each definition. Lean is both a tool set and a management system, a method for continuous improvement and employee engagement, an approach that allows us to solve the problems that are important to us as leaders and as an organization.

One succinct definition used by many instructors at the Lean Enterprise Institute is, "Lean is a set of concepts, principles and tools used to create and deliver the most value from the customers' perspective while consuming the fewest resources and fully utilizing the knowledge and skills of the people performing the work." How can healthcare deliver the most value to patients while using the least possible resources and maximizing the use of our people's skills and knowledge? That is the primary question when it comes to Lean healthcare.

Ohno's Definition of Lean

Toyota's Taiichi Ohno, who along with Shigeo Shingo was a primary creator of the Toyota Production System, defined Lean in terms of business goals that included more than the factory. Ohno wrote, "All we are doing is looking at the timeline from the moment a customer gives us an order to the point when we collect the cash. And we are reducing that timeline by removing the non-value-added wastes."[1] A hospital could view this as the time between a patient being referred by a physician through the actual care that is provided, ending at the point when the hospital gets paid.

Ohno's definition shows Lean to be a time-based approach; reducing delays leads to better quality and lower costs—these lower costs being an end result of improvements to flow. This is different from traditional cost cutting, which is often done by slashing hospital budgets and

Table 2.1 Definitions of *Lean*

Definition	Detail
Toyota Triangle[a]	Lean is an integrated system of human development, technical tools, management approaches, and philosophy that creates a Lean organizational culture.
Two pillars[b]	Lean is about the total elimination of "waste" and showing "respect for people."
"Fixing Healthcare from the Inside, Today"[c]	1. Work is designed as a series of ongoing experiments that immediately reveal problems. 2. Problems are addressed immediately through rapid experimentation. 3. Solutions are disseminated adaptively through collaborative experimentation. 4. People at all levels of the organization are taught to become experimentalists.
Lean thinking principles (Womack and Jones)[d]	The five principles of "Lean thinking" are 1. Specify *value* from the standpoint of the end customer. 2. Identify all the steps in the *value stream*, eliminating every step that does not create value. 3. Make the value-added steps occur in a tightly integrated sequence so work *flows* smoothly. 4. Let customers *pull* value. 5. Pursue *perfection* through continuous improvement.

[a] Adapted from Convis, Gary, "Role of Management in a Lean Manufacturing Environment." Society of Automotive Engineers, http://www.sae.org/manufacturing/lean/column/leanjul01.htm (accessed December 20, 2007).

[b] Adapted from Ohno, Taiichi, *Toyota Production System: Beyond Large-Scale Production* (New York: Productivity Press, 1988), xiii.

[c] Spear, Steven J., "Fixing Healthcare from the Inside, Today." *Harvard Business Review*, Reprint #1738, September 2005, 5.

[d] Marchwinski, Chet, and John Shook, ed. *Lean Lexicon: A Graphical Glossary for Lean Thinkers.* (Brookline, MA: Lean Enterprise Institute: 2003), 5.

head count. In this context, *waste* has a specific definition, being any problem that interferes with people doing their work effectively or any activity that does not provide value for the customer, as we discuss in Chapter 3.

Lean Thinking

The book *Lean Thinking* defines the term *Lean* as follows: "In short, Lean thinking is Lean, because it provides a way to do more and more with less and less—less human effort, less equipment, less time, and less space—while coming closer and closer to providing customers with exactly what they want."[2]

It is important to define Lean in terms of the goals and objectives of a hospital. Like other types of organizations, hospitals have the need to do more work with less. Providing customers (including our patients) exactly what they want includes the right care that is done right the first time. Patients want efficient, cost-effective care, but they also want perfect care that does not harm them in the course of their hospital visit. From a broader perspective, patients want to be kept healthy by their health system, providing new challenges for how hospitals integrate into the broader system. Lean is not just about the "less and less"; we should not lose sight of trying to provide more value, as appropriate, and more service to patients and our communities.

The Toyota Triangle: Tools, Culture, and Management System

Figure 2.1 shows one way of illustrating the Toyota Production System (TPS).[3] The diagram shows that Lean is an integrated system that starts with people and human development in the middle. That is surrounded by a balanced approach combining technical tools (what we do), managerial tools (how we manage), and philosophy (what we believe). All of this, taken together, will become our organizational culture, or a Lean culture.

Human Development

First, look at the middle of the triangle in Figure 2.1. It is no accident that diagrams like this from Toyota place people in the center. Toyota leaders like to use the phrase "Build people, not just cars," meaning that developing its employees is the key to improving its products and processes.[4] Human development, in the Lean approach, means putting in place "a solid framework for cultivating capable leaders and for providing employees with necessary practical skills."[5] A fundamental challenge for hospitals is developing leadership skills throughout the organization, not just our skill with Lean methods.

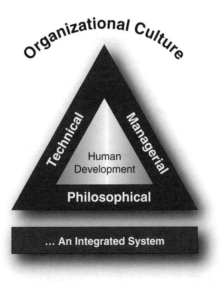

Figure 2.1   The Toyota triangle depiction of the Toyota Production System.

Philosophy

The base of the triangle is philosophy: What do we believe as an organization, and what is our purpose? What is described as the Lean philosophy often comes from what we have learned about Toyota—it is their company culture we describe. Toyota's philosophy includes commitments to their "long-term contributions to society" and to "company economic performance and growth."[6] Having a long-term focus is a frequent theme, as principle 1 of *The Toyota Way* states a company should "base your management decisions on a long-term philosophy, even at the expense of short-term financial goals."[7]

Hospital mission and values statements often sound like Toyota's, as many state that their priorities include safety, employee engagement, and stewardship toward their communities and the environment. However, can hospital employees walk through the hospital and go through their workday feeling like those values are lived and practiced every minute? Perfectly living up to those ideals can be a challenge in any organization, even Toyota, considering we are all human, and we do not always behave in accordance with our stated standards. Recognizing that, leadership has a responsibility to set a good example and to insist that others live up to the organizational ideals and philosophy, every day. If our values state that we respect and value people, how does a traditional non-Lean top-down command-and-control management system fit with that?

As a hospital, we have to make a choice: Are we going to implement Lean methods within the context of our existing culture, or are we going to examine what needs to change with our culture? Many hospitals may have a philosophy about patients and employees that is conducive to implementing the tools and management system of Lean. Other hospitals, those that do not live up to the ideals and goals of their own value statements, may struggle with Lean if they expect to find a simple cure-all for their workplace culture woes. That said, trying some of the Lean tools may lead to new ways of viewing and working with people; as the expression goes, "People are much more likely to act their way into a new way of thinking, than think their way into a new way of acting."[8] Saying "our culture is not like Toyota's" should not be an excuse for not trying Lean, but the need to change the culture will require additional time, leadership, and effort.

> Lean concepts might seem simple, but a Lean transformation takes many years. Dr. W. Edwards Deming said, pithily, "[Change] does not happen all at once. There is no instant pudding." One architect complained of hospitals that wanted quick easy answers, saying "I can't design a magically Lean hospital for them."

Technical Tools

The technical side of Lean can be described as the tools and methods that we implement and use. You may know of Lean by some of the specific methods that you have seen hospitals use, shown in Table 2.2, including *kanban*, 5S, *kaizen*, error proofing, and visual management.

Talking about a single tool or a collection of tools does not accurately define Lean. It is easier to define and copy tools, but to get the full impact of Lean, you have to work at implementing the full management system. This is just as true in hospitals as it is in any other setting or industry,

Table 2.2 Selected Lean Tools

Lean Tool	Definition
Kanban	Japanese term meaning "signal," a method for managing inventory
5S	Method for organizing workplaces to reduce wasted time and motion for employees, making problems more readily apparent
Kaizen	Japanese term meaning "continuous improvement," focused on workplace improvement by employees
Error proofing	Method for designing or improving processes so errors are less likely to occur
Visual management	Method for making problems visible, providing for fast response and problem solving

with ThedaCare (Appleton, WI) and Virginia Mason Medical Center (Seattle, WA), two leading examples of hospitals that aspire to a Lean culture throughout their organizations.

Managerial Methods

Beyond philosophy and technical tools, Lean also challenges how we manage people and systems. Leadership and management skills are important for implementing Lean methods. Without leadership, employees might not understand why improvement is necessary and why Lean methods are a path to that improvement. Once Lean methods have been implemented, sustained leadership and a management system are required to sustain those improvements.

Gary Convis, a retired Toyota senior vice president who had been one of the top-ranking Americans in the company, wrote that the "managerial culture for TPS is rooted in several factors, including developing and sustaining a sense of trust, a commitment to involving those affected by first, teamwork, equal and fair treatment for all, and finally, fact-based decision making and long-term thinking."[9] That is a mindset that hospitals can comfortably embrace in their Lean efforts.

The leaders at ThedaCare have worked diligently to create new management methods as part of their Lean culture. Part of this evolution is a shift from a command-and-control environment where "leaders talk about how to make their wishes—our commands—known to employees" to a workplace where respect is shown to each individual by listening, asking for employees' opinions, seeking their help when there are problems, and providing training so staff can drive improvement in their own areas.[10]

The "Toyota Way" Philosophy

The simplest, and possibly the most elegant, definition of Lean comes from Toyota, in two parts.[11]

1. Continuous improvement
2. Respect for people

Ohno described this as: "The most important objective of the Toyota system has been to increase production efficiency by consistently and thoroughly eliminating waste. The concept and the equally important respect for humanity that has passed down from the venerable Sakichi Toyoda (1867–1930) … are the foundation of the Toyota production system."[12] This respect extends to all stakeholders—customers, employees, suppliers, and the communities in which Toyota operates.[13]

These are not new concepts in the Lean approach; however, many organizations that have attempted to implement Lean have focused only on the elimination of waste. To be successful, we must focus on both aspects equally—continuous improvement and having respect for people. Using Lean to make quality and productivity improvements that lead to layoffs would be an example of not maintaining this balance. A growing number of healthcare organizations have publicly stated policies about not using Lean to drive layoffs.[14]

Continuous Improvement

While many associate Lean with projects or weeklong events, the greatest potential comes when every person in the organization is engaged in improving processes every day. The Japanese word *kaizen* is often used to describe continuous improvement, sometimes translated as small changes or change for the good. These improvement efforts are often focused on reducing waste from the patient's care or from people's work.

The term *waste* (also described using the Japanese word *muda*) has its own unique definition when used in association with Lean. Waste can be defined as any activity that does not help patients or does not move them toward being diagnosed, treated, or discharged. One example of waste is time spent waiting—waiting for an appointment or waiting for the next step in the patient's treatment. Another example of waste would be activities or errors that harm a patient. We take a deeper look at waste in Chapter 3.

David Sharbaugh, director of quality improvement at Shadyside Hospital (Pittsburgh, PA), said, "It's not unrealistic at all to consider 40% and 50% waste in the healthcare system."[15] Dr. Donald Berwick, former president and chief executive officer (CEO) of the Institute for Healthcare Improvement, argued that hospitals are full of waste, but the actual extent is unknown. Berwick claimed that 30–40% of the total expenditure of healthcare in the United States—about half a trillion dollars—is waste.[16] Waste, to some extent, is present in every hospital process and organization. That is not an indictment of our people; it is just recognizing the system in which we work.

Continuous improvement methodologies have generally been used in systems that are stable and relatively free of waste. Leading hospitals are using Lean principles to completely redesign or radically overhaul their processes and space. Beyond this redesign, Lean healthcare organizations then create an environment for continuous improvement through their management mindsets and their mechanisms for engaging staff members, as covered in more detail in Chapter 10.

Respect for People

When leaders at Toyota talk about having "respect for people" (or, originally, "respect for humanity"[17]), this has a different meaning than what traditional organizations might mean by respect—after all, what leader would say they do not respect his or her people? Respect does not mean that managers give employees latitude to do their jobs however they please, out of a sense of trust, as long as the results are good.[18] In a hospital that uses Lean principles, managers and leaders frequently verify the details of how work has been done. This is done out of respect for the patient (to ensure proper outcomes and quality) and can be done in a way that still shows respect for the employees.

In Lean organizations, respect does not mean that managers and leaders are always nice to their employees or that employees avoid conflict with each other. Our goal is not simply to have happy employees, as that could be accomplished in any number of superficial ways that might be costly to the hospital or might not improve patient care. Respect, in a Lean context, means a number of things, including challenging people and pushing them to perform better, in a constructive way.

Respect does not mean leaving employees alone to struggle with problems or their workload. Lean "is a system that demands employees do their best, but does not overwork them. The sense of trust created between management and the workers can promote efficiency and at the same time a relaxed feeling."[19]

The Japanese not only have a word for waste (*muda*), but also have specific words that describe overwork (*muri*) and uneven workloads (*mura*). Having respect for people means we do not allow our employees to be overworked or overburdened. Lean is not about pushing people to work too quickly or to be in two places at the same time. One hospital employee, when first hearing about Lean, joked about the need for roller skates so they could zip around faster. Lean thinkers, instead, would ask why employees have to travel such long distances and would search for ways to eliminate the need for moving faster.

Part of the approach to respect for people is that we engage and trust our employees to participate in solving problems and eliminating waste. It is not the job of leaders to solve every problem for the employees. As we discuss throughout the book and in Chapter 10, improvement needs to be a partnership between employees and managers. We are not looking to create a system in which managers do all of the thinking, problem solving, and system design, with employees just mindlessly following instructions.

Employees in hospitals report feeling more fulfilled when they are allowed to spend more time on their primary patient care work, whether this is direct patient care or work that indirectly supports patient care. We have a great systemic advantage in healthcare—the intrinsic motivation of our employees is the desire to help people, a desire that led so many to healthcare. It is our job, as leaders, to make sure that intrinsic motivation is not eroded over time through frustration and burnout. Author Peter Scholtes liked to ask about the so-called deadwood in our organizations, pointing out how we most likely hired "live wood and killed it."[20]

It is because of the notion of respect for people that we work tirelessly to create an environment in which our live wood (our employees, our most important assets) is supported and allowed to grow instead of getting frustrated and leaving the profession or jumping to a competing hospital. Live-wood employees might make a suggestion the first time they find a missing surgical instrument. When their suggestion is not taken or when the problem is not fixed, they might understandably get frustrated and give up, turning into deadwood that no longer tries to fix the source of the problem.

Both of these concepts—continuous improvement and having respect for people—are important elements of Lean. When applied to the healthcare industry, respect for people includes respect for our patients, our employees, our physicians, our community, and all stakeholders of the hospital, an environment in which it is unacceptable for anyone to treat others badly.

John Toussaint, MD, the former CEO of ThedaCare, described how Paul O'Neill, former CEO of Alcoa, taught him three key questions to ask as a test of whether your environment is conducive to respect for people:[21]

1. Are my staff and doctors treated with dignity and respect by everyone in the organization?
2. Do my staff and doctors have the training and encouragement to do work that gives their life meaning?
3. Have I recognized my staff and doctors for what they do?

Four Organizational Capabilities for Lean

Professor Steven J. Spear described Lean as a rational and scientific approach, one that hospital employees can readily relate to, as many of them are scientifically trained. If we have respect for people and fully involve them in improvement rather than relying on a few experts to come up with the ideas, this should be the case. Spear outlined four organizational capabilities in the article, "Fixing Healthcare from the Inside, Today," and elaborated on them in his book *The High-Velocity Edge*.[22,23]

Capability 1: Work Is Designed as a Series of Ongoing Experiments that Immediately Reveal Problems

There are three key elements in this statement. First, "work is designed" means that the way we do things is not random, inconsistent, or haphazard. The Lean concept of standardized work (discussed in Chapter 5) means that work should be designed, by both the employees and their leaders, rather than allowing common practices just to develop. This is not always the case in hospitals. A director of patient safety at a hospital commented, "Our blood administration system is complex and it just sort of evolved on its own. There are many inefficiencies and opportunities for error."

Hospital employees need to standardize key processes and tasks for the sake of improving patient safety, preventing time delays, making work easier for employees, and reducing costs. When different nurses treat a patient on different days, having standardized methods helps ensure a consistent experience and consistent care for that patient. A patient in an outpatient cancer treatment setting complained, "Things work differently every time I come here." Different charge nurses on different days operated differently. Some allowed late patients to be fit in immediately, while others made them wait until an open slot was available, even if the delays were not that patient's fault. This might not have necessarily impacted their clinical care or outcomes, but it caused frustration nonetheless and could have harmed patient satisfaction scores.

Second, standardizing our work does not mean procedures are carved in stone. The Lean concept of *kaizen* means that we have an obligation to find new ways of improving our work. There is a Toyota expression that says each person's job is not just to do the work but also to find a better way of doing that work. That said, we have to take care that "ongoing experiments" do not mean chaos or a shift back to everybody doing tasks their own way. For example, if we have a standardized method for inserting a central line catheter, we need to experiment with this carefully and in a controlled way.

The third point is that we need to structure work in a way that problems are made readily apparent so they can be fixed as quickly as possible. Simple methods, such as visual management, give us tools to make problems apparent. They allow us to tell when needed supplies or equipment are out of place, allowing us to more proactively solve and prevent problems. Rather than waiting for supplies, such as blankets, to run out in an inpatient unit, simple visual indicators and controls can help us see that we are running low—because we have used more than usual or because the delivery of new blankets has been delayed. We often do not have visibility to these problems because supplies are hidden behind closed cabinet doors or in drawers. When it is safe to do so, Lean concepts would call us to keep supplies visible (and to have a standardized process for checking the inventory levels), which can prevent waste, problems, and frustration. Visual management and the *kanban* system for managing supplies are discussed in Chapter 6.

Capability 2: Problems Are Addressed Immediately through Rapid Experimentation

In a Lean environment, we make problems visible and apparent because we recognize that it is acceptable to have problems, as long as we are working to fix them. There is a famous Toyota story about Japanese executives visiting American managers at their then newly opened factory in Georgetown, Kentucky. The Japanese executives asked what the top problems were, and an American manager replied, "There are no problems." The typical mindset in the automotive industry was that problems should not be revealed to your boss because either you would get yelled at or you would receive unwanted attention and management-driven "solutions" that might not help. A Japanese executive replied, "No problems is a problem."[24] In Toyota's eyes, it is very unlikely that an area would have no problems or opportunities for improvement.

When a problem is discovered, the focus is placed on solving that problem immediately, at the place the problem occurs and with the input of the people who are struggling with that problem. There is a Lean expression that problems are not solved in conference rooms; problems are solved at the *gemba*, the Japanese term for the actual place where work occurs.

For example, if there were a problem with nurses forgetting to send medications home with discharged patients, the team would not just hang signs telling nurses to be careful. Instead, the team might change where the medications are stored so they are more likely to be seen during the discharge process. The team might also develop a standard checklist for nurses to follow during each discharge, including a medication reminder. They might even print the checklist on the envelope that is used to hold information and belongings for the patient. With the Lean approach, problems are solved more quickly, and we are more likely to get to an effective countermeasure through rapid experimentation, following W. Edwards Deming's plan-do-check-act (PDCA) cycle. When problems occur, it is better to try something to see if it works rather than taking a long time to develop the "perfect" solution.

The roots of the continuous improvement approach can be traced back to the PDCA cycle (also called plan-do-study-adjust, or PDSA) that Deming taught to the Japanese after World War II. In the PDCA approach, we consider any new and improved condition to be the new starting point for future improvements, never being satisfied with our performance.[25]

The PDCA cycle, as shown in Figure 2.2, is meant to parallel the scientific method, in which any proposed change is merely a hypothesis that is presented for testing. Through small-scale trials, we are able to see if the process change leads to the expected results, and we can respond accordingly. If the expected results do not come, we can challenge our initial hypothesis and

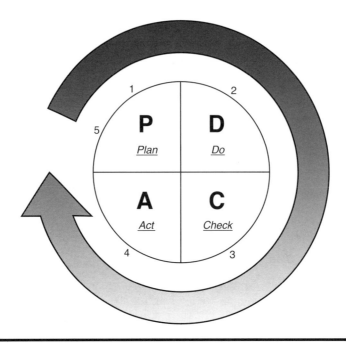

Figure 2.2   The Plan-Do-Check-Act (PDCA) cycle.

put aside the proposed change or go back to try another alternative (or we can go back to the original process). If the expected results do materialize, we can formalize that new process and spread the changes into other areas. It is important always to go back to the plan cycle, either to find a new method for improvement or to find a new problem that needs to be solved, via the PDCA process.

Traditional management approaches often assume that success is guaranteed when changes are made and either do not test to see if the expected results were achieved or will go out of their way to defend or rationalize the lack of results out of a fear of failure. A healthy Lean culture does not expect people to succeed 100% of the time. An expectation of 100% success helps lead to a risk-averse culture in which a fear of failure will lead to a lack of experimentation and a lack of improvement.

Capability 3: Solutions Are Disseminated Adaptively through Collaborative Experimentation

Local improvements made in one area need to be shared with other departments or areas to prevent everyone from having to go through the same improvement cycles on their own. We can view this in terms of our different inpatient units and floors throughout the hospital. Although we might have differences between specialized units, certain core processes can be standardized, such as how to handle pharmacy orders. When a *kaizen* improvement is made in one unit, we need a mechanism for sharing that improvement across all units.

An adaptive dissemination is different from a traditional rollout of a new best practice that was perhaps developed in one unit. People often complain of being "rolled over" when they are forced to take a new practice that might not meet the exact needs of their unit. Health systems, like ThedaCare, are learning that the Lean model leads to a more nuanced approach. Instead of each unit or hospital completely duplicating improvement efforts, the second unit might receive the process that the first unit created—considering that process to be a starting point for future improvement. The second unit does not force fit the new process without thinking; rather, it is free to adapt the process as needed for its specific patients. If the second unit finds an incrementally better way, it is obligated to share that improvement with the unit that originally developed that new method.

This collaboration and sharing could also extend to other hospitals in our system or other hospitals in the same city. The Pittsburgh Regional Healthcare Initiative is an example of hospitals working together on issues of patient safety, sharing information for the benefit of the patients and the community. The global healthcare industry has a great opportunity to create communication methods and infrastructures that allow hospitals to cooperate and share improvements across city, state, or country boundaries, for the sake of patients. More recently, the Healthcare Value Network, a collaboration of the Lean Enterprise Institute and the ThedaCare Center for Healthcare Value, has extended that sharing and learning to hospitals across North America.[26]

Capability 4: People at All Levels of the Organization Are Taught to Become Experimentalists

While Spear and other Lean thinkers talked about letting employees at the lowest level of the organization solve problems, we cannot just throw people into teams without arming them with the skills and methods for effective problem solving. Many hospital systems, such as Avera McKennan (Sioux Falls, SD), are giving initial Lean training, including that for problem-solving methods, to all employees at the hospital. Continued coaching, training, and mentoring are required, whether coming from outside consultants, internal process improvement leaders, or the direct line management and leaders themselves.

Just putting a group of employees together to come up with solutions may lead to solutions along the lines of what we have already tried in the past, or simply asking people to be more careful or try harder. The Lean methodology helps employees see their work and processes through fresh eyes, allowing them to see problems they could not have seen before and to have new ways of solving those problems. This is not meant to be a criticism of the employees' intelligence or creativity but merely a recognition that one responsibility of hospital leaders is to provide for the ongoing training and development of their employees.

Four Rules in Use for Lean

A growing number of hospitals are using concepts from Spear's earlier article, written with H. Kent Bowen, called "Decoding the DNA of the Toyota Production System."[27] The rules are also presented in the healthcare improvement methodology called "adaptive design."[28]

The rules are as follows:

Rule 1: All work shall be highly specified regarding content, sequence, timing, and outcome.

Rule 2: Every customer-supplier connection must be direct, and there must be an unambiguous yes-or-no way to send requests and receive responses.

Rule 3: The pathway for every product and service must be simple and direct.

Rule 4: Any improvement must be made in accordance with the scientific method, under the guidance of a teacher, at the lowest possible level of the organization.

Conclusion

It can be difficult to present a single definition of Lean that is succinct, yet complete. Lean is a set of concepts and tools that allow people to improve patient care (reducing harm and waiting times). Lean is a management approach and philosophy that fosters the full engagement of our employees and physicians in continuous improvement toward a goal of perfection. Lean gives us ways to precisely define how our work is done, without stifling creativity or our professional judgment. Lean organizations can improve quality and cost without asking people to work harder or to be more careful. Lean is not a silver bullet or a magic fix. As one hospital CEO said to the hospital's leadership council, "Lean is very simple, yet very complicated at the same time." That is very true, as a small set of simple-sounding principles can indeed be challenging to implement.

Lean Lessons

- While its roots may be in manufacturing, Lean can be successful in other industries, including healthcare.
- Lean is an organizational culture that develops from an integrated system of tools, management practices, and philosophy.
- Developing employees, their careers, and their talents is important for Lean to succeed.
- Eliminating waste and having respect for people are equally important.
- Work should be designed, rather than letting methods evolve.
- "No problems is a problem"—we have to be open about having problems.
- In a Lean culture, new methods are not spread by forcing them onto other units.
- All of our employees have to participate in solving problems and eliminating waste.

Points for Group Discussion

- If asked "What is Lean?" what is your best 30-second answer?
- What has to change and be implemented to create a Lean culture?
- How can we develop leadership skills in employees, from top to bottom?
- Are there ways in which people in our hospital have previously not shown respect for people?
- Why do some hospital employees get burned out or cynical over time?
- What methods or practices have just evolved in your area, rather than being designed?
- How do you strike the balance between not reinventing the wheel yet not blindly copying other units or other hospitals?

Notes

1. Ohno, Taiichi, *Toyota Production System: Beyond Large-Scale Production* (New York: Productivity Press, 1988), 6.
2. Womack, James P., and Daniel T. Jones, *Lean Thinking* (New York: Free Press, 2003), 15.
3. Convis, Gary, "Role of Management in a Lean Manufacturing Environment," Society of Automotive Engineers, http://www.sae.org/manufacturing/lean/column/leanjul01.htm (accessed April 10, 2011).
4. Liker, Jeffrey, and David Meier, *The Toyota Way Fieldbook* (New York: McGraw-Hill, 2005), 242.
5. Public Affairs Division and Operations Management Consulting Division, *The Toyota Production System, Leaner Manufacturing for a Greener Planet* (Toyota City, Japan: Toyota Motor Corporation, 1998), 7.
6. Liker, Jeffrey K., and David Meier, *The Toyota Way Fieldbook* (New York: McGraw-Hill, 2006), 26.
7. Liker, Jeffrey K., *The Toyota Way* (New York: McGraw-Hill, 2004), 71.
8. Ulrich, Dave, *Delivering Results: A New Mandate for Human Resource Professionals* (Cambridge, MA: Harvard Business School Press, 1998), 179.
9. Convis, "Role of Management."
10. Toussaint, John, and Roger Gerard, *On the Mend: Revolutionizing Healthcare to Save Lives and Transform the Industry* (Cambridge, MA: Lean Enterprise Institute, 2010), 122.
11. Liker, Jeffrey, and Michael Hoseus, *Toyota Culture: The Heart and Soul of the Toyota Way* (New York: McGraw-Hill, 2008), xxvii.
12. Ohno, *Toyota Production System*, xiii.
13. Toyota Motor Corporation, "CSR policy," corporate Web site, http://www.toyota-global.com/sustainability/csr_initiatives/csr_concepts/policy.html (accessed January 30, 2011).
14. Graban, Mark, "How Lean Management Helped Hospitals Avoid Layoffs," *Fierce Healthcare*, October 1, 2010, http://www.fiercehealthcare.com/story/how-Lean-management-helped-hospitals-avoid-layoffs/2010–10–01 (accessed January 30, 2011).
15. Savary, Louis M., and Clare Crawford-Mason, *The Nun and the Bureaucrat* (Washington, DC: CC-M Productions, 2006), 26.
16. Institute for Healthcare Improvement, "Improvement Tip: Find 'Muda' and Root It Out," http://www.ihi.org/IHI/Topics/Improvement/ImprovementMethods/ImprovementStories/ImprovementTipFindMudaandRootitOut.htm (accessed April 10, 2011).
17. Liker and Hoseus, *Toyota Culture*, 326.
18. Womack, Jim, "Respect for People," monthly e-mail letter from Lean Enterprise Institute, December 20, 2007, http://Lean.org/Community/Registered/ShowEmail.cfm?JimsEmailId=75 (accessed April 10, 2011).
19. Japanese Management Association, *Kanban Just in Time at Toyota: Management Begins at the Workplace* (New York: Productivity Press, 1986), xv.
20. Scholtes, Peter R., *The Leader's Handbook: Making Things Happen, Getting Things Done* (New York: McGraw-Hill, 1997), 331.
21. Toussaint, John, presentation, Lean Healthcare Transformation Summit, June 2009.
22. Spear, Steven J., *The High-Velocity Edge: How Market Leaders Leverage Operational Excellence to Beat the Competition* (New York: McGraw-Hill, 2010), 22.
23. Spear, Steven J., "Fixing Healthcare from the Inside, Today," *Harvard Business Review*, Reprint 1738, September 2005, 5.
24. Shook, John, presentation, First Global Lean Healthcare Summit, June 25, 2007.
25. Deming, W. Edwards, *Out of the Crisis* (Cambridge MA: MIT CAES Press, 1982), 88.
26. Healthcare Value Network, "Network," Web site, http://www.healthcarevalueleaders.org/network.cfm (accessed January 30, 2011).
27. Spear, Steven, and H. Kent Bowen, "Decoding the DNA of the Toyota Production System," *Harvard Business Review*, Sept–Oct 1999, 77, no. 5: 97–106.
28. Kenagy, Charles, *Designed to Adapt: Leading Healthcare in Challenging Times* (Bozeman, MT: Second River Healthcare Press, 2009), 1.

Chapter 3

Value and Waste

Waste Is Not the Same as Cost

Healthcare organizations have focused on trying to reduce costs for a long time, but costs keep rising. Lean provides a different way to look at cost by not directly looking at it. Patrick Hagan, chief operating officer (COO) of Seattle Children's Hospital in Washington State, said, "We rarely talk about cost. We talk about waste, quality, and safety and we find our costs go down."[1]

Lean thinkers see cost as the end result of all of our systems and processes. As an end result, cost is not something that can be directly impacted. Or at least we do not have an impact on it in the traditional "cost-cutting" ways, which typically have meant layoffs and possibly the scaling back of services provided to our community. Lean hospitals focus on reducing waste, not cutting costs. Lean organizations also focus on the customers (the patients) and the value that is being delivered to them. In this way, Lean is not focused on doing less but rather on delivering the right amount of value. If we are reducing waste, we can often provide more value while expending less effort and less cost.

What Is Waste?

What are the problems and annoyances that constantly appear, interfering with our work and patient care? In the Lean terminology, we call this *waste*. Hospital workdays are full of interruptions, miscommunications, wasted motion, and workarounds. Employees and leaders often think their job, or the value they bring to an organization, is their ability to deal with problems. When supplies are missing, we run to find them. When our workspaces are badly designed and workloads are high, we walk faster. When orders do not arrive from a physician's office, we make multiple phone calls to track them down. These are workarounds that do not prevent the same problem from reoccurring. Instead of pointing at workarounds and heroic measures as "our job," we have to look at waste as something to reduce or eliminate, so we can spend more time doing our real work—caring for patients.

Learning to separate motion (the things we do) from value (the things we do that help the patient) is a critical step in the Lean journey. Instead of defining our jobs in terms of "this is what we do," Lean gives us a framework for determining what we *should* be doing. Hospitals can learn how to free time in ways that do not cut corners on quality or care that is needed by the patient.

Hospital employees typically spend a high percentage of their time on wasteful activities. For example, medical/surgical nurses in hospitals around the world typically spend only about 30% of their time on direct patient care, including

- Checking on patient status
- Administering medication
- Answering questions
- Giving medical guidance

Seattle's Virginia Mason Medical Center has used Lean methods to increase nursing time at the bedside from about 33% to 90%.[2] The National Health Service in the United Kingdom is teaching Lean methods to nurses and hospital staff through its Releasing Time to Care program, with cases of direct patient care time nearly doubling.[3] Hospitals in the United States are using a similar approach called Transforming Care at the Bedside, which has a goal of increasing bedside time from 30% to 70%.[4] Less waste means more time for patient care, which leads to such results as fewer patient falls and shorter length of stay.

When employees, departments, or hospitals are overworked, we need to reduce waste instead of just asking for more resources and people. Reducing waste also allows us to take on more work without adding head count, doing so in a way that does not stress our employees. Reducing waste also provides time for people to do their work the right way—providing high quality and great service to patients instead of being pressured to cut corners due to a lack of time. Eliminating waste allows us to reduce costs, provide more service, improve quality, and improve employee satisfaction—it is good for all of our hospital stakeholders.

What Is Value? Start with the Customer

If waste is an activity that does not add value, what is value? In *Lean Thinking*, Womack and Jones defined five principles that describe a Lean environment, adapted slightly here for hospitals, as shown in Table 3.1.[5]

First comes the customer, as Womack and Jones stated: "Value can only be defined by the ultimate customer."[6] What does that mean for a hospital that is using Lean? We need to start by asking the question, "Who is the customer?" In a hospital setting, we might have many customers for any given activity or care that is provided. The most obvious "ultimate" customer is the patient. Most work activities and priorities should be centered on that customer.

Other customers might include the patient's family, physicians, hospital employees, and payers. Each of these different customers might define value in a different way. For example, a family member of a patient undergoing outpatient surgery might find value in knowing and understanding the exact status of the patient at all times, reducing the amount of worry during the patient's time in the hospital.

There may be times when we think of an internal customer in a process, or the person who receives our work. For instance, a physician, working on behalf of the patient, is the primary recipient of a pathologist's report. When a patient's biopsy is sent to the lab, the pathologist might also think about the physician's needs and quality criteria, as well as the patient's. The ordering

Table 3.1 *Lean Thinking* **Principles for Hospitals**

Principle	Lean Hospitals Must
Value	Specify *value* from the standpoint of the end customer (the patient).
Value stream	Identify all the value-added steps across department boundaries (the *value stream*), eliminating steps that do not create value.
Flow	Keep the process *flowing* smoothly by eliminating causes of delay, such as batches and quality problems.
Pull	Avoid pushing work on the next process or department; let work and supplies be *pulled*, as needed.
Perfection	Pursue *perfection* through continuous improvement.

Source: Adapted from Lean Enterprise Institute, "Principles of Lean," http://www.lean.org/ WhatsLean/Principles.cfm (accessed December 20, 2007).

physician might have specific requirements for how the information should be presented and structured in the pathology report.

In any process, the person doing the work should think about the ultimate end customer but can also do his or her work in a way that allows the "downstream" recipient of the work to be a more effective partner in the total patient care effort. Internal customer needs must be in alignment with the end customer, the patient. Discussion of internal customer needs should not distract from the needs of the ultimate customer, as an organization might run the risk of becoming too inwardly focused.

One of the Lean thinking principles that is questioned in hospitals, at times, is pull. Pull is good for materials management, as described in Chapter 6, about *kanban*, as supplies are pulled only when they are needed in the right quantities, as opposed to being pushed regardless of need. Hospitals already have pull in the sense that a patient might be kept in the emergency department (ED) until an inpatient room has been vacated. The empty room pulls the patient from the ED. Pull is in place, in a way, but flow might be lacking since patients wait, as discussed in Chapter 9. It might be better to think of a patient pulling on services. For example, when a patient needs a bed, the patient should be able to figuratively pull that resource, rather than having to wait, even though it is the patient who is being moved to the bed.

Some have argued that patient flow actually improves when the ED pushes patients so that they wait in the hallway of an inpatient unit instead of the hallway of the ED. Pushing a patient to a unit may create incentives for inpatient unit personnel to complete the discharge process for other patients earlier, freeing the room. That mindset assumes that employees are purposefully slowing the discharge process, which is not always true. Ultimately, bad flow is bad flow, and shifting where the patient waits does not fix the root cause of the issue.

How Do We Define Value?

Dr. Don Berwick, in his 2009 keynote address at the Institute for Healthcare Improvement annual forum, asked about our health and our healthcare, "What do we really, really, really want?" Dr. Berwick proposed he wants "safe, effective, and evidence-based medicine" for his own care. What he "really wants" is to be active and to participate in recreational activities and meaningful family events.[7] Michael Porter suggested that patients value three levels of care: survival and the degree of recovery, the time required to get back to normal activities, and the sustainability of said treatments.[8]

From a patient perspective, it can be argued that "value" means not just providing efficient, safe, and effective episodes of care when it is needed. Rather than being merely reactive, patients might value a healthcare system that helps keep them healthy and provides a longer life with a higher quality of life. The ultimate value of Lean might be to think through these high-level questions rather than just focusing on tweaking today's healthcare delivery models. Porter wrote that value at a high level should be based on results, not activity, and should be measured as "the ratio of successful patient outcomes achieved to the total cost of care for the patient's medical condition."

Within the context of these big picture questions, the Lean methodology gives us some specific rules to use in determining what activities are value-added (VA) or non-value-added (NVA). The three rules that must be met for an activity to be considered value-added are:[9]

1. The customer must be willing to pay for the activity.
2. The activity must transform the product or service in some way.
3. The activity must be done correctly the first time.

All three of these rules must be met or the activity is non-value-added, or waste.

Rule 1: The Customer Must Be Willing to Pay for the Activity

Thinkers with diverse backgrounds such as Porter and James P. Womack agreed that value must be defined from the customer's perspective.[10,11] Given the potential for different definitions of value from different customers, how can we agree on value? Often, the providers of a service assume what is valued or not valued by customers. One method for determining what customers value is to ask them. Some hospitals are beginning to formally involve patients and their families in improvement efforts, including asking patients to help define value for their care and the overall services provided by the hospital.[12]

With the first rule, we can start with the patient as customer. A medical professional might think, "Our customers do not always know enough to answer that question! They do not appreciate everything we have to do for them." That might be true; sometimes, customers or patients have to be educated. Hospital employees, caregivers, or leaders cannot assume that any activity that we do is automatically value-added because of our job title or because a certain activity has always been done or done a particular way.

A patient who comes in with a suspected hip fracture would value the steps directly required for diagnosis and treatment. Time spent directly with caregivers, such as nurses and surgeons, would be valued. The patient having to give the same triage information to three different people would be waste the second and third times. Having X-rays reviewed would be valued, but time spent waiting because the radiologist is too busy would be considered waste.

Rule 2: The Activity Must Transform the Product or Service in Some Way

The original manufacturing definition for the second rule described changing the "of the product,"[13] meaning there was a physical change that brought the product closer to its final state. For example, installing a car door changes the product in a value-added way as customers are willing to pay for doors, and the product changes from a doorless chassis to one with doors. Time spent moving doors in the factory, repairing them, or waiting to assemble them would be non-value-added because nothing is changing with the product.

Depending on the process, the "product" in a hospital might be the patient, a radiology image, a medication, or a laboratory specimen. *Product* is admittedly an insensitive term for patients and is usually avoided. Consider the process by which a patient's blood is tested for potassium levels. The product takes many different forms. The step of physician order entry changes the product from a thought in the physician's head to an order in the hospital information system.

The phlebotomist's activity of collecting the specimen changes the product from an order in the system to a tube of the patient's blood. This fits both definitions (it is valued by the patient and changes the product), so it can be called value-added, assuming the work is done properly.

The definition of the second rule can be adapted slightly when we are working with a patient instead of a product. If an activity moves the patient from one state to another, in the direction of the desired final state (such as discharge), we can say the patient has been changed in a value-added way. Merely moving the patient from point A to point B is considered non-value-added. People might question this, pointing out that patients have to be moved from their room to the radiology department to get a computed axial tomographic (CAT) scan. That is true, but we would consider the CAT scan itself to be the value-added step, as it moves the patient from the state of an undiagnosed condition to a state at which a diagnosis could be made. Moving the patient to radiology might be considered "required waste," as discussed further in this chapter.

Rule 3: The Activity Must Be Done Correctly the First Time

An activity might meet the requirements of the first two rules, but if something was done incorrectly, requiring rework and additional motion, we do not get credit for doing the same activity twice as double the value-added time.

There are many examples of things not being done right the first time in departments throughout the hospital. A physician might write a prescription for a medication for which the patient has a known allergy. This motion and time, along with the time taken by the unit clerk who entered the order and by the pharmacist who caught the error, would all be considered waste (of course, in addition to the risk of an adverse effect on the patient). The time spent writing the prescription correctly would be considered value-added.

In another example, the final minutes of a surgical procedure would not be value-added if an error occurred in the counting and verification of sponges used during the procedure. If the patient's incision is closed (what would be a value-added step) with a sponge left inside the patient, the activity of reopening the patient's incision would be considered waste. If we have to reopen the incision to remove the sponge and reclose the incision, we cannot claim the extra motion and time were value-added. It is far better for all involved to devise systems that prevent such an error.

Hospitals and surgeons have often been paid for non-value-added work because of the activity that was done, rather than the value. This is changing, through new guidelines issued by the U.S. government and the Centers for Medicare and Medicaid Services (CMS). CMS, followed by some private payers, no longer pays for certain types of rework—things not done right the first time.[14] This includes procedures that are done to remove objects left inside patients, preventable infections, air embolisms, and falls. Hospitals have previously tried to reduce these errors and the resulting rework because it is the right thing for the patient. These new payer expectations, which may spread, are an attempt to create more of an incentive for improvement.

Examples of Value-Added and Non-Value-Added Activities

Value-added and non-value-added activities can be viewed from the perspective of products, patients, employees, or caregivers. Table 3.2 shows some examples of value-added and non-value-added activity for different roles in various hospital departments.

When categorizing what people do, the distinction between value-added and non-value-added activity is not to be mistaken for a value judgment of individuals or specific roles in an organization. The intent is not to say that surgeons—the people or the role—are value-added and operating room technicians are non-value-added. The judgment of value-added versus non-value-added is based on the work being done at a given moment. We all have moments in our day that are non-value-added. If the surgeon is standing in the operating room waiting because somebody had to run off to find a missing surgical instrument, that is certainly non-value-added time. The presence of waste does not indicate that an employee is bad or not working hard. On the contrary, waste causes people to work too hard as they fight problems that interrupt their value-added work. Waste tends to be driven by the system and the design (or lack of design) of our processes.

Table 3.3 shows some examples of value-added and non-value-added activity for different departments and products in a hospital.

The distinction between value-added and non-value-added work is not always straightforward and obvious in hospitals. In one hospital, the team debated if nurses' charting activities were value-added. One side made the argument that charting did not directly care for the patient, so

Table 3.2   Value-Added (VA) and Non-Value-Added (NVA) Examples for Different Roles in Hospital Departments

Department	Role	VA Activity Example	NVA Activity Example
Operating room	Surgeon	Operating on patient	Waiting for delayed procedure or performing unnecessary steps
Pharmacy	Pharmacy technician	Creating an intravenous formulation	Reprocessing medications that were returned from patient units
Inpatient unit	Nurse	Administering medications to a patient	Copying information from one computer system into another
Radiology	Radiology technician	Performing magnetic resonance imaging procedure	Performing a medically unnecessary scan
Laboratory	Medical technologist	Interpreting a test result	Fixing a broken instrument

Table 3.3 Value-Added (VA) and Non-Value-Added (NVA) Examples for Different "Products" in Hospital Processes

Department	"Product"	VA Activity	NVA Activity
Emergency room	Patient	Being evaluated or treated	Waiting to be seen
Clinical laboratory	Patient specimen	Being centrifuged or tested	Waiting to be moved as a "batch"
Pharmacy	Prescription	Medication being formulated or prepared	Being inspected multiple times
Perioperative services	Sterilized instruments	Time when instruments are being sterilized	Instruments being sterilized repeatedly without ever being used from a standard kit
Nutrition services	Patient food tray	Time when food is being cooked or tray is being assembled	Being reworked because the tray was made incorrectly

it should be considered non-value-added. The other group argued that charting was value-added because it passed along information that helped a physician make decisions about a patient's care. A middle ground was reached that some charting was value-added (because it did have an impact on patient care), but wasted time caused by system problems was non-value-added. The practice of "overcharting" or putting more information than is necessary for patient care might also be considered waste.

Ultimately, it can be an academic exercise to categorize an activity as value or waste. Rather than arguing for hours about the classification, it is more important to ask if we can eliminate that step or find a better way. Looking for waste is meant to be a way that leads to improvement by challenging existing practices.

Learning to Identify and Describe Waste

To help identify waste, having specific shared terminology can help. Ohno defined seven types of waste, while later publications often listed eight types.[15] These definitions have been adopted as a useful framework for viewing waste in hospitals. Sometimes, the terms are used verbatim; sometimes, they are modified. Having complete agreement on the exact terms is not crucial, as Toyota did not intend this list to be all inclusive or to be something that could not be changed. Consistent terminology does, however, help us communicate within our organization and across the industry. The types of waste are summarized in Table 3.4.

Waste of Defects

Defects can be defined as any work activities that are not done right the first time. This might include a form that is not filled out properly, but more serious defects in a hospital setting can

Table 3.4   The Eight Types of Waste

Type of Waste	Brief Description	Hospital Examples
Defects	Time spent doing something incorrectly, inspecting for errors, or fixing errors	Surgical case cart missing an item; wrong medicine or wrong dose administered to patient
Overproduction	Doing more than what is needed by the customer or doing it sooner than needed	Doing unnecessary diagnostic procedures
Transportation	Unnecessary movement of the "product" (patients, specimens, materials) in a system	Poor layout, such as the catheter lab being located a long distance from the ED
Waiting	Waiting for the next event to occur or next work activity	Employees waiting because workloads are not level; patients waiting for an appointment
Inventory	Excess inventory cost through financial costs, storage and movement costs, spoilage, wastage	Expired supplies that must be disposed of, such as out-of-date medications
Motion	Unnecessary movement by employees in the system	Lab employees walking miles per day due to poor layout
Overprocessing	Doing work that is not valued by the customer or caused by definitions of quality that are not aligned with patient needs	Time/date stamps put onto forms, but the data are never used
Human potential	Waste and loss due to not engaging employees, listening to their ideas, or supporting their careers	Employees get burned out and quit giving suggestions for improvement

cause injury or death. The Institute of Medicine estimated that 400,000 "preventable drug-related injuries" occur each year;[16] each of these can be classified as a defect, with causes including illegible handwriting, misplaced decimal points, or defects in the process for getting medications to the patient. In one case that received much media attention, three babies died after they were given adult doses of heparin in the newborn intensive care unit (ICU) of Methodist Hospital (Indianapolis, IN).[17] There were numerous "process defects" that led to these deaths, including the stocking of adult doses of heparin by a pharmacy tech in the newborn ICU drug cabinet. In another process defect, nurses did not verify the proper doses before administering them, fully expecting that adult doses would not be in the newborn ICU.

The patient deaths were caused by a number of process defects, miscommunications, and errors—nothing that can be traced back to a single person or a single point of failure. Focusing on the process does not mean that people should not be held accountable. The nurse, in this case, violated hospital policies by not verifying the dose. It is overly simplistic, however, to think that firing or punishing an individual would keep this error from occurring again. This exact same set of process defects led to another high-profile overdose case, this time at Cedars-Sinai Hospital in

California.[18] Defects, and steps that can be taken to prevent them, are covered in more detail in Chapters 7 and 8.

A defect does not necessarily have to cause harm. Process defects include things that go wrong that lead to rework or workarounds. For example, if a nurse or phlebotomist draws blood from a patient and there is a problem with the specimen, the failed draw attempt and the time required to have drawn the specimen are considered waste. The defect slows the product (the patient specimen and the test result) and wastes time for the employees.

Waste of Overproduction

Waste of overproduction can be defined more easily using a manufacturing scenario. Overproduction can be defined as producing too much of a product (more than the customer desires) or producing earlier than it is needed by the customer. If you are in the market for a new car and visit a dealer, much of the inventory you see sitting on the lot is overproduction—and you often get a discount as a result.

The pharmacy is one hospital department that produces (by formulation or delivery) medications for internal customers (nurses and patients). Delivering medications too early can be considered overproduction when some medications end up being returned to the pharmacy. Reasons for this might include patients being discharged or orders being changed by the physician. In one hospital, prior to implementing Lean, about 250 medications were returned to the pharmacy each day (more than 1 per admitted patient). The overproduction led to other types of waste, as pharmacy employees spent a total of 11 hours per day processing returned medications. The improved process aimed to deliver medications more frequently during the day, adding more transportation and motion, but with the trade-off of reducing the reprocessing work and helping ensure the right medications were available when needed.

In many cases, hospitals can avoid the overproduction of doing more than necessary for effective patient care. Some laboratories have phlebotomists draw "just-in-case" tubes from inpatients to have extra specimens in case unplanned testing is required after the draw. Labs often find the extra tubes are rarely used (less than 10% of the time), resulting in wasted time, motion, and materials. Looking at trade-offs with the types of waste, it might be easier to rationalize the just-in-case tubes when a trauma patient arrives at the ED, as having the tubes already drawn can prevent waiting time in providing care. Or, it is possible that drawing a "rainbow" of tubes in advance of orders being written is a workaround for laboratory turnaround times being longer than desired. A better systemic fix might be to improve the flow of the lab testing to reduce the need for that overproduction.

Some hospitals, including Virginia Mason Medical Center (Seattle, WA), have made attempts to reduce the overproduction of radiology and other diagnostic procedures. Virginia Mason started a program in which clinicians decided they would first refer patients with certain types of conditions to physical therapy before approving radiology procedures. This less-expensive therapy was expected to be more beneficial than a diagnostic procedure. Unfortunately, Virginia Mason sacrificed revenue because the insurance payers would have likely paid for the magnetic resonance imaging (MRI) or other radiology procedure. This illustrates one of the dysfunctions of a payer system in which hospitals are often paid for their activity (piecework) instead of for patient outcomes. Virginia Mason was trying to be responsible in how it spent other people's money, but reducing that overproduction harmed the hospital in the short term. Virginia Mason responded by proposing a savings-sharing arrangement with insurers and payers, getting higher reimbursements for physical therapy so both parties could benefit from the waste reduction.[19]

One could argue that the overutilization of diagnostic procedures should be categorized as overprocessing instead of overproduction. But again, it is less important to have 100% agreement on the classification than it is to develop patient-focused process improvements as a result of discovering that waste.

Waste of Transportation

Waste of transportation refers to excess movement of the product through a system. Some amount of transportation might well be necessary given the context of the current hospital layout. In the long term, we might reconfigure the hospital layout in a way that reduces transportation distance for patients or specimens. More likely, we might use our understanding of transportation waste during the design and construction phases of building a new hospital or site.

The waste of transportation can apply even to patients. One hospital was using Lean methods to improve patient flow through its operating rooms and followed patients from arrival to surgery. During the course of her visit for a procedure, one 74-year-old woman walked the equivalent of 5½ football fields. The redesign of the hospital was going to more carefully take patient walking distances into account to reduce that waste.

Park Nicollet Health Services in Minnesota built its new Frauenshuh Cancer Center based on the idea of reducing patient transportation time and distance. Rather than making sick patients expend their limited energy by walking, the new center was designed so that patients remain in a single room for their nurse and doctor visits, lab draws, treatment, and other support services. "Where care comes to you" becomes both an operating principle and a marketing slogan.[20]

Waste of Waiting

Waiting time can be defined, simply, as time when nothing productive is happening. It is easy for most to see the lack of activity as a type of waste. Patients wait for the next step in their patient pathway. Employees wait because of systemic problems or because of uneven workloads. Lean methods can help reduce the waste of waiting in both cases.

Patients and Products Waiting

Patients often wait for appointments in physician clinics or for procedures, such as chemotherapy or radiology, due to poor flow or poor scheduling. Hospitals might not have previously focused on reducing this waste if they had been more concerned about maximizing the use of particular hospital resources, such as MRI machines, beds, or physicians. For example, the old practice of having all surgical patients arrive at 6:30 a.m. for "as follows" procedures helps ensure the surgeons and operating rooms are fully utilized, without delays between procedures, but Lean helps us see that this is not a patient-focused approach. Hospitals might move to giving each procedure a scheduled time and having a patient arrive 90 or 120 minutes before that time. This reduces patient waiting and improves patient satisfaction, while creating some risk of lower surgical utilization.

Waiting time for a product might include time when a patient is waiting for the next clinical encounter or value-added step in the patient journey. Patients are not the only product that waits in a hospital process. Other physical products, such as tubes of blood for the laboratory, pharmacy orders and medications, and instruments to be sterilized also spend a high percentage of time waiting instead of having value-added work performed on them. This waiting is often due to batching within or between departments; lack of first in, first out (FIFO) flow; or the product waiting on employees who have multiple responsibilities.

Employees Waiting

Employees are often put in the position of waiting instead of being able to perform value-added work. Common causes of employee waits can include process defects, delays in upstream processes, uneven workloads, and low patient volumes.

Many departments have uneven workloads, including radiology, the ED, or operating rooms. While we want to level workloads and prevent process defects that lead to employee waiting time, there are some cases when the waste of waiting is necessary, or at least preferable to other types of waiting. When we have unpredictable or unscheduled demand, such as in an ED, the prudent approach might be to err on the side of having employees waiting, being ready to go when needed. Hospitals need to evaluate employee waiting on a case-by-case basis, understanding which waiting has a root cause that can be eliminated and which is helpful in preventing patient care delays. In many cases, waiting time can be replaced with productive activities, such as problem solving and improvement work instead of just sending people home.

Waste of Inventory

All inventory, such as materials, supplies, and equipment, is not inherently wasteful. Excessive inventory is waste, meaning we have more inventory than is needed to perform our work properly. When inventories are too high, the hospital's cash is tied up in the inventory sitting on shelves, or excess inventory may expire, including supplies and medications.

Many manufacturing companies harmed themselves by thinking Lean meant keeping inventory low as a primary goal. A Lean approach first takes care of customer and patient needs but does so with the lowest possible inventory levels, given the current system. We should not take the current system as given; we want to look for root causes that lead us to hold inventory so we can eliminate those problems. One root cause might be unreliable vendors whose time required to replenish inventory varies (due to transportation delays or infrequent shortages).

Having too much inventory wastes space and cash, but running out of inventory can lead to additional wasted motion, costs, and expediting. Employees might have to make additional unplanned trips to stockrooms, or they might have to place expensive expedited orders from vendors, sent via overnight shipping. In a Lean environment, keeping the right supplies and inventory on hand ensures the right patient care can be delivered while reducing costs and waste for the hospital. It is not uncommon to see million dollar cost reductions in hospital-wide inventory improvement efforts while also increasing the availability of supplies, as discussed in Chapter 6.

In some cases, improved inventory management can help reduce other types of waste. One hospital was working on improving the adherence to their method for inserting central lines, with the goal of reducing infections. To properly perform the work, a technician or nurse had to gather and bring 10 separate items to the patient's room, including drapes, gloves, the line, and sutures. If one item, such as a drape, were forgotten, there would be a temptation not to walk back to the inventory storage area. This would reduce the waste of motion but might also increase the chances of a defect (an infection). By purchasing a single stock item, a central line kit, the risk of forgetting or not being able to find an item was eliminated. This eliminated the need for extra motion that would have been needed to insert the central line and encouraged staff to use the best-known methods for the benefit of patient safety. In addition to benefitting patients, it is likely that the increased cost of buying a kit would be more than offset by the cost savings of not having to treat these avoided infections.

Waste of Motion

While the waste of transportation focuses on the product (including the patient), the waste of motion refers to those doing the work. Hospitals should reduce the amount of motion required by employees to get the work done. This provides numerous benefits, including reducing the physical fatigue of employees and freeing more time for value-added work, including patient care. As one hospital chief executive officer (CEO) said, "Nobody should go home hurting at the end of the day."

Wasted motion in a hospital setting is often most obviously seen as unnecessary walking. Walking is often considered part of the job, but it is rarely a value-added activity. One example might be a nurse or technician walking with a rehabilitating patient down a hospital corridor. More often, the walking is waste that can be reduced by improving the layout and organization of supplies and equipment. Our search for wasted motion should not be limited to walking, but walking is usually a good place to start. The goal is not to have stationary employees who never move but to reduce or eliminate unnecessary motion and walking.

At one hospital, a finance director had an employee who would constantly run back and forth through the billing office. The director used to think, "We need more people like that," meaning highly motivated employees willing to go above and beyond to get work done. After starting to implement Lean, the director realized that the running was a sign of waste in the process. The director started to ask the employee to identify root causes of the running, discovering it was a combination of bad layout (certain frequently needed files were located across the office) and overburden, or *muri*. By adjusting workloads and changing layouts, the employee no longer had the need, or felt the time pressure, to run.

Waste of Nursing Motion

Direct observation of nurses show that they typically walk many miles per day. This can be seen in settings as varied as EDs, inpatient units, and cancer treatment centers. Data collected, with electronic pedometers, at one hospital showed a medical/surgical unit nurse consistently walked 3.5–4.5 miles per 12-hour shift. Data collected at an outpatient cancer treatment center showed that nurses walked at a pace of 4.2 miles per day.

Walking is often driven by the layout of the area. If the nurses station is at the end of a long hallway, nurses will walk more than if the station were in the center of a cluster of rooms (or the nurses will avoid walking, staying at the nurses station, which can negatively impact patient care). Keeping nurses closer to the patients not only reduces walking but also allows for faster response and closer monitoring of patient needs. For example, Avera McKennan hospital (Sioux Falls, SD), has built a new ED layout, driven by Lean principles, that has all the patient rooms located around a central nursing station.

Nurses in one inpatient unit reported having to walk more because of a change in the location of supplies. In the past, many frequently needed supplies had been kept in multiple locations throughout the unit or in patient rooms, where it was convenient for nurses (and prevented patient waiting time). In the name of materials efficiency, a central automated supply cabinet was installed, and most of the supplies were consolidated in that cabinet.

While the hospital kept a tighter control on inventory levels and the single cabinet made it easier for the materials department to restock supplies (saving money in that department's silo), the nurses disliked walking to the far end of the hallway every time they needed an item. This suboptimization often leads to nurses hoarding supplies in drawers, lockers, or pockets, a practice that can create other problems. The hospital started reconsidering the value of the central supply cabinets, rationalizing which items really needed to be under such tight control and which items could be stocked in more convenient locations, as they had been before. Once again, we can see trade-offs in different types of waste. If items are inexpensive and do not take up much space, it might reduce the total waste in the system to store them in more locations or in each patient room.

Nurses (and other employees) are often good at reducing their own walking but often in ways that may, unfortunately, cut corners with safety. At one hospital, lift assists for patients were located in a closet on a different floor because the unit did not have enough storage space. Because it was inconvenient and time consuming to go get one, nurses often lifted patients without the assist, which increased the risk of employee injuries and patient falls. To reduce walking and to ensure that proper practices were followed, the unit freed space, using the 5S process, and relocated the lifts to the unit.

Waste of Overprocessing

Waste of overprocessing is described with many different names and is sometimes called the waste of processing itself. *Overprocessing* refers to doing something to a higher level of quality than required by the customer or doing unnecessary work. One example might be found in the laboratory. Many blood specimens need to be centrifuged before they can be analyzed. At some point in the cycle, the blood has separated into its components (plasma, red cells, and white cells). After this separation is complete, additional centrifugation provides no additional separation, or value. The blood is no longer being transformed; it is just being spun longer. Laboratories sometimes find that centrifuges are set at times that are longer than recommended or required, either due to an error or from habit.

Often, overprocessing results from miscommunications in the handoffs between people or departments. In one hospital, a surgery project uncovered that one employee spent three hours a day folding towels after they came back from the laundry, unaware that nurses upstairs were immediately unfolding them and laying them flat. The wasteful folding step was discontinued.

The billing department division of one home health product could be characterized as a classic batch-and-queue process. Individual employees each did small portions of work in the overall flow; a patient record would be handled by seven or eight employees from the receipt of the order to the receipt of cash from the payer. Piles of charts, or batches, were usually passed between workers, leading to the waste of waiting and long delays between steps.

The entire process was observed by a Lean coach. The coach watched the first employee go through the chart, taking out duplicate paperwork and placing it in a bin to be shredded. That employee said the extra copies were unnecessary, just making the chart thicker, so they were removed to save storage space. The coach then observed the next worker and noticed that the first step was to go make a few copies of some of the forms in the chart, walking right past the employee who had thrown out the "extras." It was obvious that each employee meant well, but neither understood how her work fit into the entire process. The coach asked them to stop their work and to explain to each other what they did. They soon realized the waste—that throwing away and re-creating copies was overprocessing. Immediately, the employees changed their process to avoid this waste.

Waste of Talent

Waste of talent, the eighth type, is not always recognized in Lean literature. Some sources only list the first seven and justify this by saying the waste of human potential is embedded in the other types of waste. If highly skilled employees are forced to search for supplies, we are not getting the most out of their potential, and they are not doing any work that can develop their skills or career.

Those who do list this as a separate category of waste emphasize the importance of people in the system. Lean is not just about managing equipment or processes; it is about managing, leading, developing, and inspiring people. This is particularly true in a hospital, when our people (and their performance) are our primary product to the patients. Employees are our primary cost driver (typically more than 50% of a hospital's revenue)[21] and a major driver of patient satisfaction through their daily interactions.

The waste involved in "not utilizing the talent inherent in your workers" harms patients, the organization, and the employees themselves.[22] It is a common lament in the manufacturing world that management told workers to "check their brains at the door" or implied that they should. Employees may fall into a cycle in which they feel like they are not listened to, so they quit trying to improve the system in which they work. There is incalculable waste when employees just show up, do their jobs (as told to or as they have always done it), and go home.

Unfortunately, these same types of comments are heard in hospitals. At the start of one implementation, a laboratory technologist complained, "Nowadays, I feel like a robot." Having more than 25 years of experience in the field, the employee complained that what used to be challenging, scientific work had become an exercise in loading tubes into a machine and hitting the start button. Ironically, employees are often concerned that Lean efforts, including standardized work, will turn them into unthinking robots. In this case, though, the employee had been playing no role in improving the process. Managers rarely asked employees their opinions or ideas on improving the department. Through Lean management approaches, employees can have their intelligence and creativity utilized in a productive way, even if the details of the work itself have become highly automated.

One aspect of respect for people is engaging employees' minds in continuous improvement. How many problems could be solved permanently if we just asked our employees what we should do? At one hospital, a nurse commented that their initial Lean work led to "the first time in six years that anybody has asked me what I think about anything." Many organizations are stuck in the outdated philosophy that managers must design the system, and workers should just execute the process, no questions asked. Managers often fear losing control or power by engaging employees in improvement. But our patients and our healthcare systems deserve no less than to have everybody working on improvements, "every person, every day," as the common Lean expression goes.

What Non-Value-Added Activities Are Required?

In the course of a given day, time spent walking might fall into a category called "non-value-added, but required." A nurse might have to walk 100 feet to a medicine cart, but that does not make that walking time value-added. What if the medicine cart were relocated so that it reduced walking time for all nurses in the unit? What if a second cart was added? What if more patient-specific medications were kept in a locked cabinet in the patient's room?

We might look at nurses and decide what portion of their walking is necessary in the current system and how much can be eliminated. Ideally, all of a nurse's patients would be in adjoining rooms, reducing the need to walk between far ends of the unit. Keeping patients clustered together would also allow faster nurse response. There are conflicting objectives that keep this from happening, such as the need to fairly distribute patient acuity levels and nursing workloads. It might be preferred to have a nurse work with the same patients as much as possible to reduce the number of handoffs and for the comfort of the patient; however, as patients are discharged, newly admitted or transferred patients might be put wherever a room is available. Quickly, we might end up with scattered patient assignments. Moving patients creates additional work and might be disruptive to the patient. Reassigning patients might require additional work for the nurses and creates risks for errors due to miscommunication.

Some people call this activity category "enabling waste" or "enabling activities," rather than non-value-added. The enabling terminology somewhat skirts the issue and might make the activity seem more acceptable. It is preferable to call this non-value-added, but required or "required waste" because the negative connotation helps emphasize that this waste should be reduced or eliminated if possible. Leaders need to emphasize to their employees that identifying non-value-added activities is not a criticism of the people doing the work.

There are many common hospital activities that are certainly required but cannot be considered value from the patient's perspective. For example, registration and billing paperwork does nothing to directly diagnose or treat a patient; however, the paperwork is required so the hospital can get paid, and it might be necessary to get payer authorizations to provide certain care to the patient. This paperwork might be very necessary, but that does not mean we should categorize it as value. When staff members say "we have to do that step," it may very well be required waste— having to do it does not equal value. Finally, categorizing something as waste does not mean we can eliminate that step.

One common controversy that arises in discussions of value-added or non-value-added activity involves quality inspections. Granted, inspection steps are intended to protect the patient from harm. The medication administration process has multiple inspection steps, such as

- Pharmacists verifying prescriptions for proper dosing and interactions
- Pharmacists double-checking the work of pharmacy technicians who pulled medications to match the order
- Nurses double-checking that the right medication is being given to the right patient

From a Lean perspective, these inspection steps are most often categorized as required waste. Why would a process step that is intended to help the patient be considered non-value-added? Rather than saying we should stop doing those inspections, Lean thinkers would consider them to be non-value-added because they are only necessary given the existing process is not perfect and might be prone to error. Lean thinkers would always challenge the process to find ways of preventing errors from occurring rather than using inspections or double-checks to find them after the fact. Hospitals should not eliminate the inspection steps until error proofing is put in place, as described in Chapter 8. If the error proofing cannot be deemed 100% effective, then inspection steps might still be used to protect the patients.

Non-Value-Added, Pure Waste

Beyond the required waste, some non-value-added activities are so unproductive that we refer to them as pure waste, such as waiting time or time spent dealing with errors or process defects. Time spent fixing errors or doing rework is also considered pure waste because we need to focus on preventing future problems, reducing the need for rework. We are not suggesting that employees avoid fixing problems to avoid the non-value-added time involved. Rather, when a problem occurs, we need to recognize that rework is pure waste and focus on improvement and prevention, rather than just tolerating the rework activity as part of our normal work.

Conclusion

Learning to identify waste, through our definitions of waste and the types of waste, and going to the *gemba* to identify waste are good starting points. Training people and making lists of waste might create awareness, but we need the courage to take action and lead efforts to improve the system and eliminate that waste.

We say "courage" because the mere act of identifying waste can be risky behavior, given the wrong environment. Often, when we point out waste, people take it personally, especially if they created the existing system or have been working in it long enough. We have to be careful how we point out waste so we do not turn people against our efforts. Focusing on the waste and describing waste in terms such as "This process seems to have a lot of wasted motion" brings a different response than saying "You are walking too much." When we personalize the waste, intentionally or not, people will get defensive and often attempt to rationalize the existing process. People usually have pride in the way they do their work, even if it is full of waste. Managers might also take it personally if they perceive their department is being criticized, which can interfere with acceptance of improvements.

Employees often define their value as their skill in working around broken processes and making things happen, being the hero, if you will. The nurse who knows where to run to find a blanket when they seem to be unavailable might be praised as a hero for making that extra effort to get the job done. When focusing on waste, we would ask why the same nurse is making the same heroic run every day. We would improve the system so that blankets were available at the right place and in the right quantities, thus avoiding the need for heroic efforts. The nurse might resent this improvement, as it has robbed the individual of a source of pride and recognition.

Recognizing all of this, we cannot dance around the topic of waste. We must point it out. We cannot accept excuses for the waste that is in the system. Keeping with the theme of respect for people, we should not point fingers of blame, asking, "Whose fault is it that the system is this way?" It is helpful to state that we do not care why the system is the way it is today, but we need to focus on the future and work together on improvements.

Lean Lessons

- Waste interferes with us doing our work.
- Not all activity is value.
- Waste tends to be driven by the system and the design in our processes.
- Not all waste can be eliminated; some of it is required to make the system function.

- Just because we have to do something does not make it value.
- Quality is a primary goal of Lean.
- Patients should not have to pay for defects or rework.
- The primary goal is not low inventory, but rather having enough inventory to efficiently do our work, without having too much.
- To drive problem solving and continuous improvement, focus on the process.

Points for Group Discussion

- Who are our customers? Is the customer always right in a hospital setting?
- How can we reduce delays in one part of the process without negatively impacting another part?
- Which types of waste are most prevalent in your department or hospital? Can you find an example of each?
- Are there times when we make the patient wait for the benefit or convenience of everyone else in the system?
- Are there times when the desires of "internal customers" are out of alignment with patient needs?
- How far are our employees walking on an average day? What can do we do to reduce that?
- What are some reasons we might err on the side of having too much inventory rather than too little?

Notes

1. Hagan, Patrick, Presentation to Healthcare Value Network visitors February 3, 2011.
2. Kenney, Charles, *Transforming Healthcare: Virginia Mason Medical Center's Pursuit of the Perfect Patient Experience* (New York: Productivity Press, 2010), 122.
3. National Health Service, *"The Productive Ward: Releasing Time to Care,"* http://www.institute.nhs.uk/ quality_and_value/productive_ward/case_studies.html (accessed January 30, 2011).
4. Robert Wood Johnson Foundation, "Transforming Care at the Bedside," http://www.rwjf.org/quality equality/product.jsp?id=30052 (accessed January 30, 2011).
5. Lean Enterprise Institute, "Principles of Lean," http://www.lean.org/WhatsLean/Principles.cfm (accessed December 20, 2007).
6. Womack, James P., and Daniel T. Jones, *Lean Thinking* (New York: Free Press, 2003), 16.
7. Berwick, Donald, "2009 National Forum Keynote Video On Demand," http://www.ihi.org/IHI/ Programs/AudioAndWebProgrms/BerwickForumKeynote2009.htm (accessed July 4, 2011).
8. Porter, Michael, "What Is Value in Health Care?" *New England Journal of Medicine*, December 8, 2010, http://healthpolicyandreform.nejm.org/?p=13328 (accessed April 8, 2011).
9. Sayer, Natalie J., and Bruce Williams, *Lean for Dummies* (Hoboken, NJ: Wiley, 2007), 51.
10. Porter, "What Is Value."
11. Womack and Jones, *Lean Thinking*, 28.
12. Laura Landro, "Hospitals Boost Patient Power as Advisors," *Wall Street Journal*, August 8, 2007, http:// online.wsj.com/public/article/SB118652860268491024.html (accessed April 10, 2011).
13. Flinchbaugh, Jamie, and Andy Carlino, *The Hitchhiker's Guide to Lean: Lessons from the Road* (Dearborn, MI: Society for Manufacturing Engineers, 2005), 14.
14. Studer Group, "It's Now or Never: Resources to Ensure that Never Events Never Happen Again," http:// www.studergroup.com/never (accessed January 30, 2011).

15. Liker, Jeffrey K., *The Toyota Way: 14 Management Principles from the World's Greatest Automaker* (New York: McGraw-Hill, 2004), 28–29.
16. Stencel, Christine, "Medication Errors Injure 1.5 Million People and Cost Billions of Dollars Annually; Report Offers Comprehensive Strategies for Reducing Drug-Related Mistakes," National Academy of Sciences, July 20, 2006, http://www8.nationalacademies.org/onpinews/newsitem.aspx?RecordID=11623 (accessed April 10, 2011).
17. Davies, Tom, "Fatal Drug Mix-up Exposes Hospital Flaws," *Washington Post*, September 22, 2006, http://www.washingtonpost.com/wp-dyn/content/article/2006/09/22/AR2006092200815.html?nav=hcmodule (accessed April 10, 2011).
18. Tiernon, Anne Marie, "Families Upset over New Heparin Overdose Cases," *MSNBC Online*, November 22, 2007, http://www.wthr.com/story/7394819/families-upset-over-new-heparin-over-dose-cases (accessed April 10, 2011).
19. Pham, Hoangmai H., Paul B. Ginsburg, Kelly McKenzie, and Arnold Milstein, "Redesigning Care Delivery in Response to a High-Performance Network: The Virginia Mason Medical Center," Health Affairs Web Exclusive, *Health Affairs,* 2006, 26: w532–44, http://content.healthaffairs.org/cgi/reprint/hlthaff.26.4.w532v1.pdf (accessed April 10, 2011).
20. Park Nicollet Health Services, "Everything to You at Park Nicollet Frauenshuh Cancer Center," video, http://www.youtube.com/watch?v=PUre7cMDYd4 (accessed January 30, 2011).
21. Berger, Steven, "Analyzing Your Hospital's Labor Productivity," *Healthcare Financial Management*, April 2005, http://findarticles.com/p/articles/mi_m3257/is_4_59/ai_n13621288 (accessed April 10, 2011).
22. Bodek, Norman, *Kaikaku: The Power and Magic of Lean* (Vancouver, WA: PCS Press, 2004), 115.

Chapter 4

Observing the Process and Value Streams

How Do We Find Waste? Go and See

Once we know the definitions of waste, we have to take action. We have to "go and see" (*genchi genbutsu*, in Japanese), as Toyota would tell us. Ohno was famous for training engineers and managers to look for waste by chalk drawing what came to be known as an "Ohno circle" on the floor.[1] The trainee was told to stand in the circle (just a few feet in diameter) and watch the process for hours, looking for waste. That is an extreme method and not one that is commonly used, but there are lessons to be drawn from it. First, you have to go and see with your own eyes, as meeting in a conference room to discuss the process is not as effective. Leaders at all levels have to go to the *gemba* (the place where work is actually done) to see what really happens.

In any organization, including hospitals, there are three forms of any process:

1. What the process *really* is
2. What we *think* the process is
3. What the process *should* be

Leaders cannot rely exclusively on reports, data, or metrics, especially early in the Lean journey. You might ask, "How long are patients waiting in the emergency department before seeing a doctor?" The hospital might already have measures and reports in place, but the most effective way to actually improve the process is to go and see for yourself to identify waste. This takes time, but that time will prove to be an extremely good investment for you and your team.

What Is a Value Stream?

As we see in many industries, hospitals and health systems are designed around specialized functions or departments. These departments or sites have their own physical space, their own budgets, their own employees, and their own management structures. Each department has its own job to do, but also plays a role in the overall patient experience and care. Problems and waste in hospitals are often found in the interactions or handoffs between those departments because of a lack of focus on patient pathways, or what are called "value streams" in the Lean methodology.

For a hospital to provide waste-free patient care, it is not enough for each department to be great on its own. Dr. Paul Batalden, former president of the Institute for Healthcare Improvement, once said, "We have the very best pharmacy sitting right next to the very best laboratory, sitting right next to the very best x-ray department, sitting right next to the very best nursing department … and the hospital doesn't work."[2]

Womack and Jones defined the value stream as "the set of all the specific actions required to bring a specific product (whether a good, service, or increasingly a combination of the two) through the three critical management tasks of any business: the problem-solving task, the information management task, and the physical transformation task."[3]

For a hospital and a patient, the general value stream definition holds true. For example, when a patient arrives in the emergency department (ED), we have problem solving (finding what is wrong with the patient), information management (demographic or diagnostic information that guides or assists treatment), and the physical treatment path through the hospital. The value stream is that end-to-end patient journey from door to door, not just what happens in the ED. A value stream can also encompass the time and steps that occur between the patient's referral for treatment and the hospital being paid for that care.

Value Stream Mapping

Value stream mapping has been a popular tool to help hospital leaders see the entire picture across departmental boundaries. A value stream map (VSM) is a structured diagram that originated with Toyota, as a tool called material and information flow mapping.[4]

A VSM may seem similar to other quality improvement tools, such as the process mapping method used in the total quality management and Six Sigma approaches. Both process maps and VSMs document the steps in a process, the activities that take place, but VSMs take this further by capturing time elements. VSMs identify how long each process step typically takes to complete and, more important, the amount of waiting time between process steps. The maps typically reveal and illustrate that most of the time in the system, from a patient's perspective, is time spent waiting for the next process, time that is wasted. The book *Value Stream Mapping for Healthcare Made Easy* (Jimmerson) is an excellent resource for a more in-depth examination of this method.[5]

Creating a Current-State Value Stream Map

Value stream maps are typically created by a cross-functional team of people who are dedicated to the mapping effort for anywhere from two days (for a smaller, limited-scope VSM) to two weeks (for a full patient journey VSM). When mapping, it is important to have representatives from all departments and functions that work in that value stream. For example, the team for a patient discharge VSM might include physicians, nurses, unit clerks, social workers, patient transporters, and others from multiple departments.

Avoid the temptation to create VSMs without leaving a conference room. If we only talk about the process rather than seeing it firsthand, we run the risk of capturing the "what we think it is" version of the process instead of "how it really is." Even the most knowledgeable employees will forget steps in the process or underestimate how often a step, such as rework, actually occurs. People also tend to underestimate or overestimate the process times or, more likely, the waiting times between process steps. The steps and times captured on a VSM must be verified through data collection and actual process observation to make sure we have an accurate current-state map that reflects how things work today.

Figure 4.1 shows a high-level value stream for a patient journey for outpatient surgery. Looking at the VSM, we see the information flows on top, showing what communication takes place among different people, departments, and information systems. The information flows, in this case, highlight the waste involved in three separate roles (registration, scheduling, and assessment), all contacting the patient, creating extra work for the hospital and confusion on the patient's part. Patients who were interviewed in the course of this mapping complained that they received multiple voice mails and did not always realize they needed to call all three people back. This often led to a patient arriving for a scheduled procedure without having completed needed lab work or preauthorizations.

In the bottom part of the VSM, we see the patient pathway, as the boxes represent the different departments or steps in the process. The black triangles represent the patient's waiting time between the process steps. This product or material flow might also represent the flow of a discharge order, a lab specimen, or supplies that have been ordered from a vendor.

When creating a current-state VSM, the team needs to identify problems that need fixing, such as a long waiting time between steps in the process or high amounts of rework. These are often drawn onto the map as "*kaizen* bursts." At this point, we do not necessarily need to jump to solutions, but the team needs to start prioritizing problems based on the impact on patients or other stakeholders. Sometimes, problems can be solved quickly, right after the VSM is drawn. In other cases, specific follow-up on problems may need to be defined as a formal improvement project to be done later. It is important to recognize that some value stream problems cannot be fixed

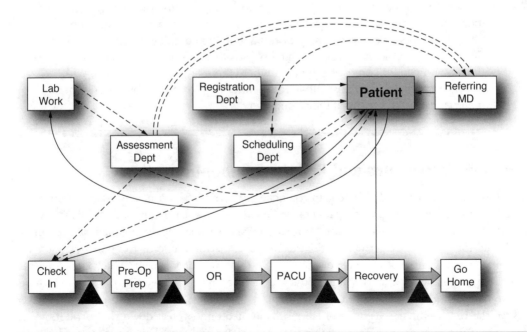

Figure 4.1   High-level value stream map for an outpatient surgery patient, simplified view. OR, operating room; PACU, postanesthesia care unit.

in the short term due to cost, timing, or technology constraints. But, those short-term constraints should not be used as excuses for not improving.

The Future-State Maps

Drawing the current-state VSM is just a starting point. The maps themselves are not useful unless we, as an organization, use them to prioritize or drive improvements. In the example VSM, the hospital cross-trained the people who made patient contact calls so that everything could be handled in a single interaction—reducing the total number of calls, the duplicative information, and the missed calls that led to missing information.

After identifying improvements, the team also creates a future-state VSM that illustrates how the process should work or could work if redesigned. Typically, a future-state VSM shows a dramatically smaller number of process steps (as we simplify the process), less complexity in the information flows, and shorter waiting times between steps (as we improve flow). Teams sometimes create two versions of the future-state VSM—an ideal state (looking at the long term and how things should work) and a practical state (what short-term improvements can be made).

It is tempting for value stream mapping facilitators to create electronic VSMs using standard office software or specialized software created specifically for VSM purposes. As with many things, just because you can draw a map electronically does not mean that you should. Many teams prefer to create maps in a very analog way, using sticky notes on large pieces of butcher paper. This allows a group to create a map in a far more collaborative way compared to one person controlling the mouse and keyboard. Instead of creating the waste of overprocessing or redrawing the completed manual maps in software, consider the use of digital photos that can be easily shared with those who cannot come visit the area where the map was drawn. Even with a photo or digital map, insist that your leaders "go and see" by visiting the *gemba* instead of staying at their computer.

Breaking Down Silos and Reducing Suboptimization

One Lean transformation challenge is to reconcile our vertical departmental organization structures with the horizontal flow of a patient's treatment, as shown in Figure 4.2. While this vertical organization structure makes sense for many reasons (such as the development of specialized skills and for employee career paths), this functional silo structure leads to many dysfunctions. Often, employees only know people or processes in their own department, which contributes to poor cooperation across departmental boundaries and delays for patients at the handoff points between departments. In one hospital, for example, key members of the laboratory staff had never visited the ED, a primary customer of lab results located only 50 feet down the corridor. Many hospitals suffer from poor communication between the lab and the ED, with most communication coming in the form of the ED calling the lab to ask (or sometimes yell) about delayed test results. This generally is not a collaborative, problem-solving form of communication. Through

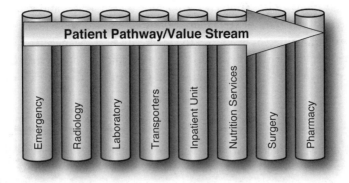

Figure 4.2 Illustration of vertical department silos and horizontal patient flow through a hospital.

Lean efforts, we want to increase the collaboration and teamwork across department boundaries, as cross-functional VSM or project teams can help.

To treat patients more effectively, we need to start looking at end-to-end processes (the value streams) rather than just improving our isolated departments. Making isolated improvements within our own departmental boundaries runs the risk of suboptimization that helps the individual department but harms the overall system.

For example, a laboratory might decide, for the sake of cost and efficiency, to only run a certain specialized test two times per week, on Tuesdays and Thursdays. This local efficiency, however, might lead to delays in patient care or delays in discharging a patient, a delay that might cost the hospital far more (due to the increased length of stay) than was saved in lower laboratory staffing levels or the decreased cost of running larger test batches. Hospital leadership plays an important role in ensuring that the overall system is optimized and that individual departments are not punished, through their metrics and incentives, for actions or policies that help improve the overall system. The best solution for the hospital might be to increase lab staffing (or better yet, eliminate waste to free up time) so they can run the test more frequently.

Another hospital discovered, through the structured analysis of its own value stream, that the orthopedics department only performed trauma surgery two days a week. Considering that patients suffer trauma every day of the week, it was difficult for the hospital to justify how it was patient centered to perform two procedures on a patient—one to stabilize the patient until the second and final procedure could be done on one of the two scheduled days.

Observing the Process

In the course of value stream mapping, *kaizen* events, or other less-structured Lean activities, an important fundamental skill is structured process observation. By *structured*, we mean more than just walking through a department or watching without a particular aim or goal.

To identify waste and improvements, firsthand observation is critical. There are two lenses through which we can observe the process and work. First is what we generically call the "activity of the product." Here, we ask what is happening (or, more often, not happening) to the product (or patient) at every step in the value stream. Second, we can view the process with the perspective of nurses, technologists, pharmacists, or others, something we generically call the "activity of the employee."

This direct observation can be extremely eye opening for employees and managers. Employees are often too mired in the details of their daily work to see waste, so stepping back and observing the process, watching different people do the work, can help. Managers, physicians, or other outsiders often have not had firsthand visibility of the problems that others struggle with every day because they are too focused on their own individual work or because they are stuck in meetings all day.

In some cases, managers who were shown summaries of the waste their employees had directly observed responded by saying, "I don't believe you." Managers often do not want to believe that lab specimens sit for hours between batched steps or that employees are spending so much time on inspection and rework. We often have an idealized view of what we think is happening that does not line up with reality. Those skeptical managers saw reality when their own direct observation confirmed what had been reported to them.

Activity of the Product

The product in a process can be a patient, an order, or a specimen, among other things. When we are observing through the lens of the product, we have to choose starting and ending points for the observation, which will vary based on the type of problem we are looking to solve. Depending on the value stream we are following, we might choose to start and end our observation at different points, as shown in Table 4.1. Observers will follow and directly observe the patient through that part of the value stream.

We may limit the scope of an analysis because the total overall time frame might be too long to observe from beginning to end. If a patient is arriving for a scheduled procedure that will result in a planned inpatient stay, we might stop the observation at the point when the patient is physically in the hospital room. On the outbound side of the stay, we might do a different analysis, this time of the discharge process (with the same patient or a different set of patients). It is sometimes possible to piece together separate independent analyses to paint a picture of the entire door-to-door journey for a representative patient.

In any of these studies, we are looking for times when value-added work is being performed, times when non-value-added work is being performed, and times when the patient is just waiting (an example of non-value-added, pure waste). Some short waiting time might be required in even the best processes; any waiting is consciously designed into the process for the sake of the overall value stream flow, but our goal is to minimize this waiting.

When observing, we track the start and stop times of new events. This can be facilitated with a range of tools, from simple to complex, including

- Digital watch and notepad
- Digital camera with time/date stamp and notepad
- Video camera with time/date stamp
- Specialized software for mobile devices

Table 4.1   Possible Start and End Points for Analysis of the Activity of the Product

Product/Value Stream	Possible Starting Points	Possible Ending Points
Laboratory testing	MD giving stat order	Arrival at laboratory
	Collection of specimen	Start of testing
	Arrival at laboratory	Release of test result
Pharmacy medications	Signal for replenishment is given	Medication sent to unit
	Order written by MD	Medication delivered to unit for storage
		Medication administered to patient
Pathology	First call to schedule biopsy procedure	Specimen delivered to histology
	Specimen taken from patient	Slide delivered to pathologist for reading
		Pathologist report sent to physician
Information systems (IS) call center support	Initial problem call to IS	Resolution of IS issue

Cameras, while a useful tool for capturing the context and timing of events, may make patients uncomfortable when there is direct patient observation. Use your own judgment and consider hospital policies and releases that might be required. Video may be more appropriate for use in nonpatient areas. Having an observer scribbling notes down may lose some detail, compared to taping, but any method of direct observation will typically uncover many types of waste and opportunities for improvement.

The same methodology and tools can be applied when observing nonpatient products through a process. We also need to choose starting and stopping points, depending on what process we are observing and our improvement goals, as shown in Table 4.2.

The department or hospital might, but not always, have data on turnaround times or process flow times from start to finish. These data might be collected automatically through computer system event logs or bar code scans. For example, a lab might generate turnaround time data on every single test result by comparing the time when the patient's wristband bar code was scanned until the logged time when the result is released to the hospital's information system. These data do not give us direct insight into how that time breaks down into value-added and non-value-added components. We need direct observation to identify waste, waiting time, and other problems that can be fixed with Lean.

Activity of the product analysis is helpful because it helps us focus on the waste (the waiting time) in the process. Traditional process improvement often focuses on doing the value-added work in a faster or more efficient way. In the Lean approach, we first focus on the waste since there can be a greater, and more realistic, opportunity to reduce large portions of the waiting time instead of trying to reduce the value-added time. If 90% of the total value stream time is waiting,

Table 4.2 Possible Start and End Points for Patient Flow Analysis

Patient Pathway/Value Stream	Possible Starting Points	Possible Ending Points
Emergency department	Phone call made for ambulance	ED discharge
	Arrival at door	Start of cath lab procedure
		Moved into room
		Discharge from inpatient care
Outpatient surgery	Arrival at door	Start of procedure
	First call for scheduling procedure	Start of postanesthesia care unit (PACU)
	First referral from general practitioner	Discharge
Outpatient cancer treatment	Arrival at door	Start of treatment
		Discharge
Scheduled inpatient surgery	Arrival at door	Start of procedure
	First call for scheduling procedure	Start of PACU
	First referral from general practitioner	Movement into room
		Discharge
Patient discharge process	MD writing discharge order	Patient ready to leave
		Patient physically out door
		Room physically ready for next patient
Radiology	Order for procedure	Start of procedure
	Arrival at outpatient center	End of procedure
	Start of procedure	Report verified

we are better off reducing that by half, as opposed to doing the value-added activity twice as quickly, if that were even possible.

Activity of the Product—Laboratory

The product flow in a value stream can be illustrated by a timeline that shows elapsed time and where the value-added and non-value-added time occurs. In the example in Figure 4.3, a team

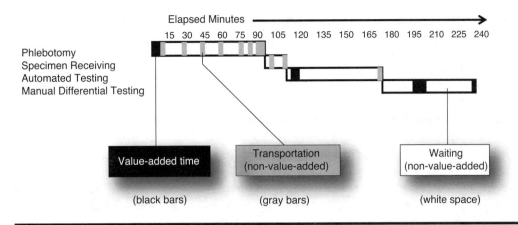

Figure 4.3 **Product flow timeline illustration for a tube of blood, from phlebotomy draw until the result is ready for the ordering physician to view.**

followed a tube of blood from the time the specimen was collected by a phlebotomist until the test result was released. The lab might have already had reports that would show average turnaround times, but this example shows one particular case for which the time was about 230 minutes, which was a fairly representative result.

After the phlebotomist drew the blood (the first value-added activity), the specimen was not put on the automated test instrument (the second value-added activity) until over an hour later. The final value-added activity was completed after about three hours (a technologist reading a slide for cell counts), and there was a further delay until the result was entered and verified in the information system (the final value-added activity). All of the other time was waste, including 87% of the time that was spent waiting—a tube of blood on the phlebotomist cart, sitting in a rack in the lab, or a printout sitting on a printer waiting to be verified.

Examples like those illustrate the potential for improving performance by eliminating the delays and "white space" in between the value-added steps. Finding faster ways to draw blood or purchasing faster test equipment would not yield the benefits of reducing waiting time, as we discuss more in Chapter 9 in our discussion on flow.

Activity of the Employee

The same direct observation method can be applied to the employees in a process. When working on a process or a value stream, we can choose a variety of roles to observe. Observers follow the employee as the employee conducts normal work, looking for waste in the process and problems the employee encounters.

Videotape is particularly helpful when observing employees; we might not have the same privacy restrictions or concerns we would have with patients, depending on the setting. Videotaping is helpful for a number of reasons:

- It accurately captures employee activities, movement, and timing.
- It captures walking patterns and distances to be documented.
- Observers can review and replay the videotape to capture detailed observations.

■ An observed employee can watch the tape to see the waste in the process and give suggestions for improvements.

Observing employees (and being observed) can be uncomfortable, even if handled with sensitivity. Care must be exercised so the activity of the employee observation is done with the respect for people principle in mind. Leaders must communicate to their employees, in advance, that observation is going to be done. Employees need to understand that observers are looking for waste and delays in the process and problems that interfere with employees doing their value-added work. The observation is not done to catch employees doing something wrong or to see who is the fastest employee. Employees will typically be on their best behavior, knowing they are being observed, but errors may occur as a result of nervousness. There is also the risk that observers see an ideal version of the process as opposed to seeing shortcuts or other problems with the way work is normally done.

Observers should strive to build rapport with the employee and allow the employee to concentrate on performing high-quality work. If the observer sees an error or mistake being made that would have an impact on a patient, the observer has a responsibility to help the employee (and patient) by saying something about the error. Employees who have done the actual work should conduct the employee observations, making it a peer-to-peer interaction. If outsiders or supervisors do the observation, employees might be more nervous about negative outcomes, or clinicians might be understandably upset if engineering interns are timing how long they are in the restroom.[6] Staff members at any level deserve to be involved as a partner in this observation and improvement—to be a scientist, not merely a subject.[7]

In addition, having coworkers observe work will lead to more accurate analysis and identification of waste. They are also more likely to know when observed employees are using methods that are inconsistent with others or standard practices. This realization serves as the first step in determining what the best work method should be. The observation and analysis can also uncover activities that those in certain roles should not be doing. For example, if a pharmacist is doing manual work (such as entering medication orders into the computer system) that a pharmacy technician could be doing at a lower cost, we might change the roles and responsibilities to better match tasks with skill levels.

Looking at walking patterns can help identify opportunities for layout improvements. Point-to-point diagrams (often called spaghetti diagrams because they look like you threw a handful of cooked spaghetti on the page) can help identify equipment and supplies that can be moved, based on how people actually work. Walking is not the only waste that can be identified through observation. Observers can see rework or workarounds that are normally hidden to supervisors and higher managers.

During many Lean projects, employees get an opportunity to watch video of themselves or their colleagues doing their daily work. Employees often say, "I never knew I did that!" In one example, three people from the same department, with seniority of 1, 7, and 20 years, all watched video of someone else doing the work, and they each realized they did it different ways. They had been working together for years but until that moment had never realized how different their methods were. The team was also able to see the impact the variation had on the timing or the outcome of the process. Observation also allows professionals who are normally busy in their own silos of work to see and appreciate the work that others do as part of a team.

Activity of the Employee—Nursing

One hospital and its outpatient cancer treatment center undertook an assessment to identify opportunities for improvements. The staff knew they spent too much time walking and searching for supplies, but the formal activity of the employee activity uncovered the full extent of the waste.

The chemotherapy area had nurses whose jobs and tasks included

- Taking patients to their chair or bed and prepping them for treatment
- Getting medications and starting injections and drips
- Responding to patient requests for pain, comfort, or other needs
- Answering questions about the treatment and process for patients and families
- Stopping the treatment and preparing the patient to go home

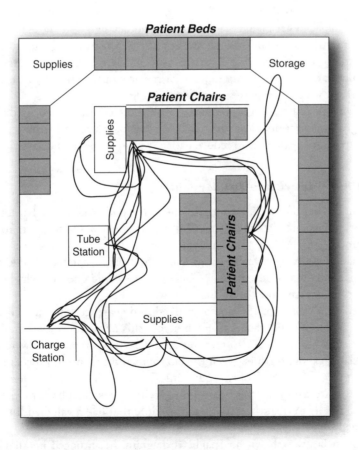

Figure 4.4   Walking pattern of one nurse in a chemotherapy center.

One observed nurse walked 1,825 feet in 50 minutes, a pace of more than four miles per day. The spaghetti diagram of the walking is shown in Figure 4.4. For the observed time period, 32% of the nurse's time was spent walking. Only 30% of the time was spent on value-added activities, which were defined loosely as any time with direct patient contact.

As we often do with Lean, our first response should be to ask why the nurse has to walk so far. Some of the walking is driven by the assignment of patients to chairs. Chemotherapy nurses would prefer that all of their patients be located together, but this is not always practical. When patients arrive they tend to get whatever chair is available and any nurse who happens to be available. If a patient requests a certain nurse, the only available chair might be far away from that nurse's other patients.

More walking is caused by the location of other frequently visited areas, including supply closets and the tube station where medications are delivered from the pharmacy. This can all be challenged and questioned. Each patient chair and bed had a supply cart that was supposed to have standard supplies. The carts were not standardized, however, meaning nurses sometimes had to walk to the main supply room when supplies were not in a cart. Some items on the carts were not restocked properly, so drawers or slots were empty, necessitating a walk to a different supply cart or to the supply closet. When we directly observe a nurse walking from cart to cart, searching for hard-to-find supplies, that clearly identifies a problem that can be fixed. Before Lean, the nurses might consider that walking and searching to be part of their normal daily work rather than viewing it as non-value-added activity that can be fixed. The nurse was seen frequently walking to a storage cabinet to get blankets for patients, another sign that those blankets should be stored in more convenient locations throughout the center. Other walking leads to questions about what nurses should be doing and what assistants or technicians should do. Nurses might not be the best ones to walk around collecting supplies or medications, as this distracts them from the value-added work for which they have specialized training.

After identifying the waste, part of the department's Lean efforts were focused on standardization and improved organization, all in the name of reducing waste and freeing nurse time. This was in addition to separate attempts to reduce patient waiting times and delays.

Activity of the Employee—Primary Care

On four different days of the week, a young hardworking podiatrist worked at four rural clinics that were part of an integrated health system. One day, a patient was in his exam room for a quick minor toenail procedure. The doctor left the exam room and the patient to gather his supplies and instruments, including a scalpel, freeze spray, gauze, and other material. Thinking back to the Gilbreths' lessons from 1915, as discussed in Chapter 1, one could question why he was having to use his valuable time in such a non-value-adding way.

As illustrated in Figure 4.5, the doctor walked and searched—he hunted and gathered, as some would say. He walked back and forth across this clinic for a total of about 670 feet, delaying the patient's care for about 10 minutes (and delaying patients who were in the waiting room). He walked back and forth between the lab room and the minor procedures room, muttering a bit about forgetting which of the four clinics stored supplies in what location; there was a clear lack of standardization that hurt his productivity. He walked back to his office, back to the lab, and then finally to treat the patient, a procedure that had a value-adding time of about 30 seconds perhaps.

When the physician was shown his spaghetti diagram, he shrugged his shoulders and said calmly, "Well, that's how it has always been." The team in the clinic realized things could be better. Before the doctor arrived the next week, the staff took an empty unused crash cart and

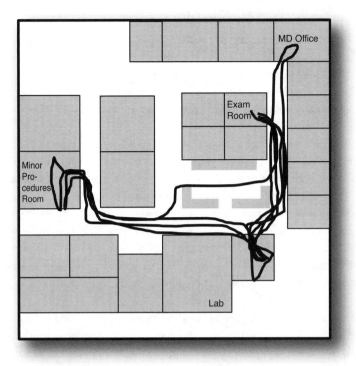

Figure 4.5 Walking pattern of a podiatrist in a primary care clinic prepping for one patient procedure.

gathered all of the supplies that the podiatrist normally used (or their best first attempt at this). They created a checklist that could be used to restock the cart the evening before the doctor was in the clinic. The cart was rolled to the room where the physician worked that next time.

The physician loved the cart, making just a few small suggestions to tweak what was in the cart and where. The waste in his daily work had been hidden because it was "normal," and the clinic was not accustomed to looking at their work as a process. "The way it has always been" turned into a new and improved process that made the physician very happy, wasting less of his time and preventing delays for patients. The podiatrist's next question was to ask how quickly the other three clinics could put together the same standardized cart and checklist so he could be equally efficient all four days of the week.

In this same clinic, a physician assistant (PA) went into an exam room. She walked out of the room to find a supply that she need for the exam. She was in and out of the room five times within the span of a few minutes because the room had not been stocked properly, a problem that is addressed in Chapter 6. On each successive trip into the room, the PA had been putting on a fresh pair of gloves. After the last trip, she came out of the room and sighed, saying that she had to go and get a new box of gloves for the room because she had used them all up with her trips in and out of the room.

Activity of the Employee—Perioperative Services

In one hospital's perioperative services department, technicians and nurses built case carts that were later rolled into an operating room for surgery. These employees were observed to identify waste and excess walking, identifying process improvements for building carts more efficiently. In two observed cases, a technician and a nurse walked more than 1,000 feet to build each of their carts. In the two cart builds, walking made up 44% of the technician's time and 36% of the nurse's time.

A spaghetti diagram representative of the case cart builds can be seen in Figure 4.6. Each star represents a location where the technician walked to get an item for the case cart.

In this case, some of the walking was caused by needed items not being stored in the case cart prep room. The technician had to walk to an operating room to get an item from a storage cabinet (an item that would then have to be transported back into an operating room). The Lean improvement team could investigate and determine which supplies should be stored in the case cart area and which could be left off carts because they were part of the standard operating room inventory. There were also frequent trips to the copier to copy the surgeon's case card, which specified what went on the cart. This walking could be reduced by putting a small copier in the case cart area.

Within the case cart room itself, the layout and organization of supplies on the shelves led to the walking. The team identified that high-volume supplies and items were scattered throughout the case cart room. Because the cart room was congested with more than a dozen empty, partially, or fully completed carts, employees had little room to work and could not move the cart to the shelves. This was also a waste of overproduction issue, where the carts were sometimes built up

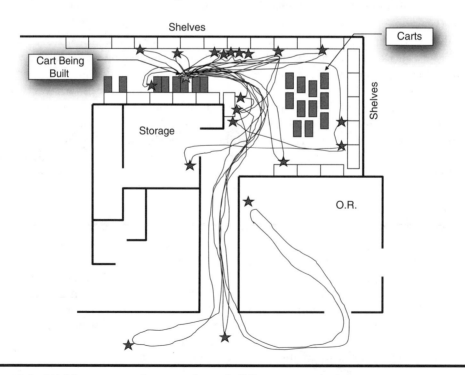

Figure 4.6 Walking pattern of one employee building one surgical case cart.

to 24 hours before a planned procedure, partially to leave time for multiple cart inspections (the waste of defects). The overproduction could have been reduced by building the carts closer to the time of the procedure, helping prevent the need to tear down carts after a procedure was canceled.

Direct observation and study of the existing work can lead to process improvements that can help a hospital avoid expensive capital improvements. Akron Children's Hospital spent $20,000 to overhaul their instrument sterilization process, allowing them to avoid a $3.5 million capital expansion project. Other patient flow improvements reduced the average time spent waiting for nonemergent magnetic resonance imaging exams from 25 days to less than 2 days.[8]

Conclusion

To improve our hospitals, there is no substitute for direct observation. Leaders need to see the waste that their employees and physicians have to deal with on a daily basis. We need to see what the patient experiences to help identify causes of delay, rework, and other waste. Data may show that product flows through the laboratory, pharmacy, or other support departments are on par with benchmarks, but direct observation will show the amount of waste and the opportunity for further improvement. With Lean, our goal is not to be better than our peers, but rather to be as good as we can be, aiming for the goal of a perfect, waste-free process.

Lean Lessons

- Managers have to go and see where the work is actually done, as observation can help identify waste.
- It is not enough for each department to be great; the pieces have to work together as a whole (the value stream).
- VSMs must be used to drive improvement; documenting the current state is not enough.
- It is important to observe products (including patients) and employees in the process.
- Walking and wasted motion are due to poor physical layouts and system design, not individuals.

Points for Group Discussion

- How can we avoid having people take waste identification personally?
- Why must we observe processes firsthand to identify waste?
- Why are we sometimes surprised by what we see when observing the process?
- Can you think of an example where part of the entire value stream was suboptimized? Why did that happen? What can be done about that?
- Why do products and patients spend so much time waiting in the value stream?

- Pick a process you are accountable for. Could you sit down right now and diagram it for one of your customers?
- What keeps nurses away from the bedside?

Notes

1. May, Matthew, *The Elegant Solution: Toyota's Formula for Mastering Innovation* (New York: Free Press, 2006), 72.
2. CC-M Productions, "The Deming Library: A Study in Continual Improvement, Parts 1 and 2 Discussion Guide," http://forecast.umkc.edu/ftppub/ba541/DEMINGLIBRARY/DLVol26-27.PDF (accessed April 8, 2011).
3. Womack, James P., and Daniel T. Jones, *Lean Thinking* (New York: Free Press, 2003), 19.
4. Rother, Mike, and John Shook, *Learning to See* (Brookline, MA: Lean Enterprise Institute, 2003), introduction.
5. Jimmerson, Cindy, *Value Stream Mapping for Healthcare Made Easy* (New York, NY: Productivity Press, 2010), 19,
6. Kim, CS, W. Lovejoy, et al, "Hospitalist Time Usage and Cyclicality: Opportunities to Improve Efficiency," *Journal of Hospital Medicine*, Jul–Aug 2010, 5, no. 6: 329–34.
7. Graban, Mark, and Amit Prachand, "Hospitalists: Lean Leaders for Hospitals," *Journal of Hospital Medicine*, Jul–Aug 2010, 5, no. 6: 317–19.
8. Weed, Julie, "Factory Efficiency Comes to the Hospital," *New York Times*, July 10, 2010, http://www.nytimes.com/2010/07/11/business/11seattle.html, (accessed April 8, 2011).

Chapter 5

Standardized Work as a Foundation of Lean

The Need for Standardized Work

In hospitals, even with all of the standard operating procedures (SOPs), binders, and policies, it is far too easy to find different people doing the same work in different ways, sometimes harming patients as a result. For example, teams working in operating room settings often discover there are no standardized methods for presurgical procedures, leading to higher preventable infection rates. Individuals should not be blamed for this. Instead, the hospital and its leaders need to look at the environment that has been created and the culture that has allowed different work methods to develop.

Job instructions and policies are often communicated informally in hospital settings. Communication about process changes is often ineffective when it happens through informal channels, including posted signs and verbal handoff communications. A typical nursing unit might have dozens of signs and postings, communicating new policies on hand hygiene, changes to the information system, and new practices involving medications. The visual noise can be overwhelming, as signs are posted on top of notices, in front of reminders. It is too easy for employees to miss or tune out the cacophony of signs. Hospitals are dynamic environments that operate with many people rotating in and out of jobs, 24 hours a day, 7 days a week. We need a formalized method for managing and improving the way we do our work and how those methods are communicated. We can better support patient care and our employees with a standardized work system based on Lean practices.

The Toyota House Metaphor

One common illustration of the Toyota Production System is the house model, adapted just slightly for hospitals. As with other Lean illustrations, it begins with people at its core, as shown in one version of the house in Figure 5.1. The diagram representing the "Park Nicollet System of Care"

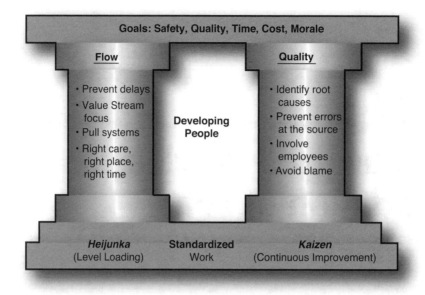

Figure 5.1 The Lean house.

is an example of how this house is often customized for the particular needs of an organization, shown in Figure 5.2.[1]

In this chapter, we discuss the three foundations of Lean and the two "equally important" pillars that help create the structure for Lean: improved quality and improved flow.[2]

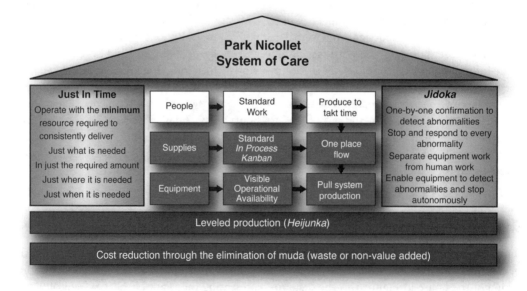

Figure 5.2 The Park Nicollet System of Care. Copyright 1999–2011 John Black and Associates LLC—Used with permission by Park Nicollet Health Services and Mark Graban.

Overview of the Lean Foundations

The foundation of the Lean house consists of three core principles. Standardized work is the method for developing best practices and methods in the hospital. *Heijunka* is a Japanese word for "level loading" workloads or demand for services, smoothing the workflow and patient flow throughout the hospital, as discussed in Chapter 9. *Kaizen* is another Japanese word that can be translated as "continuous improvement," as discussed in Chapter 10.

All three of these concepts are interconnected and necessary for a Lean system to thrive. Standardized work without *kaizen* would be a stagnant workplace that never improved. *Kaizen* without a basis of standardized work might be a chaotic environment where people randomly try new methods that do not necessarily improve the overall system. Standardized work without *heijunka* means employees will still be stressed, and patients will suffer long waiting times. Standardized work, *heijunka*, and *kaizen* all work together to support the concepts of eliminating waste and respecting people.

Lean Foundations: Standardized Work

Standardized work starts with a simple premise: People should analyze their work and define the way that best meets the needs of all stakeholders. Many of the problems in hospitals can be traced back to a root cause that involves the lack of standardization. For example, one commonly occurring preventable patient injury is pressure ulcers, or bedsores. To avoid these, one method requires staff to reposition at-risk patients every 2 hours. Many hospitals struggle with making sure this is done in the proper way and at the proper frequency. Instead of responding to this challenge by blaming our employees and exhorting them to do better (or by posting more signs), we need to instead look at a method for documenting standardized work and managing the work to ensure it is followed consistently. The bedsores example is revisited in this chapter.

The idea of standardized work is not new. Henry Ford, whose words had a great influence on Toyota, wrote, "Our own attitude is that we are charged with discovering the best way of doing everything."[3] Toyota helped extend this discovery into more of an ongoing process, through *kaizen*.

The concept of standardized work is certainly not new within hospitals or medicine, tracing back to the industrial engineers Frank and Lillian Gilbreth and their research in the early 1900s. Their observations showed that a surgeon spent more time searching for instruments in the operating room than actually performing the operation. The Gilbreths recommended that trays be better organized and that a "surgical caddy" should hand the instruments to the surgeon as needed.[4] But, change often comes slowly in healthcare, as these new ideas were not accepted by the American Medical Association until 1930—having been proposed by the Gilbreths in 1914.

Definition of Standardized Work

So, what is *standardized work*? One definition might be *the current one best way to safely complete an activity with the proper outcome and the highest quality, using the fewest possible resources.* We can break this definition down into its component words and phrases.

"Current"

Today's standardized work is merely the best method currently defined. A standard is not meant to be permanent or inflexible, as SOPs and binders tend to be. Standardized work can (and must) be improved on as the people doing the work have ideas for new and improved methods.

Toyota called standardized work "the basis for *kaizen*."[5] Without a standard, you cannot have sustainable improvement. If employees do things in different ways, an improvement idea from one employee might either add to the variation in the current system or get lost because we do not have a standard method for transferring that new idea to other employees.

Do not confuse "current" as meaning that we simply need to document the way work is currently done. In the process of developing standardized work, employees must look for waste and challenge all aspects of how work is currently done. Far too often, traditional documentation just captures all of the waste in the current method, without stopping to make improvements, or *kaizen*.

"Proper Outcome and the Highest Quality"

A Toyota guidebook began explaining standardized work by starting with the end goal in mind, saying, "Standardized Work is a tool for maintaining productivity, quality, and safety at high levels."[6] Hospitals must keep this in mind and not standardize for the sake of standardizing. There are a countless number of tasks and procedures that our employees face every day. Trying to standardize all of our methods would seem like an overwhelming challenge. Hospitals must ensure that their standardized work benefits the patients, the employees, the physicians, and the hospital itself. We must prioritize our improvement and standardization activity so our initial efforts can have the largest impact on all of our stakeholders. We might ask, for example, "Does standardizing this method improve quality?"

Quality is continually emphasized as a core Lean principle, and our standardized work should reflect that. Standardized work is not an approach that emphasizes speed over quality. Our standardized work documentation must reflect the amount of time required to do the work in the proper way to avoid overburdening employees or inadvertently pressuring them to cut corners. This is one example of how standardized work can benefit employees and embodies the respect for the people aspect of Lean.

Standardizing methods that have an impact on patient safety is a great place to start. These are areas in which hospitals have typically already made an effort at standardizing, including

- Hand washing and hygiene
- Preparation steps for cardiac surgery
- Labeling of patient specimens
- Medication administration processes
- Communication with patient on outpatient or primary care appointment
- Proper cleaning and disinfection of patient rooms

Keep in mind that having a written procedure in place does not mean that a standardized method is always going to be followed. It is widely reported that hand-washing policy compliance is low in hospitals, with few studies or estimates showing at least 50% compliance.[7] Standardizing the best method for cleaning an operating room can reduce rates of hospital-acquired infections, as one study found that employees overlooked more than half the objects that should have been disinfected.[8] The root cause of the problem could have been a poorly defined standard, or it could have been a case of managers not checking to see if the standard was being followed. The idea of a standardized work system and leadership's role in overseeing standards are discussed later in this chapter.

"To Safely Complete"

"To safely complete" further emphasizes the focus on outcomes and benefits from standardized work. As we discussed with quality, standardized work does not encourage speed or efficiency over safety. Safety practices, for both patients and employees, should be considered nonnegotiable aspects of our standardized work practices. The old adage comes to mind that says: "You can have it quick, correct, or cheap—pick two out of three, but you can't have them all." In this case, we are striving to find a method that achieves all of the objectives in the best way we know. So, it is possible to have good, faster, and cost-effective service at the same time—not by cutting corners, but by taking out waste.

"One Best Way"

For different types of work, is there truly "one best way"? It is important to ensure that the proper level of detail and specificity is documented in our standardized work. When medical technologists in the microbiology lab, for example, inoculate and streak patient specimens onto petri dish media, there might be variation in how that work is done. Certain details, such as the exact pattern of streaking the specimen across the plate, might make a big difference in how the culture grows and the resulting medical decisions. *Toyota Talent* refers to this as work of "critical importance"— the 20% of tasks for which work must be highly consistent.[9] The standardized work documentation might be detailed for this method, with pictures and examples used for initial training and continual refreshers on how the work should be done.

On the other hand, there might be details of the work that do not have an impact on safety, quality, or outcomes. Does it matter which hand a technologist uses to streak the plate? Probably not, so our standardized work documentation would not be that specific. Left-handed techs might disregard an overly specific standardized work method as an unjust standard. This creates an environment in which, unfortunately, individual employees feel like they are given choices over which standards to follow, contributing to inconsistent quality and outcomes. Standardized work methods cannot be considered optional by employees or managers if the methods truly have an impact on patient outcomes.

Other work tasks and methods might not require such detailed specification in the method. It would be a waste of resources to try to standardize every possible task. For some activities, there is room for some variation in the way the work is done (what *Toyota Talent* called the important tasks), and there might be other activities (the low-importance tasks) for which varying methods are not likely to have any impact on the quality or outcomes of the process.

At the outpatient clinic at one children's hospital, it was easy for staff to blame parents for their late arrival or for having children who violated orders for nothing by mouth (NPO) orders. When a team looked deeply into the process, the team learned that each person in the scheduling office had a unique way of communicating to parents in the reminder call. Some explained that "no clear liquids" also meant that milk was forbidden, but others did not. Some staff were careful to explain that the hospital and the clinic were two different locations, to avoid mix-ups. The staff standardized their calls to parents, emphasizing certain key points in a consistent way, without having every single word scripted. Late patients and NPO violations dropped dramatically. It was not a matter of "bad parents"—it was "bad process."

"Fewest Possible Resources"

While safety and quality are nonnegotiable priorities in the Lean mindset, we are also concerned and making the best use of our resources: minimizing waste. "Resources" include our people and their time, supplies, equipment, physical space, anything that costs money. We should also consider resources that do not directly cost the hospital anything, such as the patient's time. Many attempts at productivity make minimizing resources the primary goal. Some managers have traditionally tried to limit resources, hoping that people will, of necessity, figure out a better way to do their work. The direct labor cost may drop in the short term, but quality becomes worse if people do not have enough time or people available to do high-quality work in that system. This often leads to a cycle of discouragement, making improvement even less likely to occur.

That is why in the Lean approach we first improve quality and productivity, only then taking an opportunity to reduce head count. Lean leaders keep in mind the idea that we respect people and retrain or redeploy them to do other work rather than laying them off.

Standardized, Not Identical

It is often tempting to say *standard* instead of *standardized*, but there is a distinction between the two words and concepts. *Standard* can sound like an absolute, a method with zero variation or zero flexibility. It starts sounding like the word *identical*, which makes employees concerned that they are being turned into robots. Most employees—not just in healthcare—value their ability to use judgment to make decisions on the job. There is a balance to be struck somewhere between complete chaos, with everybody doing things differently, and mindless conformity. Employees who are constantly thinking through "How should I do this?" or "What do I do next?" may find themselves drained and worn out mentally by the end of the day. Standardized work is the plan that frees us from having to make hundreds of small decisions throughout our day, thus freeing brain capacity and reserving energy to deal with the smaller number of more important decisions that arise.

Bill Marriott, CEO of Marriott Hotels, explained the company is not trying to turn employees into robots through the company's SOPs. Standardization has long been a part of the Marriott culture and management system. Marriott explained: "Mindless conformity and the thoughtful setting of standards should never be confused. What solid SOPs do is nip common problems in the bud so that staff can focus instead on solving uncommon problems."[10] These ideas are very compatible with the Lean philosophy.

If Toyota wanted its employees to be mindless robots, it seems likely Toyota would call its system identical work instead of standardized work. The *-ized* in *standardized* implies that some effort is made toward total standardization, but the effort often stops before 100% standardization is achieved. One might wonder if 100% standardization is even possible in any environment, yet alone in complex hospital settings.

Written by Those Who Do the Work

Standardized work is not a command-and-control approach that is dictated from managers or experts to their employees. A key difference with standardized work, compared to other process documentation models, is that Lean documents are written by the people who do the work. Toyota's Taiichi Ohno wrote, "Standards should not be forced down from above but rather set by the production workers themselves."[11] The assumption is that the employees know the work best and are in a better position to write accurate and effective documentation.

While the employees are the experts on the current methods, the process of writing standardized work must force a reevaluation of how things are done, rather than just documenting the current method. Before writing standardized work documents, teams spend time observing, videotaping, and examining their current methods in detail, as described in Chapter 4. Having to talk through and write down methods, with coworkers, can lead to waste reduction, as Frank Gilbreth wrote about hospitals in 1914: "You will be surprised what improvements will suggest themselves to you as a result of seeing in cold ink exactly what you are doing now in your department."[12] Initial improvements will come from this documentation effort, with more improvements, or *kaizen*, to follow over time.

In a large department setting, it might not be practical to have everybody directly involved in the writing of the documents. A smaller group, such as a Lean project team, can write documents that are considered initial drafts. The entire department can review these drafts so that everybody has a chance to give input.

A major challenge with standardized work is getting everybody to agree on a standardized approach, particularly when people have been left to their own approaches in the past. It is not a cure-all, but employees are more likely to accept standardized work (and to follow it) if they have had the opportunity to provide input.

The radiology department at one hospital inadvertently learned the value of standardized work as they implemented Lean. Different people, including technicians, nurses, assistants, and radiologists, were formed into teams on different days, depending on the scheduling rotation. One particular combination had worked together, the exact same people every day, for about two weeks straight. "Things were working really well. We all knew exactly who was doing what and everything went smoothly," said one technician, showing pride in their efficiency (and their ability to get home on time).

Things worked well until the schedule changed, and the team was broken up. Employees now complained that since "everybody does things differently," the new combination would not be as productive as that previous group. The employees started to ask why that had to be. With proper standardized work in place, the department expected to have that same productive feeling every day, regardless of who was working on the team, since each team would not have to reinvent its own methods and team roles.

Considering How Long Tasks Take

Hospitals already have process documentation and SOPs, listing steps for completing many work tasks. Standardized work documents also show the expected duration for tasks or activities. On a Toyota assembly line, it would be unfair to employees, as well as being bad for flow and quality, to give employees more work than can be done in their repetitive job cycles.

Granted, most hospital jobs are not repetitive in nature, like assembly line jobs, but the same general principle should hold true. It should apply from the standpoint of not expecting 10 hours of work content to be done in an 8-hour shift. It should also apply within the day, such as not expecting employees to do two tasks at the same time or not overburdening an employee during a peak hour in the day.

With the variability found in hospital work, determining precise workloads can be difficult. Departments should do their best to estimate workloads, trying to balance work evenly across employees. Better yet, a department can draft standardized work that allows for employees to be cross-trained and to help each other as workloads demand. A hospital department is unlikely to have a script that is followed as precisely as an assembly line job that repeats every 60 seconds. The standardized work document can be considered a plan, more than a script.

Staffing Based on Data

In many hospital settings, staffing levels are set by benchmarking data, rules of thumb, habit, or financial constraints. Ideally, staffing levels should be based on actual workloads, driven by patient demand, and the standardized work that suggests the pace at which people can work without jeopardizing quality or safety.

Takt is a German word that should be familiar to readers who are musicians as it signifies a pace or tempo, as in a piece of music. *Takt* is a Lean term for expressing the pace of customer demand for a value stream or a process. An auto assembly factory might have a *takt* of 50 seconds, meaning a customer buys a car every 50 seconds during the hours the factory is running. *Takt* is calculated as the number of available working hours (or minutes or seconds) divided by the customer demand.

In healthcare settings, applications of *takt* can be difficult to find or can be more complex than in manufacturing. Instead of having a level-loaded production rate for a month, based on average *takt*, a hospital must do work in response to varying patient demand, as hospitals cannot build a parking lot full of cars to sell later. That said, there are some cases for which *takt* is useful in understanding our workload to drive staffing decisions.

For example, a hospital laboratory might need to draw 360 patient specimens in a 4-hour window each morning. *Takt* is then 14,400 seconds divided by 360 specimens, or 40 seconds per specimen. As we develop standardized work (having eliminated waste from the process), we might learn that it takes a phlebotomist (at worst) 8 minutes to properly draw a specimen and then walk to the next patient. One person drawing a specimen every 480 seconds cannot meet the patient demand of a specimen every 40 seconds.

Simple math tells us we would need a minimum of 12 phlebotomists to meet *takt*. Practically speaking, we would want 13 or 14 to account for variation in the time it takes to draw specimens. In this case, and in other settings, we would likely have different *takt* time and different staffing requirements throughout the day and throughout the week. We should do our best to use data to match staffing to demand, out of respect for our patients and for our employees.

Types of Standardized Work Documents

So far, most of our focus has been on the concepts and philosophy of standardized work. What do these documents look like in practice? There is no single magic format; many types of standardized work documents can fit different situations. Some of the common formats are listed in Table 5.1, with examples of where those formats might be applied in a hospital.[13]

Table 5.1   Types of Standardized Work Documents

Tool or Document	Purpose	Hospital Example
Standardized work chart	Primary document that shows job responsibilities, common work tasks, and how long they should take. Often shows a diagram of where work is done.	Daily routine for lab employees, nurses, pharmacy employees
Work combination sheet	Analyzes relationships between an operator and a machine to synchronize work and eliminate operator waiting time. Used to determine how multiple people could divide that work.	Clinical laboratory "core cell" automated area
Process capacity sheet	Analyze capacity of equipment, rooms, other resources; considers changeover or set time and other planned downtime.	Analyzing operating room capacity and changeover time
Operator work instructions	Details important cyclical and noncyclical tasks; used as a reference or training document and is not posted in the work area; describes "key points" for quality and safety.	Clinical laboratory core cell, pharmacy technician duties for responding to first-dose orders
Cycle balance chart	Used to balance work on an assembly line across workers, and matching up production rate with rate of customer demand.	Nutrition services (sandwich production line)

In some instances, hospital departments have implemented the detailed work instructions as a posted document in the workplace. These documents spell out, in the appropriate level of detail, tasks, sequence, timing, and "key points" that are important for safety or quality.[14] The documents can be used for training or reference, or they can be used as checklists that help ensure that important steps are not forgotten or deviated from. The exact format of standardized work documents, as with other Lean practices, should be considered guidelines that can be adopted and adapted, depending on your situation.

Standardizing Daily Routines

While standardized work often looks at the details of specific methods, we can also use the concepts to plan daily schedules and timing. For example, a laboratory team might have certain activities (such as instrument maintenance or weekly inspections) that are routinely done. Departments often find benefits in determining the best time (or timeframe) for certain activities to be done, with the goals of avoiding time conflicts and smoothing out workloads. Some labs, out of routine, have the first-shift technologist start machine maintenance when beginning his or her shift at 7 a.m., even if that is a peak busy period. Since the maintenance has to be done daily, the exact time does not matter, as long as it is consistent. Through the Lean process, teams quickly identify that tasks like machine maintenance can be done during slower periods, having less of an impact on testing turnaround time.

In another case, the radiology department at one hospital had a team of three employees working at the front registration desk to sign in patients. Before Lean, two of the employees went to lunch at 11 A.M. each day, even if large numbers of patients were arriving, leaving the remaining one clerk with a heavy workload. This clerk felt this was unfair, and it delayed patients (which also delayed imaging procedures). With Lean, the team started with a patient focus and instituted flexible lunchtimes. The employees would delay their lunch if patient volumes mandated it. The team also had to reconsider the staggering of lunch breaks, sending only one clerk at a time instead of the two together. This was not an easy change to make, but it was fair for all the employees and beneficial for the patients. The role of leadership was to emphasize why the changes were necessary and beneficial.

This approach of specifying when breaks are taken might seem to go against the idea that Lean is good for the employees. It is true that some employees may be asked to change their habits and schedules, but only if it is for the benefit of the patients. The team should ask, "Is there a benefit to standardizing lunch- and break times?" In some areas, employees might have more leeway in choosing their own break times. Managers need to explain why such standardization is necessary, rather than mandating it through their position of formal authority.

Defining Roles and Responsibilities

Standardized work goes beyond the details of completing tasks and scheduling one's day. The writing of standardized work also gives hospitals an opportunity to reconsider which tasks are done by which employees. This is not a new question in hospitals, as a 1924 journal article highlighted, "I have seen competent nurses scrubbing floors, and doing other things which to the lay mind are functions of service not requiring the high skill and training so essential to the nursing profession."[15]

One example can be found in the laboratory. Since medical technologists are often in short supply and have specialized scientific education and skills, the hospital must use those skills wisely. We cannot afford to waste the time of technologists by having them do work that does not require their expertise or skills.

If technologists are performing manual tasks, such as replenishing supplies from the storeroom or moving specimens within the lab, we have to challenge that assignment of work. The fact that work "has always been done that way" should not be an excuse for not changing. Some labs have gone as far as to have laboratory assistants load specimens into automated instruments since the skill of the technologist is needed for interpreting results and troubleshooting the process. Loading a tube into an instrument is sometimes just a manual material-handling function that laboratory assistants can do, given the proper training and having standardized work in place. The ability to shift this work may depend on legal or regulatory restrictions in a given state or country, so caution is advised.

Allowing technologists to focus on their skilled work fits with the philosophy of respect for people, as it values their special abilities. In one laboratory, prior to Lean implementation, a technologist with 25 years of experience complained that the work had become "robotic." This was due to new automated lab technology, for which all the technologist did was "move tubes, load them, and press a few buttons," compared to the manual methods used decades earlier. In a Lean environment, we can allow technologists to focus more on the work that requires their scientific training. In addition, as we engage employees in *kaizen* efforts, technologists and assistants can use their creativity to solve problems, a decidedly unrobotic activity.

The same concepts can be applied to the highest-skilled professionals in other departments. A pharmacy can ask which tasks currently done by pharmacists should be done by pharmacy technicians. An inpatient unit can evaluate which activities should be done by technicians or nurse assistants instead of registered nurses. There may be instances, however, for which we have somebody working below his or her level in the name of teamwork or improved flow. For example, in some pharmacies, the pharmacist will load a medication into a tube system carrier immediately after verifying and inspecting the medication. This does not require pharmacist training, but it requires only a few seconds and prevents a potential delay in waiting for a technician to send the medication to the patient.

Quick Changeover as Standardized Work

One variation on standardized work is the methodology for quick changeover, also known as setup time reduction. Toyota's innovation, under the leadership of Shigeo Shingo, was to reduce press changeover times from multiple hours to less than 10 minutes, via what was called single-minute exchange of dies (SMED). Setup times were often reduced by a factor of 40 in a 10-year period.[16] A hospital equivalent example would be the time required to change over an operating room between patients, including all of the cleanup, sterilization, and preparation for the next case.

Rather than accepting that changeover times inherently had to be long, Shingo taught a methodology that included analyzing the way work was done to find a better way. Typically, a lot of work, including walking to get the new dies, would occur after the machine was shut down. Tasks that could be done in advance of machine shutdown were "externalized," leaving only those "internal" tasks that absolutely had to be done while the machine was down.

In the operating room setting, a hospital might have team members help stage everything that would be needed for the next case outside the room while the previous case was finishing, rather than taking that time between cases. Roles and responsibilities for room cleaning and prep are highly specified, leading to faster room turns. Quality often improves as certain surfaces or sections of the room are no longer forgotten by previously hurried staff. In some circumstances, having additional prep staff might increase cost in a way that is more than paid for by the increased operating room utilization and revenue.

The pit crews for professional auto racing are another inspiration for quick changeover work, with pit crews often teaching hospitals their methods.[17] Pit crews have highly orchestrated methods that are practiced frequently, with the goal of maximizing the time the driver is on the road, while also doing their work in the safest possible way. Hospitals can have a similar goal of maximizing the amount of time a surgeon and the surgical team can operate, thereby reducing the amount of time that surgeons or patients wait.

Explaining Why through Standardized Work

An innovation of the Lean approach to standardized work is the extra effort taken to explain why certain steps are necessary or why things should be done a certain way. Instead of telling employees to perform a task a certain way because a manager said so, the approach shows respect for people by treating them like thinking adults. Detailed work instruction documents typically have two columns to the right of the list of steps and time durations. The first column highlights key points that are critical to safety or quality, and the second column explains why those key points should be followed.[18] Employees are more likely to follow the standardized work when they understand the reasoning behind the key point. If we rely on formal authority to enforce standardized work adherence, it is likely that employees will do things their own way when nobody is watching.

When managers are directive, we must explain why the policies, goals, or decisions are necessary. This shows respect for people. It is often said that people hate change. It might be more accurate to say people hate being told what to do. At any level in the organization, people dislike decisions that are forced on them, especially those that seem arbitrary. Signs or notices, when used, should not just be directive; they should explain why.

In one lab that was implementing Lean, a manager taped a sign to the centrifuge that read, "DO NOT CHANGE SPIN TIME. Should be 6 minutes." This was a command-and-control action; the employee was expected to follow the sign (an order) because of the manager's formal authority. Sure enough, a technologist soon walked by, saw the sign, and asked, "Why is that?" before moving on. The manager realized the error in not explaining why. A new sign was made that explained that the time was now 6 minutes rather than the old 10 minutes because they were using a new type of tube that required less centrifuge time. It was not, as the employee might have feared, an attempt to save time (at the expense of quality) by arbitrarily shortening the time.

The idea of explaining why can also apply to interactions with patients. In one hospital, instead of just telling patients, "You must wear masks," the signs were more informative and made it more likely that patients might follow the instructions. Signs explained that hematology-oncology patients must wear masks because of the construction for the new patient tower and how construction dust increased the risk of fungal infections if it was breathed. Another hospital changed its directive "no food or drink" signs in the waiting room to a slightly longer sign that explained that banning food was a courtesy to patients who were not allowed to eat before their procedures. The number of people who brought food into the waiting room dropped as a result.

Standardized Work Documents and the Standardized Work System

Lean implementers often initially think of standardized work in terms of the documents we produce. The standardized work documents themselves are an important starting point, as it is difficult to say an organization or department has a standard if it has never been written down.

Even if we have fully documented methods and procedures, leaders cannot guarantee that all employees will always perform the work in that consistent manner. You might ask, "If we have been talking about standard methods for more than 100 years and we have shelves full of binders, why are we still struggling with standardized work? Why are we implementing this as a new concept?" Standardized work is a deceptively simple concept, but one that is difficult to implement and sustain. Managers have to do more than just assume that procedures or standardized work will be followed. We have to check, audit, or inspect that these are being followed consistently, with the right results.

All too often, we have focused on standardized work as a documentation exercise instead of viewing it as an ongoing management exercise. It is typical for organizations to go through waves and cycles of standardization and procedure writing, often corresponding with cycles of inspection and certification by outside bodies. We become excited about documenting our processes and devote employee time to the effort, but to what effect and results?

There is a phrase that we use that attempts to capture the responsibility of leaders in overseeing standardized work: "You get what you expect and you deserve what you tolerate." As leaders, if you expect that employees will follow the standardized work, you have to take time to go and see, to verify that the standardized work is actually being followed. If you tolerate people not following the standardized work, you deserve the outcomes that result from the standardized work not being followed.

Coming back to our bedsores example, traditional management approaches might measure the number of bedsore occurrences in different wards or under each nurse's responsibility. There might be two different areas in which the employees are not following the standardized work of properly repositioning patients every two hours. Due to variation in our patients and, to some extent, pure luck, one area might have a patient who develops a bedsore, while the other area does not. Would it be right to praise the area where zero bedsores developed? Through the same actions (or inaction), they might have a patient develop a bedsore the next week. As leaders, we need to focus on the process and hold people accountable for doing the right things the right way, rather than just focusing on outcomes. Lean leaders believe that the right process will lead to the right results.

Measuring and Observing for Standardized Work Adherence

Rather than waiting for measures or other reports, leaders can also spend time directly inspecting and observing the process to see if the standardized work is being followed. We can shadow employees on a regular basis. We can develop checklists or visual indicators that leaders can use throughout the day to see if routine or scheduled tasks are getting done.

For example, patients who are at risk for bedsores might have a checklist posted in their room, where staff members who reposition the patient every two hours initial or mark the list. Charge nurses, team leaders, or other managers would, on a schedule, do rounds and verify that the standardized work is being followed at the right frequency. Managers would also occasionally directly observe to see if patients were being repositioned according to the standardized work.

With checklists and other records, leaders have to be alert to employees going back and filling them out at the end of their shift. This could mean the standardized work was not getting done, and employees were fudging the checklist. Or, it could mean they are doing the work but not filling out the form until the end of the shift. Checklists and standardized work timing must be followed throughout the day.

In a non-Lean culture, this might be seen as hounding the employees or not trusting them. The key is how we react to the standardized work not being followed and how we engage with employees. Leaders need to ensure that standardized work is being followed for the sake of the patients, not because we like telling people what to do.

Frontline employees are not the only employees to have their standardized work audited. The first-level supervisors have standardized work that indicates they audit their area once a day. That supervisor's manager will also conduct regular audits and check that the audits are getting done, as accountability does not stop with the first-level supervisor. More detail about this process is given in Chapter 10.

Leaders must have discipline to keep auditing standardized work. A case in point involves the experience of a radiology department with process audits before Lean. New Joint Commission rules required a radiologist to sign oral contrast orders before the contrast was administered to a patient. Managers and the director had been doing audits but stopped after about 3 months. Predictably enough, after the audits stopped, 100% compliance with the orders no longer occurred.

"Resistance" to Standardized Work?

While standardized work has clear benefits for the patients and the employees, it is common for some people in the organization to resist the idea. Some employees might resist, feeling insulted that they need to be told how to do their jobs. Of course, that is not the intent. Especially for many long-time employees, "We already know how to do our jobs" is a common complaint, but does everybody do their job the same way? Employees might also fear being unable to learn the new standardized work method. Employees should be reassured that they will be trained properly and given time to learn the new method, without being criticized.

It is often easier to gain acceptance to the general concept, to get people to agree that we should standardize. The real challenge often comes in the details of deciding whose standard or which combination of standardized methods is the best way. Building consensus can be time consuming, but it is the best way to gain acceptance. If there is disagreement over which way is the one best way, we should rely on data rather than opinions. Teams can try different methods, measuring for the impact on safety, quality, time, or cost. Decisions on standardized work should be based on more than who is influential or who argues the loudest. If there are two equally good methods, a leader can help decide which method should be used.

Asking Why When Standardized Work Is Not Followed

When a leader sees that standardized work is not followed, the first question needs to be: "Why is the standard not being followed?" This question needs to be asked sincerely rather than in an accusatory manner. The question could be asked in a tone that really says, "You must follow the standard work," which might intimidate an employee into falling back in line.

Asking why can also encourage *kaizen*. Some managers get focused on making sure employees are following the standard methods, no matter what. In this zeal to enforce standardized work, we might lose potential opportunities for *kaizen* if we are not careful. Again, standardized work is not meant to be permanent; it is to be improved on, over time, by the employees doing the work. If managers reacted negatively every time they saw someone not following the standardized work, *kaizen* and creativity would be stifled.

We ask why because there might be legitimate reasons the current standard is not being followed; there might be a problem in the process that necessitates changing the standardized work. As leaders, we need to encourage people to bring those problems to the surface so we can work on fixing them. If the employee is employing a workaround, we can encourage the individual to find and fix the root cause of the problem, as discussed more thoroughly in Chapter 7. Second, the employee might be trying a new method, a potential *kaizen* that could be incorporated into the new standardized work. If we are not open to hearing what the new method is and why it might be better, we will lose that opportunity. As leaders, we have to be open to *kaizen* instead of merely policing the standardized work.

In the example from Chapter 3, in which staff members were not using the proper lift assists, managers responded by hanging a sign on the wall that berated staff for not using that equipment. Again, the inconvenient storage location was a barrier to doing the right thing. A chastising "thou shalt" sign is more often the symptom of a problem than an effective root cause solution.

Many hospitals, for example, have portable computer carts for nurses and techs to use. The intent is to allow nurses to chart in the patient rooms. This would provide more patient access to the nurses, compared to the nurse going back to the central nurse station to chart at a fixed computer station. The portable computer also should allow the nurse to chart throughout the day, rather than batching charting until the end of the day. These all sound like objectives everyone could agree on, but not all nurses use the portable computers. When we as managers introduce new technology, do we assume it will be used, or do we observe firsthand?

If we get reports that nurses are not using newly purchased portable computers (or better yet, when we observe it firsthand), we have to ask, "What prevents you from wanting to use the portable computers?" Some answers might be related to technology glitches, such as batteries that do not hold a charge or computers that reboot without warning. Nurses are busy enough, so the first time they have to repeat work or waste time because of a technology-related problem, it is understandable they might be leery of the tool. Some nurses question the assumption that they have time to chart as they go through their morning rounds. If a nurse is told, on the one hand, to see all their patients promptly, that may come into conflict with the objective of charting as they go. "If I charted as I went, there is a patient I wouldn't get to until a few hours into my shift. I don't have the time to chart as I go," a nurse may explain. Proper standardized work design for a nurse would include time estimates for how long daily routine tasks actually take, given technology tools, department layouts, and patient loads, among other factors. Employees are less likely to be able to follow standardized work if there is not enough time in their day to follow it as written.

Other nurses may question if the technology saves them any time. Principle 8 of the *Toyota Way* states: "Use only reliable, thoroughly tested technology that serves your people and processes." Effective technology would make things faster or easier for nurses, but many nurses report that charting in the computer system takes much longer than the old bedside paper charts; this is due to software design, screens that load slowly, or a system that requires many clicks to enter basic information. Resistance to computer systems is heightened by perceptions that the ultimate users were not consulted in the software selection process or that systems are not designed around how they work.

To a Lean thinker, those are all very understandable reasons for not being able to follow the process that is desired by management. Forcing people to follow a process, to force them to chart via computer at the bedside as they go, will most likely damage nurse morale.

This does not mean we can necessarily accept a suggestion to go back to paper charts. Leadership has a responsibility to articulate the many reasons why information systems and electronic charting are necessary. If leaders have to resort to telling nurses to follow the process because the bosses said so, they have an obligation to explain why in terms of benefit to the patients, physicians, and the hospital.

Employees might also be ignoring the standardized work as a way of testing new boundaries or management's commitment to the process. Supervisors and managers should be trained to coach employees and to assume, at least initially, that noncompliance is an issue of awareness or training. Only after multiple attempts to coach and train should we rely on formal disciplinary processes. If we start threatening to write people up at the first sign of noncompliance, we will likely get compliance—but only when we are watching. Since employees cannot be monitored 100% of the time, we have to build real support for standardized work to ensure that employees will follow the method all of the time through their intrinsic motivation.

Standardized Work Can Apply to Physicians

From the earliest days of the Gilbreths and their industrial engineering studies of hospitals in the early 1900s, the question has been asked: Does standardized work apply to physicians and surgeons? The same guidelines and rules of thumb, as described previously, can also apply to physicians.

Physicians would seem the most likely to resist the idea, countering that every patient is unique, and therefore their work cannot be standardized. Remember, though, that standardized does not mean identical, as in the feared "cookie cutter" medicine. As in any Lean endeavor, we should standardize only those activities, tasks, and sequences that are proven to have an impact on safety, quality, waiting time, or other strategic factors. Physicians should not be forced to set aside their professional judgment in the case of a particular patient. Nor should standardization be forced on physicians from experts, outsiders, or managers. Physicians deserve the same respect that Lean principles demand for anyone in the system.

In many cases where standardized work has been successful in direct patient-physician interaction, the method has been created by those who do the work, in this instance, the physicians. Geisinger Health System (Pennsylvania) recognized the need to decrease patient mortality after elective heart bypass surgery.[19] Rather than dictating standards of care, they enlisted cardiac surgeons to study their own methods and define their own standardized work, a system they call ProvenCare. Although this was not done using the Lean terminology, the approach is strikingly familiar.

The cardiac surgeons discovered there were different protocols being followed by different surgeons before, during, and after surgery. "We realized there were seven ways to do something," said Dr. Alfred S. Casale, the director of cardiothoracic surgery at Geisinger. The surgeons, getting past their prior belief that they each had the best way, reviewed the literature and guidelines to document 40 steps that should always happen, including presurgical antibiotics and postsurgical beta-blockers.

The surgeons established the expectations that any of them could choose not to follow some aspect of the standardized work for a particular patient if circumstances demanded it, but they "rarely do so," said Dr. Casale. In any standardized work situation, employees deserve this right, but if people frequently deviate from the standardized work, we should take it as a sign that there may be a problem with the current documented method. The surgeons also follow the guideline that their standardized work can be improved if new research or evidence emerges.

The standardization efforts at Geisinger, now called ProvenCare, led to improved patient outcomes, including

- Length of stay reduction from 6.2 to 5.7 days
- 44% reduction in readmission rates
- 21% reduction in patients with at least one complication
- 55% reduction in cases of reoperation due to bleeding
- 25% reduction in deep sternal wound infections.[20]

Dr. John B. Tebbetts, a cosmetic surgeon in Dallas, Texas, took it on himself to study and use Lean methods in the name of reducing patient recovery times.[21] His goals included minimizing the time the patient was under anesthesia not by working faster but by eliminating waste in motion and delays in the procedure itself. Dr. Tebbetts even experimented with his own surgical methods and instruments, finding methods that caused less trauma to the patient, thus reducing recovery time. Motivated by his patient's recovery time and comfort, the surgeon gained personal efficiency without sacrificing quality. Using the improved and standardized methods, 96% of patients were able to return to full normal activities within 24 hours, a goal deemed impossible by most.

Lean and Checklists

In recent years, an increasing number of hospitals are using checklists, as inspired by pilots in the aviation industry, to improve quality and patient safety. Books by Dr. Atul Gawande and Dr. Peter Pronovost explained the transference and applicability of these methods for reducing central line–associated bloodstream infections (CLABIs), surgical errors, and other problems.[22,23] A group of 100 intensive care units in Michigan completely eliminated catheter-associated bloodstream infections within 18 months of using a simple five-item checklist to ensure the best-known care was given to every patient.[24] Similar efforts led to a 70% reduction of ventilator-associated pneumonia (VAP) cases in these same hospitals.[25] Dr. Richard Shannon has also been a leader of applying checklists and other Lean methods to reduce hospital-acquired infections, in Pennsylvania first at Allegheny General Hospital and then at the University of Pennsylvania Medical Center. At Allegheny in 2004, the hospital reduced CLABI occurrences by 87% and VAP by 83%.[26]

There are many direct parallels between the checklists methodology and Lean standardized work, including

- Checklists are written by the people who do the work.
- Clinicians have the ability to deviate from a checklist when necessary for a specific patient.
- Checklists are meant to be improved on over time, given new medical evidence.
- Checklists are not only a document, but also about discipline, attention to detail, and organizational culture.

As a physician wrote to a newspaper in England, "The checklist in itself is not really the point. What is important is the quality of its implementation."[27] This includes factors such as communication and having a proper team environment in which everybody is allowed to speak up if they see a problem.

Standardized Work Can Apply to Managers

Increasingly, healthcare managers at all levels are realizing that standardized work does not just apply to frontline staff. Frontline supervisors might have up to 80% of their day driven by standardized work, including their plan for the day and the checklists they use to help manage their team.[28] As we move higher in the organization chart, less time is typically spent in a standardized work mode, with relatively more time being unstructured.

Some organizations, including ThedaCare (Appleton, WI), are instituting "no meeting zones" for the first two hours of the day, creating time for leaders to do structured rounding or *gemba* walks.[29] Supervisors and leaders at ThedaCare have checklists and standardized work documents that prompt how they spend their time and which questions they ask at the *gemba*. Even vice presidents have a standardized sheet that they carry with them to remind them to start all team discussions with a discussion about employee and patient safety. Leaders might also carry with them guidelines for effective problem solving, as discussed in Chapter 7.

As with other roles, standardized work for managers is not meant to be restrictive or to limit people to simple check-the-box thinking. Standardized work provides helpful structure, planning those management tasks that can be standardized while freeing mental bandwidth for times when creativity is necessary.

Training through Standardized Work

Standardized work documents can be used to support effective training of new employees, compared to informal, verbal training. In one hospital microbiology lab, before Lean, students were given unstructured, verbal training that forced the student to scribble notes to serve as individual process documentation. Verbal training brings many risks, including miscommunications and inconsistency among employees.

In another example, a new pharmacy technician was given the responsibility of delivering medications to multiple units, being told, "figure out your own best route." This approach slows the learning curve for the employee, as he or she experiments with different routes. It is fine to ask the employee to find the best way, but only after starting with a standardized work plan for what the current one best route has already been determined to be. Each new employee should be able to build on the accumulated knowledge of previous employees. A new employee who discovers a better route needs to share it with the rest of the team through the *kaizen* process.

Some hospitals have once again started utilizing the training approach from the Training Within Industry (TWI) program that was so influential at Toyota.[30] Following a standardized approach to training can help ensure practices that are more consistent and will lead to quality that is more consistent. The job instruction training approach follows four steps.

Step 1: Prepare the employee. Start by discussing the need for standardized work and by talking through the formal documents. This is best done offline when the employee does not also have to do his or her regular work and so can focus on learning the method. The expectation should be set that the employee can challenge the standardized work and improve it if he or she finds a better method.

Step 2: Demonstrate the job. Have the trainer demonstrate the standardized work, allowing the employee to observe and follow along in the documentation. The trainer should emphasize the key points in the standardized work to highlight quality and safety considerations.

Step 3: Observe the job being done. Trainers must observe the employee trying the new job, coaching and providing guidance or clarification as they go. It is the trainer's job to confirm that the employee understands and can perform the standardized work. In the TWI approach, a frequently used phrase is, "If the worker hasn't learned, the instructor hasn't taught."[31]

Step 4: Follow up. The trainer (and supervisors) must follow up periodically to ensure that the standardized work is followed. After the new employee has some experience with the job, the trainer can follow up to see what *kaizen* ideas they might have, for the sake of improving the standardized work.

Having a formal training approach brings much better results than haphazard methods. A department should consider training supervisors and other senior employees in how to train others, as it is a bad assumption to think that the best employees would necessarily make good instructors. Often, the opposite is true, when experienced employees have little patience for those who are new to a role.

The histopathology lab at Yuma Regional Hospital (Yuma, AZ) struggled with finding a person to effectively perform an order entry role, having "chewed up" six people over the course of three years.[32] Each new person made order entry mistakes, so the lab blamed the individuals or the inability of the lab to attract a careful person. Through their early Lean efforts, they were introduced to the TWI method for training, and they started looking at the system. The disciplined use of the job instruction approach of TWI to train the next new person led to a reduction of errors from 33.5% to 2.5%. The lab learned that the problem was not the person; it was the system.

Conclusion

Standardized work is a method that can benefit all hospital stakeholders. Consistent methods can lead to improved quality and reduced delays for patients, while being fair and respectful to employees. Part of being fair and respectful is that we do not force inflexible standardized work methods on people, rather, we let them develop and refine their own standardized work. That is the only way to ensure that staff want to follow the standardized work, based on their own intrinsic motivation to provide the best care for their patients. The goal is not to standardize. The goal is improvement and the best possible results for the organization. Standardized work is just a means to that end.

Lean Lessons

- The foundations of Lean are standardized work, *heijunka*, and *kaizen*.
- Practices that are more consistent lead to quality that is more consistent.
- Standardized work should reflect an emphasis on quality and safety, not speed.
- Standardized work is written by those who do the work.
- Do not standardize for the sake of standardizing.
- Standardized work frees people to be creative problem solvers, rather than turning them into robots.
- Explaining why shows respect for people.
- Standardized work is not just a one-time documentation exercise.
- Managers must directly observe and audit to see if standardized work is being followed.
- Standardized work is not permanent; it must be improved over time.

Points for Group Discussion

- How is patient safety impacted by standardizing methods?
- How do irregular or unexpected circumstances fit into standardized work?
- Why is it important that the people who do the work author standardized work documentation?
- How does standardized work apply to physicians and surgeons?
- How can standardized work be helpful for your supervisors and leaders?
- How can we gain acceptance of standardized work?
- In your workplace, what might be some examples of critical tasks, important tasks, and nonimportant tasks?
- What methods do you currently have in place to verify if work methods are being followed?
- What would be an example of overly specified work in your area? What problems would this cause?

Notes

1. Hetzel, Joe, and Andy Brook, "Kanban at Park Nicollet Health Services," presentation, http://www.premierinc.com/about/events-education/breakthroughs/2009/presentations/web/concurrent/LST5–209A-hetzel-brook-v2.pdf (accessed April 8, 2011).
2. Ohno, Taiichi, *Toyota Production System: Beyond Large-Scale Production* (New York: Productivity Press, 1998), xiii.
3. Ford, Henry, *Today and Tomorrow* (Garden City, NY: Garden City Publishing, 1926), 51.
4. Baumgart, A., and D. Neuhauser, "Frank and Lillian Gilbreth: Scientific Management in the Operating Room," *Quality and Safety in Health Care*, 2009, 18:413–15; doi:10.1136/qshc.2009.032409.
5. Public Affairs Division and Operations Management Consulting Division, *The Toyota Production System, Leaner Manufacturing for a Greener Planet* (Toyota City, Japan: Toyota Motor Corporation, 1998), 32.
6. Ibid.
7. Pittet, Didier, "Improving Compliance with Hand Hygiene in Hospitals," *Infection Control and Hospital Epidemiology* 2000, 21: 381–86.
8. Carling, P., N. Church, and J. Jefferson, "Operating Room Environmental Cleaning—An Evaluation Using a New Targeting Method," *American Journal of Infection Control* June 2007, 35: E26–27.
9. Liker, Jeffrey K., and David P. Meier, *Toyota Talent* (New York: McGraw-Hill, 2007), 143.
10. Marriott, J. W., and Adrian Zackheim, *The Spirit to Serve Marriott's Way* (New York: HarperCollins, 2001), 17.
11. Ohno, Taiichi, *Toyota Production System: Beyond Large-Scale Production* (New York: Productivity Press, 1988), 98.
12. Gilbreth, Frank B., "Scientific Management in the Hospital," *The Modern Hospital*, February, 1914, 2: 87–88.
13. Liker and Meier, *Toyota Talent*, 119.
14. Dinero, Donald A., *Training Within Industry: The Foundation of Lean* (New York: Productivity Press, 2005), 175.
15. Brown, Percy S., "A Few Facts about Scientific Management in Industry," *American Journal of Nursing* 1927, 27: 828–32.
16. Shingo, Shigeo, *A Revolution in Manufacturing: The SMED System* (New York: Productivity Press, 1985), 113.
17. American Society for Quality, "Ferrari's Formula One Handovers and Handovers from Surgery to Intensive Care," Quality in Healthcare Web site, http://asq.org/healthcare-use/why-quality/great-ormond-street-hospital.html (accessed April 4, 2011).
18. Liker and Meier, *Toyota Talent*, 173.
19. Abelson, Reed, "In Bid for Better Care, Surgery with a Warranty," *New York Times*, May 17, 2007, http://www.nytimes.com/2007/05/17/business/17quality.html?_r=1&ref=policy&oref=slogin (accessed April 10, 2011).
20. Geisinger Health System, "ProvenCare by the Numbers," http://www.geisinger.org/provencare/numbers.html (accessed April 8, 2011).
21. Tebbetts, John B., "Achieving a Predictable 24-Hour Return to Normal Activities after Breast Augmentation. Part I. Refining Practices by Using Motion and Time Study Principles," *Plastic and Reconstructive Surgery*, January 2002, 273–90.
22. Gawande, Atul, *The Checklist Manifesto: How to Get Things Right*, (New York: Metropolitan Books, 2009), 136.
23. Pronovost, Peter, and Eric Vohr, *Safe Patients, Smart Hospitals: How One Doctor's Checklist Can Help Us Change Health Care from the Inside Out* (New York: Hudson Street Press, 2010), 1.
24. Brody, Jane E., "A Basic Hospital To-Do List Saves Lives," *New York Times*, January 22, 2008, http://www.nytimes.com/2008/01/22/health/22brod.html (accessed April 4, 2011).
25. Henry, Tanya Albert, "Hospital Checklist Helps Pneumonia Rates Tumble by 70%," *American Medical News*, March 11, 2011, http://www.ama-assn.org/amednews/2011/03/07/prse0311.htm (accessed April 4, 2011).

26. Institute for Healthcare Improvement, "Allegheny General Hospital: Lower Infection Rates Have Lowered Costs," Institute for Healthcare Improvement, January 20, 2006, http://www.ihi.org/IHI/Topics/CriticalCare/IntensiveCare/ImprovementStories/AlleghenyGeneralHospitalLowerInfectionRatesHaveLoweredCosts.htm (accessed April 4, 2011).
27. Bleakley, Alan, Letter to the editor, *The Independent*, July 2, 2008, http://www.independent.co.uk/opinion/letters/letters-interfering-state-858284.html, (accessed April 5, 2011).
28. Mann, David, *Creating a Lean Culture* (New York: Productivity Press, 2005), 33.
29. Toussaint, John, and Roger Gerard, *On the Mend: Revolutionizing Healthcare to Save Lives and Transform the Industry* (Cambridge, MA: Lean Enterprise Institute, 2010), 174.
30. Liker and Meier, *Toyota Talent*, 40.
31. United States, *Hospital Adaptation for the Job Instruction Manual*, August 1944, Subgroup 211.22.3 General Records of the Training Within Industry Service, Records of the War Manpower Commission (WMC), Record Group 211, National Archives Building, Washington, DC, http://chapters.sme.org/204/TWI_Materials/National_Archives_March_2006/Job_Instruction/Hospitals/Materials-Hospitals.pdf (accessed December 20, 2007).
32. Chuy, Jesus, and Peter P. Patterson, "A Breakthrough in Training—Call it Near-TWI," Lean Blog, June 30, 2009, http://leanblog.org/2009/06/breakthrough-in-training-call-it-near/ (accessed April 4, 2011).

Chapter 6

Lean Methods: Visual Management, 5S, and *Kanban*

Lean Is More than Tools, but Tools Can Help

Looking back to the Toyota triangle from Chapter 2, technical tools are just one component of the integrated system of Lean. Rather than documenting all of the details of how to implement these methods, this chapter focuses on some of the hospital-specific examples of the use of visual management, 5S, and *kanban*. We also focus on the management methods and philosophical concepts that are embedded in the effective use of these methods. This chapter is by no means an all-inclusive list of tools, but these are some more commonly used in the early stages of hospital implementations. Many of the existing guidebooks or manuals for these methods, published for manufacturing, can be adapted for a hospital setting. In addition, healthcare-specific books are now being published on some of these methods, including 5S and *kanban*.[1,2]

Reducing Waste through Visual Management

Another form of standardized work is the method of visual management. The goal of visual management is to make waste, problems, and abnormal conditions readily apparent to employees and managers. Our aim should be to expose problems so they can be fixed, as opposed to the old approach of hiding problems to make things look good. Visual management is a mindset, more than a specific technology. Our goal, as managers, should be to ask ourselves how we can make our process more visual and our problems more apparent.

Gwendolyn Galsworth wrote that the purpose of visual management is to reduce "information deficits" in the workplace.[3] She wrote that, "In an information-scarce workplace, people ask lots of questions and lots of the same questions, repeatedly—or they make stuff up."[4] We can see this throughout hospitals. Listen to the questions employees ask, such as:

- Does this patient have any more tests, or can he go home?
- Have these medications been double-checked?
- Which patient should be brought back next?
- Are these tubes ready to load into the test instrument?
- Is this pump clean?
- Who is the physician for this patient?
- Which patients are assigned to that nurse?
- Is this room open?

These questions are rooted in a lack of information, information that either does not exist or is not readily apparent—thus the need for visual management. Visual management can also, ideally, be used for real-time decision making—a major improvement over waiting for monthly, or even daily, reports and metrics to gauge the performance of a process.

Examples of Visual Management for Patient Flow

In the radiology department of one children's hospital, some of the children are scheduled for multiple imaging appointments, such as a sonogram and magnetic resonance imaging (MRI). Because most patients just have one appointment and employees can only see the schedule for their modality, it is common for a technologist or nurse to say, "You're done now" after the first procedure. Because many young children do not know what they are in for and some parents might not fully understand the plan for their child's care, some patients leave without having their second imaging completed. This leads to wasted equipment time, rework for the scheduling staff, and wasted transportation and time for the patient and parents.

The front desk staff in the radiology department came up with a simple visual management tool to prevent this waste from occurring. When a child has two modalities to visit, the desk staff clips together two color-coded laminated cards and attaches them to the patient's shirt. This gives a clear indicator to the staff of the first modality that the patient has to move to a second procedure. This is also a form of error proofing, as discussed in Chapter 8. Rather than managers browbeating employees to be careful, the team took a more effective, simple, and visual approach to solving that information deficit.

Hospitals often use visual management to identify the status of patients or their needs, facilitating real-time decision making. Tracking boards (either low-tech whiteboards or high-tech plasma screens) are used to identify which rooms are open or to share with families where patients are currently located in the value stream. One outpatient orthopedic clinic, instead of their previous practice of stacking patient charts on a desk, now places charts in wall holders that create a clear visual of how many patients are waiting for each physician. In addition, there are clear visual signals that indicate if the patient is ready or is still getting an X-ray. The registration desk staff can easily look down the hallway and use this visual information to prioritize the registration of patients who might arrive at the same time, first registering a patient whose physician is currently available rather than the patient who will be waiting until the other patients have been seen by a different physician.

Many hospitals have used software systems that display patient status on large flat-panel televisions. It is a common Lean principle to use technology and automation only after the process has been piloted in a manual way. Principle 8 of *The Toyota Way* says to "use only reliable, thoroughly tested technology that serves your people and processes."[5] Lean thinkers are not antitechnology, but they tend not to jump immediately to technology solutions. One large children's hospital created a large whiteboard with color-coded magnets laid over a drawing of the inpatient unit layout. While the board was intended to be a prototype to help them choose an electronic system, the hospital decided the whiteboard worked just fine and was flexible enough to be changed quickly as their needs evolved. Another hospital built a prototype of a patient tracker in a shared network spreadsheet that could be displayed on screens throughout the hospital. They were surprised to conclude that their inexpensive home-grown solution also eliminated the need to buy the commercial system. Homegrown visual systems (analog or digital) have the advantage of being completely customized to your own situation.

Examples of Visual Management to Prevent Process Problems

Visual management can also be used to create awareness or prevent problems. In one hospital laboratory, simple visual management methods were used to prevent specimen testing delays. Certain specimens were transported from the main lab site to microbiology through a pass-through box built into the wall that divided the departments. Once used by microbiology, the specimen was placed back in the box for the main laboratory to continue testing. Often, the specimen would sit up to 1 hour in the pass-through box, waiting to be taken back out by the main lab. The delay was caused partly by the ambiguous signal that was sent by the visual indicator that a specimen could be seen in the box. The main lab employees could easily, and incorrectly, assume the specimen was still on its way into microbiology. The Lean team came up with a simple visual control—a laminated sheet that microbiology could place in the lab side of the pass-through window when a specimen was coming back in that direction. When the main lab took the specimen back, they could take the sign down until it was needed the next time.

Care must be taken that visual controls or indicators are standardized across units or even across hospitals. Patients' color-coded wristbands help identify special needs or DNR (do not resuscitate) requests. Unfortunately, wristbands are not always standardized among different hospitals in the same community, leading to opportunities for confusion when nurses or physicians work at different sites. What might indicate allergies in one hospital might indicate DNR in another, creating an opportunity for catastrophic errors.[6]

5S: Sort, Store, Shine, Standardize, and Sustain

Another example of workplace waste or an information deficit might be evident when questions such as these are asked:

- Where are the blankets?
- Why did we run out of syringes?
- Where did those medications go?
- Why are we walking so far within the department?
- Why do we spend so much time looking for things we need?

The 5S (sort, store, shine, standardize, and sustain) methodology reduces waste through improved workplace organization and visual management. Implementing 5S is not about looking neat and orderly, and it should not be confused with a one-time or annual "spring cleaning" exercise. The primary goal of 5S is to prevent problems and to create a work environment that allows people to provide the best patient care in the most effective way. For example, John Touissant, chief executive officer (CEO) of ThedaCare (Appleton, WI), estimated that 5S improvements had helped reduce the amount of wasted time in an average nurse's 8-hour shift from 3.5 hours a day to just 1 hour per day.[7] 5S is often used as an early Lean method as a way to start engaging staff in small improvements as a precursor to addressing bigger challenges, leading to the "revitalization of the workplace."[8]

The surest way to alienate medical professionals is to push the 5S methods in a top-down way that does not seem to be solving any meaningful problems. 5S (and Lean) might become dirty words if your first efforts involve a specialist moving around other people's stuff and putting tape around things. Nurses at one hospital were trying to engage leadership on patient safety issues, yet they rightfully complained about "being told to reduce the number of pens and pencils" at the nurses station."[9] 5S needs to engage everybody and needs to focus on important problems, rather than the trivial.

The term *5S* comes from the origins of the method in five Japanese words. Rather than forcing more Japanese words on employees, most hospitals refer to some variations of English translations, as shown in Table 6.1, but the principles behind the 5Ss are the important thing.

First S: Sort

The first 5S activity is to go through the department or area, looking for items or equipment that are no longer needed, items that are just taking up space. In one laboratory, for example, the team conducting the initial 5S sorting activity found things such as

- Old, yellowed stationery and forms with a 1970s hospital logo
- Expired reagents or slides dating back decades
- Broken computers and keyboards
- Specimen collection tubes that expired months ago in the bottom of drawers

Table 6.1 5S Term Translation

Japanese Term	Translation 1	Translation 2	Description
Seiri	Sort	Sort	Sort out unneeded items, keep items based on frequency of use
Seiton	Store	Straighten	Organize for the reduction of waste
Seiso	Shine	Shine	Keeping the workplace clean, daily
Seiketsu	Standardize	Systemize	Developing a consistently organized workplace
Shitsuke	Sustain	Sustain	A system for ongoing support of the first 4Ss

Items that can be clearly thrown away without controversy or the risk of someone later saying "I needed that" can be immediately disposed of, recycled, or donated. When unneeded items take up valuable workspace, the department ends up being larger than it needs to be, which results in excess construction and maintenance costs. These larger departments and workspaces lead to excess employee walking and other types of waste. Broken equipment and expired supplies take up space that could otherwise be used for supplies and tools that are used more frequently or for value-adding activities.[10] Before 5S, Seattle Children's Hospital (Washington) had an operating room that served as a cluttered storage room or "boneyard." Thanks to 5S, they were able to convert that room back into usable clinical space in just three days.[11]

One medical laboratory found a box of slides that, to the employees' best estimates, dated to the 1960s. The slides were found in the new building, opened in the 1990s, meaning they had been moved from the old building to the new building, just to clutter up the new space. Any new construction, major renovation, or department move should be preceded by a major 5S activity.

If there is some question about items that *might* be needed, a buffer zone—a 5S sort area—is set up somewhere in the department. Since not all employees can be present during the sort activity, holding items for a week allows everyone to review what the team is planning to throw away. This prevents rash decision making and the waste of disposing of items that would have to be repurchased. At the same time, we have to prevent people from reclaiming all items just because they think they might need the item someday. If there is disagreement over what is needed, a supervisor can facilitate or intervene. Items that might possibly be needed could be kept in a central supply or off-site storage location (with good records kept about what is being stored off site).

5S should not be viewed as only being about throwing items away. As part of this initial sort process, a team should also identify needed items that are not readily available in their workplace.

Second S: Store

Some organizations make the error of stopping after the first S, sort. While it is beneficial to get unneeded items out of the way, the most ongoing waste elimination will come from properly organizing the material and equipment that remain and "new" items that had been previously missing or unavailable, leading to the store phase.

In the store phase, employees identify how frequently each item is used. Items used most often should be stored closest to the point of use. If items are used by multiple people in an area, such as latex gloves in an emergency department (ED) or laboratory, consider having multiple storage points. There is a trade-off between reducing the waste of motion (keeping supplies close by) and the increase in inventory that might result with additional storage points. If supplies are inexpensive and take up little space, it is better to err on the side of more locations to avoid employee walking and wasted time.

The guidelines in Table 6.2 are only a suggestion. Common sense should prevail over hard-set rules. If an item is used infrequently but takes up little space, or if it is needed urgently (such as a crash cart or maintenance items for an instrument), it should be kept closer to where it is needed.

Table 6.2   5S Guidelines for Storing Items Based on Frequency of Use

Frequency of Use	Storage Proximity
Hourly	Within arm's reach
Every shift	Within a short walk
Daily	Further away
Monthly	Department storage
Annually	Hospital storage

Items that are used most frequently should be kept in good ergonomic zones, on top of benchtops or on shelves that are not too high or low. Employees waste motion, and can get hurt, by bending to get commonly used supplies out of low drawers. They also exert unnecessary motion opening doors to reach for supplies.

Before Lean, most supplies are kept in closed cabinets or drawers, which create waste as employees search for items and cannot see what is located where. With improved organization, employees will no longer waste time opening multiple cabinets or drawers, searching for what they need. When determining storage locations, Lean leaders challenge the need to store items in closed cabinets or drawers. Well-organized departments are not afraid to keep supplies visible and in the open since there no longer are the piles of disorganized supplies that used to hide behind doors, as pictured in Figures 6.1 and 6.2. Hiding the old mess behind closed doors was often a workaround to the problem of not keeping things organized.

In the case of the hospital unit where the lift assist was not being used, it was stored upstairs on a different floor. The room in the unit with equipment and supplies was overcrowded with broken walkers and way too many old commodes. The 5S process then became an effective way to get people to use the correct equipment. Freeing space allowed the unit to bring its lift assist to the second floor, where it was much more convenient and became used much more regularly. This countermeasure was more effective than hanging signs.

Third S: Shine

After removing unneeded items and determining the best storage location for those that remain, the 5S focus turns to cleanliness. Hospital departments often rely on the centralized housekeeping department, a group that often only does major cleaning, such as floors and trash cans. Dust often accumulates on top of instruments and behind equipment in the pharmacy or laboratory. In the 5S approach, people who work in the area take responsibility for their own light cleaning and the overall cleanliness of the department.

Figure 6.1 In an inpatient unit storage area, supplies were disorganized in drawers and storage space.

In manufacturing settings, the focus on shine was typically related to oil that might leak from machines. Floors that are always oily not only would be unsafe but also make it hard to determine if machines were leaking. Clean floors are safer and let you immediately detect problems with equipment. In healthcare settings, the focus on shine is more correctly oriented toward infection control.

Cleaning should not be considered a "make-work" activity but rather an opportunity for the team to show pride in their workplace by keeping it clean at all times. A side benefit is an opportunity to inspect the equipment and benches that are being wiped down. If problems such as frayed wires are seen, they can be reported immediately.

Fourth S: Standardize

The fourth stage of 5S is often the most visible when you visit a Lean hospital or a department. Once we have determined the best locations for needed items, it is time to ensure that items are always kept in the defined locations. We can standardize in a department, or we can standardize across departments, bringing benefits to employees or physicians who work in multiple units. At one hospital, the automated supply cabinets in different inpatient units were each organized differently, with no attempt made to standardize. This frustrated nurses who worked in different units,

Figure 6.2 In a nursing station, disorganization was hidden behind closed cabinet doors.

as they wasted time reorienting themselves when in a different unit. Standardized cabinets might have 80% of items that are the same across units, with customized space based on the needs of a particular unit. Again, standardized does not have to mean completely identical.

We often standardize through visual methods, the marking of "home locations" with vinyl tape or shadow outlines, as shown in Figures 6.3–6.5. Marking the locations of items brings many benefits, including

- Being able to see instantly when an item is missing or out of place
- Less wasted time looking for items
- Subtle psychological incentives for employees to return items to their home locations

In a workplace, we often find an item is missing just when it is most urgently needed. This can be true for tools (such as pipettes in a lab or wheelchairs in an ED) and information (such as maintenance manuals or a patient's plan of care). By using 5S and visual methods to mark standard locations, it is obvious when something is missing. Instead of just seeing a blank space, we see an outline labeled with what is supposed to be in that space. This allows for more proactive problem solving.

In one hospital lab, a collection of binders contained important maintenance and troubleshooting information for a test instrument. Over a weekend, the instrument malfunctioned, and the employees could not find the binder. This led to delays in getting the instrument back in working order, extra work for the team, and increased stress. It turned out that an employee with good intentions had taken the binder home to study it. A clear expectation had not been set that the binder needed to stay in place. The group responded by putting a diagonal

Figure 6.3   A laboratory bench shows clearly marked locations for specimen drop-off and supply storage.

tape stripe across their binders, so it became apparent when one was missing, as shown in Figure 6.6. In the future, a supervisor might be able to find the missing binder proactively before it is desperately needed.

In addition to using inexpensive vinyl tape, the practice of "shadowing" the location of items can be helpful. A shadow is a physical outline or photo of an item that is supposed to be in a location. These can be created with digital pictures or by tracing the outline of the item. A laminated plastic shadow can be attached to the location. Some orthopedic surgical trays already use this approach, using photos on the bottom of the tray to indicate which tool goes where. The photos are so realistic that it can be, at times, difficult to tell from a distance if the tool is actually there or not. In cases like that, a solid shadow showing the shape might be more useful than a realistic image.

As with other methods, we need to take care that we are not using the tool (5S) without thinking about the problem that is being solved or the waste that is being prevented. In some implementations, people go overboard by labeling or outlining everything they can. If an item is heavy and not likely to move, such as a large desktop printer, there is no value in putting a tape outline around it. There is no problem being solved by outlining the printer. We are, in fact, wasting tape. Likewise, putting printed labels on obvious items, such as a label that says "Printer" on the machine, adds no value and does not prevent a problem; however, a label may be helpful to identify the specific use of a printer. Asking people to do 5S for an individual office desk that is not a shared workspace might also bring little benefit to patients or the organization. Common sense should drive the use of this method. If people start questioning the benefit of the approach, it might be a sign that we have gone overboard with the tool.

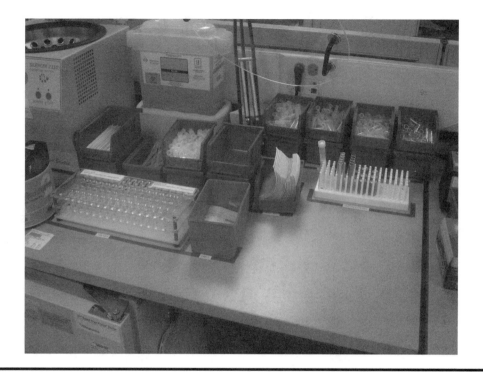

Figure 6.4 A laboratory bench shows clearly marked and labeled storage locations for tools and supplies.

Fifth S: Sustain

To prevent 5S from becoming a one-time event, we need a plan for sustaining and continually improving our workplace organization. The department needs a formal audit plan so supervisors and leaders can see if the new standards are being followed. As with standardized work audits, this can be done on a scheduled basis. The visual management methods also make it possible for leaders to scan the department as they are walking through. If something seems out of place or missing, they can ask a few questions and coach employees about maintaining the proper setup. If an item is out of place, it might be because an employee has found a better or more convenient location. For situations like this, the 5S tools (outlining tape and label makers) should be kept available so employees can update their own workplace organization.

Safety as a Sixth S?

Some organizations add a sixth S to the methodology—safety. Detractors point out that safety should be an underlying philosophy of the organization, not something to be tacked on to 5S just because it also starts with the letter *s*. Attention to safety should be the focus of all 5S stages as it should be a focus on any regular day. For example, removing unneeded equipment can reduce tripping hazards that might result from cluttered spaces. Having the right supplies and equipment in nearby locations can help improve patient safety, as well, as the case study at the end of this chapter illustrates. Excluding safety as a formal *S* does not mean that safety is not important; instead, it signifies that safety is not something that can be delegated only to those implementing

Figure 6.5   A laboratory benchtop shows clearly marked and labeled locations for the drop-off and temporary holding of different specimen types.

Lean. A culture of safety is owned by executive-level administrators and all other leaders in the organization.

Kanban: A Lean Approach to Managing Materials

Kanban is a method that builds on the concepts of standardized work, 5S, and visual management to give hospitals a simple yet effective method for managing supplies and inventory. *Kanban* is a Japanese term that can be translated as "signal," "card," or "sign."[12] A *kanban* is most often a physical signal, often a paper card or a plastic bin, that indicates when it is time to order more, from whom, and in what quantity; it can also be an electronic signal that is sent by a cabinet or computer system.

> Creating *kanban* cards can require a significant time investment just to get the system up and running. One hospital pharmacy created 1,600 laminated cards to manage medication inventory. After a few months, inventory levels had fallen from $600,000 to $350,000 by preventing the accidental overordering that occurred under the old method—not a bad return on that time investment!

Figure 6.6 Laboratory documentation binders set up so that a missing binder is visually apparent.

The *kanban* approach is sometimes mistakenly thought of as a system that just focuses on low inventory levels when its goals are actually to support the patients and the employees by ensuring needed supplies are in the right place, in the right quantity, and at the right time and to ensure the availability of material with the lowest required inventory levels. *Kanban* systems typically have fewer stock outs and better availability of materials than traditional materials management methods.

Problems with Traditional Materials Systems

Before Lean implementation, inventory management in hospital departments is often an informal process. Responsibility for ordering supplies might fall on a single person. When that key person is on vacation, or in the hypothetical case of that person winning the lottery and quitting, the system often falls apart, leading to stock outs on key supplies or other employees mistakenly ordering large amounts of inventory.

Even with a capable person managing supplies, if there is not a standardized, quantitative methodology for managing materials, there is a risk that the hospital is not minimizing its total inventory management costs. One method is the standing order; a vendor sends a predetermined amount each period (weekly, monthly, or quarterly). Standing orders are indeed easy to manage (the material arrives automatically), but it is a "push" system that is not responsive to variation in material usage. Since hospitals and departments have demand that changes for many reasons (seasonality, population changes, broader health trends), the standing order method sets us up for holding excess inventory (when usage of an item drops) or stock outs (when usage increases).

Reactions to inventory levels tend to be late and overreactive. When an item is out of stock, the department spends money unnecessarily to expedite the order. This takes up employee time, and the expedited shipment costs more. We might see the same reactive approach every time an items runs out instead of using the stock out to drive a potential systemic change to the ordering method.

The common practice of "par levels" is generally an advance over standing orders; par levels create a "pull" system, as items are replenished only in the quantities in which they are being used. Par level systems are, unfortunately, full of wasted motion as each individual item must be counted every time restocking occurs—a lot of extra motion, time, and cost. If the par level of an item is 15, a physical count must be done each time. If there are 4 items remaining, then 11 are restocked. This number is likely to vary, and restocking 11 items might require breaking open a box of 20, which is additional time and motion.

A more modern hospital practice is the automated inventory supply cabinet. These cabinets promise easy restocking if staff members press a button each time they remove an item. While this is a pull system that works in theory, people often forget to press buttons in the haste of their waste-filled days or buttons do not properly register each time. When the buttons are not pressed, the computer system thinks inventory levels are higher than in reality, so items run out, and staff are left to scramble to find supplies elsewhere. Because staff have to log in to the system, each encounter with the machine consumes precious time; furthermore, only one person can use the cabinet at a time, leading to a queue of nurses waiting to access the cabinet.

In one hospital pharmacy, the automated medication cabinets in the nursing units were set, in the computer system, to send a restocking signal when inventory reached zero. This was too late, as nurses and patients would not have medications available for many hours, requiring an expedited "missing med" order that generated more work for the pharmacy. In a Lean process, the restocking signals have to be sent before inventory is completely depleted to allow for the time it takes for more material to arrive.

Seattle Children's Hospital (Washington) realized a *kanban* system with open wire shelves could work better while allowing more than one person to take items at a time. They went from 100 of these cabinets to just 6, reducing their maintenance costs. Since items were at "zero inventory" 40% of the time with the automated cabinet, the *kanban* system provided higher service levels. In addition, the hospital found that a vast majority of "chargeable" items were not actually charged to patients, eliminating another common justification for the cabinets. The only items left in these locked automated cabinets are expensive items that are actually charged to a specific patient or items for which there is a safety concern.

Trade-offs with Inventory

In any system, there are trade-offs between high availability of materials and increased inventory costs, especially when the use of supplies is not perfectly predictable or steady. This is certainly the case in hospitals.

Generally speaking, the cost of inventory rises as we want to be more certain that we never run out. Industrial engineering and supply chain management principles teach us that inventory levels must unfortunately increase exponentially if we are to approach a guarantee of 100% availability for an item.

While our primary goal is to keep patient care flowing, we have to look at the trade-offs and costs involved. This trade-off can be seen with expired or obsolete inventory. We cannot expect constant availability yet also insist there be zero wasted inventory. For example, if a hospital's blood bank needs to ensure that it never runs out of O-negative blood, it is inevitable that some waste will occur since it might be difficult to perfectly predict blood usage. While other industries, such as manufacturing, might not want to run out of a particular item, the cost of shutting down an automotive assembly line for an hour, while high, does not compare to the cost of a lost life because a critical blood component, medication, or supply was not available. When the cost of stock outs is high, we have to err on the side of excess inventory. For items that are less critical, or have a close substitute, we can more easily allow some risk of stock outs.

Another trade-off to consider is the frequency of ordering from outside vendors. As we order less often, we can order in larger quantities. This often leads to volume discounts from vendors, or we can spread out fixed ordering costs (such as the labor cost of cutting a purchase order and the often fixed shipping cost from the vendor) across more material. The trade-off with ordering less frequently is that we have higher inventory management costs, which include

- Cash tied up in inventory
- Space required for storage
- Labor required to move, count, and maintain inventory
- Risk of damage, obsolescence, or expiration

Keeping inventory low by ordering more frequently is not always the approach that minimizes the total system cost. For example, the laboratory at Henry Ford Hospital (Detroit, MI) had been ordering some reagents and quality control materials in six-month batches. Rather than moving to an extreme of ordering weekly or monthly, they found the optimal point was to order somewhere between every three and six months. This was because each time they ordered reagents, technologists had to do time-consuming calibration, time and cost that could be considered part of the cost of ordering. So, the lowest inventory (ordering monthly) would not have led to the lowest total cost.[13]

Ordering more frequently also reduces the overall risk of stock outs because we can reevaluate actual usage and respond more quickly if we are ordering small amounts weekly instead of large amounts quarterly.

The *kanban* method allows us to quantify an optimal reorder point for supplies. This formula considers a number of factors, including

- Average usage or demand for an item
- How frequently we consider reordering (often daily or weekly)
- The vendor's lead time for replenishing items

■ Safety stock, considering the variation of usage and variation in replenishment time and the cost of stocking out

The amount of safety stock required will depend on the amount of variation involved with a given part. If an item is critically important, has highly variable usage, and comes from an unreliable vendor who might deliver more in 2 days or 2 weeks, the hospital would hold a relatively high amount of safety stock.

Using *Kanban* to Replenish Supplies

Kanban can be used to pull materials from a central hospital supply room or a departmental stockroom to the point of use. Or, we can have a series of pulls, each with its own *kanban* signal and reorder points, as shown in Figure 6.7. The *kanban* pull signal is meant to be simple and visual, such as an empty bin, a card, or a message sent by a bar-code scanner.

Park Nicollet Health Services has implemented *kanban* across 68 hospital departments and 33 clinic departments since 2004. They have created and maintained over 60,000 *kanban* cards that are used to signal replenishment of their supplies. Between 800 and 1,000 items are replenished via *kanban* on any given day.[14] The central materials department works with departments to setup *kanban*, with the central materials specialists placing orders and restocks from the main storeroom. Park Nicollet estimates it has saved $1.1 million in the past 3 years with this method.

One visual way of managing inventory, especially in a department, is a style of *kanban* called a two-bin system. This method uses two plastic bins at the point of use, bins that can stack together or sit in front of or behind each other on a shelf, as pictured in Figure 6.8. For an employee who uses the items, the system is simple. Anyone can take items for use, but when the first bin is empty,

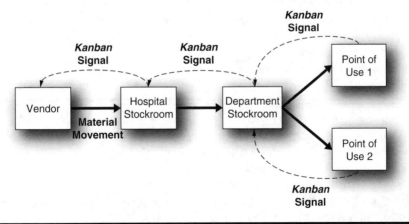

Figure 6.7   Illustration of the flow of supplies through a multistage *kanban* system in which each downstream area (to the right) pulls material from an upstream location vendor.

Figure 6.8   A laboratory benchtop with multiple items set up on a two-bin *kanban* replenishment system.

that empty bin becomes a visual signal to order more. With the two-bin system, when one bin is empty, we still have enough with which to continue working. This system does not require the manual counting of a par-level system. The empty bin, which is labeled with information such as the item name, number, and source of more material, can be set in a designated area (properly labeled in a 5S and visual management manner). At Seattle Children's Hospital, 95% of supplies are replenished using bins, with anything too large to fit in bins being triggered by *kanban* cards.[15]

The *kanban* bins or cards are collected by a single person on a regular basis (typically every shift or every day). Instead of multiple unplanned trips to the stockroom, one person makes one trip. Hospitals, generally, should not pay highly skilled and highly trained individuals, including technologists, nurses, and pharmacists, to do manual material-handling work. The goal of the *kanban* system and the materials management department should be to properly support the highly skilled employees who do the value-added work in an area.

In one hospital's operating room project, implementing *kanban* helped reduce the time required to restock the rooms. Before Lean, nurses would spend 10 minutes at the end of each day counting inventory and replenishing each item in its proper location. With the *kanban* process, the Lean implementation manager highlighted the ease and time savings, saying, "Now, the nurses just throw empty bins into a basket, and people refill them during their downtime. It doesn't seem like a big deal until you add it up and realize that we're saving 600 nursing hours over the course of a year."

One benefit of a *kanban* approach is that we no longer wait until we are very low on (or completely out of) an item to order more, as might commonly happen before *kanban*. This minimizes the number of interruptions to employees and the flow of work, whether it is testing specimens, processing medication orders, or caring for patients. In traditional materials systems, an employee, such as a medical technologist, sees that the supply of an item is dangerously low. Because inventory levels have gotten so low, the technologist might interrupt work to immediately run to a stock area or immediately stop to get an expedited purchase order issued. This time away delays the primary workflow in the area, and the reactive nature of the interruptions causes stress and frustration, especially when conditions like this are the norm.

The systematic *kanban* method not only minimizes stock outs, but also prevents an accumulation of excess inventory. Often, when we run out of a needed item, the natural reaction is an overreaction to order more inventory to protect against running out again. In a *kanban* system, any stock out needs to be investigated to identify the root cause. Was this a one-time event or a consistent shift in the usage of an item? Instead of just reacting by ordering more, the person responsible for the *kanban* system needs to determine if the reorder point needs to be changed. This systematic analysis prevents an emotional reaction to what might have been an unforeseen one-time event. At Seattle Children's, supplies that are ordered more or less frequently than expected have their *kanban* bin sizes adjusted to account for this demand change.[16]

During operating room improvement projects, the variation of supplies on physician preference cards often comes up for discussion. Some surgical teams have worked to standardize the use of sutures and other supplies if a variation that does not necessarily benefit the patient can be costly to the hospital. The department can shift from personal preference to what is proven to be best for all stakeholders. Changes like these are most effectively initiated and driven by the surgeons, rather than being forced on them by operating room business directors.

Before *kanban* is put in place, we often find that employees hide or hoard needed supplies, often in response to a materials replenishment system they cannot trust. A nurse at another hospital admitted to the author that she hid supplies above ceiling tiles to ensure her own supply. One laboratory found there were eight different storage locations for a particular type of blood tube, all right within the phlebotomy department. Different drawers and shelves were full, with tubes tucked away in many hidden places. This took up excess space and increased the risk that tubes in the bottom of drawers would expire before getting used.

By installing an effective *kanban* system, the department better organized its supplies into a single stock location on exposed shelves for all to see. Because the *kanban* system was reliable, employees no longer felt the need to hoard supplies. Instead of just mandating that employees quit hoarding supplies (a mandate that would force the practice further underground), the need to hoard was eliminated. Making the proper supplies available with high reliability also creates conditions that make it easier for staff to properly use gloves and other protective equipment.

In a very advanced case, Seattle Children's has essentially eliminated its central supply room by restocking directly from vendors to departments, in most cases, leading to lower inventory and better response to the units or departments that pull materials.[17]

The New York Health and Hospital Corporation (HHC) is using "just-in-time" ordering to replenish materials, as part of their Lean program called Breakthrough. As many organizations do in conjunction with their supply chain redesign efforts, HHC rationalized the variety of rubber gloves that are available. Instead of 20 different colors and thicknesses, there are now just 2 options available (in different sizes, of course). This saves HHC $4 million a year on gloves alone.[18] In keeping with the principle of respect for people, changes like this should be made with significant staff and clinician participation, rather than being mandated from the top.

A *Kanban* Case Study

Northampton General Hospital NHS Trust (Northampton, England) is a 695-bed acute hospital that can trace its history to an infirmary that was built in 1743. The pathology department struggled with inventory management prior their use of Lean methods, starting in 2008. "We were under increasing pressure from Hospital Management to improve our level of service," says then-pathology directorate manager Peter Martin.[20] The environment was often stressful, with high absenteeism due to illness. Lean was a method aimed at improving the service provided to physicians and patients, while also being a way to reduce stress and overtime for staff.

One cause of stress and interruptions during the day was the waste caused by problems with the existing materials management system. Some supply storage points would run empty and some items were replenished from a somewhat inconvenient location, a lower level called the "undercroft." In other cases, the newest supply of specimen collection tubes would be poured on top of the old supply, causing some tubes at the bottom of the bin to expire. This represented either wasted money or the risk that an old tube would be used to collect a patient specimen, causing problems with test results.

Describing the old process, Samantha Martin, Biomedical Support Worker, said, "We had several storerooms, some on the other side of the hospital," adding, "You'd look at what you had and think, 'I need a bit more of this, some more of that.' We'd end up with loads of things we don't use and not enough of the things we do use." It wasn't always clear, from a visual management or process perspective, when items should be restocked, so staff often over-ordered on a "just-in-case basis."[21]

Pathology staff members worked to implement a *kanban* system, first auditing the quantity used of each item in a year, and then calculating daily and monthly usage rates. The team created and utilized laminated *kanban* cards, as pictured in Figure 6.9, that display the full product information, stock level, and required ordering volumes for an item. The cards then visually marked the re-order point for items, as shown in Figure 6.10. When it was time to restock items, pathology staff would place the appropriate card in a pocket, as pictured in Figure 6.11. In some cases, the two-bin *kanban* approach was used for small items that could be kept in plastic bins. For items that ran the risk of expiration, the two-bin system ensured that stock could be properly rotated, so the oldest supply was always used before the new.

New standardized work was created to help ensure that the processes for using the *kanban* system were clear and that staff were well-trained in their role in using or maintaining the *kanban* system.

After the initial implementation in the blood sciences area, the *kanban* system was also put in place in histopathology. Now, 80 to 90% of their stock is managing using *kanban*, says Clare Wood, Biomedical Scientist. Wood adds, "We have definitely improved the tidiness of our stock and we have had a reduction of stock outs for some items. People like *kanban* in histology, so

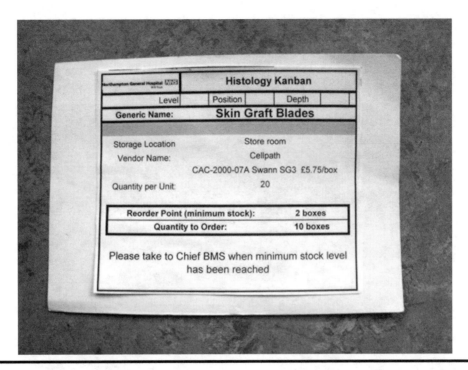

Figure 6.9   Example *kanban* **card.**

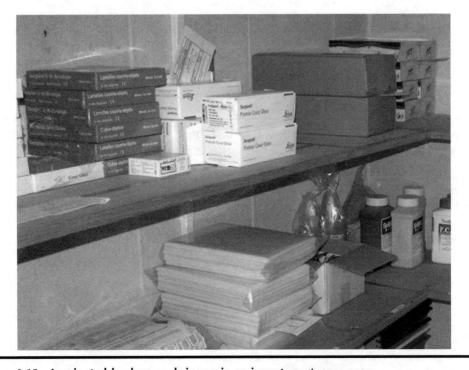

Figure 6.10   Laminated *kanban* **cards in use in an inventory storage area.**

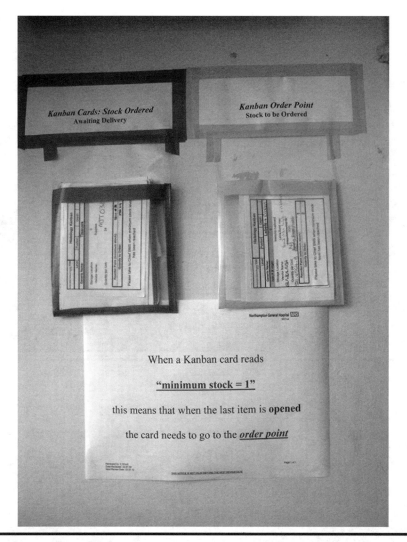

Figure 6.11 *Kanban* **card collection point for items that need to be ordered or have already been ordered.**

much so, that I have just had a look in the pocket and we have a post-it note for a rare item of stock, something that doesn't have a *kanban* card. So, people like them enough to make their own!" Wood says the only difficulties with *kanban* are managing items that don't stack neatly, cards going missing, or cards not being returned to shelves when new stock arrives , but these problems happen rarely.

With all of their initial Lean improvements, the pathology department avoided a total of £158,000 in labor, storage, and inventory costs with the *kanban* system, as well as improvements to the physical layout and standardized work. *Kanban*, specifically, enabled them to save money by maintaining a smaller standing inventory. More importantly, staff had what they needed to perform their vital work for patients and fewer people are involved in the management of stock. "We've had no stockouts in a year," says Samantha Martin.[22]

Reflecting on the overall improvements to the layout and workflow, including the *kanban* system, Peter Martin reflected, "Thanks to Lean, we can absorb the added work. We are finishing on time now and on good days, slightly early. We've taken the stress out of the process."[23]

Case Example: The Use of Lean Methods to Prevent Patient Harm

At a large children's hospital, a young patient, having been sedated, started vomiting while secured inside the machine for head and neck MRI. The MRI tech detected this situation and interrupted the scan to go care for the patient, an action that might be considered first-order problem solving: make sure the patient's airway is clear.

In her attempt to rescue the patient, the tech looked to the MRI-safe clips that were on the wall inside the room—but there were no suction tubes available as there should have been. This created a second-order problem to solve: the lack of needed equipment to solve the first-order problem.

The MRI tech, in a rush, walked back to the control room to get suction tubes from the high-tech inventory cabinet—except that the cabinet also had zero stock, another problem. The tech then ran and interrupted another MRI procedure, taking suction tubes from the other room back to her patient. The child was, ultimately, unharmed, and the first-order problem was solved: The patient's airway was cleared, without injury.

Problems in this case:

- First order: Patient in distress
- Second order: No suction tubes available
- Third order: No reliable, consistent process to ensure needed supplies are available in the cabinet or the MRI rooms
- Fourth order: Lack of a robust management system to more quickly react to or prevent problems like this

What happened next? When asked about this the next day (after she volunteered the story), the MRI tech answered, "We completed the scan." There was no immediate problem solving around the second-order problem—the absence of suction tubes. After the scan was completed, the team brought in the next patient (since they were now behind schedule). Even without working on the third-order problem (fixing the system that led to missing supplies), one might have expected that somebody would have simply gone and gotten more tubes (via the proper channels, not robbing them from another room), just in case that patient (or the next one) also started vomiting.

We should not blame the individual MRI tech for her reaction or lack of immediate problem solving, as she was working within the culture and management systems of the radiology department and the hospital. She had no "support chain" to ask for help to resolve even the second-order problem: Why was there no help to immediately restock the needed supplies?

If the MRI suite had been a Lean setting, such as an outstanding Lean factory, the MRI tech would have been able to pull a physical "andon cord," which would have immediately drawn a helpful response from a supervisor[19] to assist with the recovery of the patient or to get more suction tubes so the MRI tech could focus on her work and the patients.

In this case, the MRI tech also did not have a process or a mechanism for getting a response about the third-order problem: the lack of a reliable, consistent system. She said nothing to her supervisor and did not escalate the issue until the next day, when she discussed it with the outside consultant who was in the area (as opposed to the supervisor, who was usually in meetings). The team almost missed the opportunity to investigate, to learn, and to improve.

In a Lean setting, a group would be quickly convened from the natural work team, including representatives of roles including MRI techs, respiratory therapists, anesthesiologists, nurses, and managers. This team might come together during a gap in the schedule for the day or at the end of the cases scheduled that day. In the most serious patient safety situations, the manager and team might consider fully stopping procedures until the underlying root causes and risks had been eliminated.

In this case, we could ask why suction tubes were missing from the room. It turned out that there was no clear responsibility or consistent standardized work regarding who restocked the MRI rooms and at what interval. This showed an opportunity to define the standardized work for restocking the rooms, including clear responsibility for who would restock the room after an item was used and what escalation process could be used if that could not occur—to prevent putting another patient in harm's way.

Looking at the supposedly "automated" inventory cabinet that had no suction tubes, the team discussed some of the limitations of that technology. If staff did not press the proper button when taking supplies, the right restocking signals were not sent electronically to materials management. The closed cabinet did not lend itself to easy visual management of the inventory levels; if inventory were low or zero, it was hard to see behind the glass doors. The team started to discuss a simple, visual, two-bin *kanban* system for inexpensive items that were not charged to patients—a process that might work better, and at a lower cost, than the cabinet.

In addition, the team, having learned about 5S and visual management, realized that there were not enough wall clips for all needed items, including suction tubes. Some items were stuffed into plastic drawers, making it difficult to determine, at a glance, if any items were missing. The manager responded by ordering more MRI-safe clips in place of the drawers, an improvement that would also reduce the time required to rescue a patient in distress.

While the team consistently performed a pre-MRI checklist to help ensure, for example, that the patient did not have metal on or inside his or her body, the team did not have a similar checklist to ensure, with a visual scan, that all needed safety supplies were stocked and in place before each procedure started, a clear opportunity for improvement to the system.

Finally, this situation provided an opportunity for managers, directors, and senior leaders to talk about their culture and management system. Why did employees feel uncomfortable asking for help or raising concerns about patient care? Why were supervisors and managers unavailable to provide help as problems occurred? Why did the culture emphasize and tolerate immediate first-order "firefighting" without also focusing on identifying root causes and improving systems? What could senior leadership do to create an environment for continuous quality improvement?

This scenario was used in ongoing Lean efforts in the department to emphasize the importance of 5S, visual management, *kanban* replenishment, and standardized work and how these methods could solve real problems that previously affected patient care and created unnecessary stress for staff members. The MRI tech who told the story to an outside consultant (not her supervisor) 24 hours after it occurred was upset for two reasons: The patient could have been harmed, and the technician was afraid that these problems could easily happen again, with unfortunate results, without improvements to the process. It is in this way that Lean improvements and waste reduction serve patients and employees in a respectful way.

Conclusion

As with any Lean tools or methods, hospitals should not implement visual management, 5S, or *kanban* because a book says so or to be part of a trend. The point of any of these tools is to create a culture for solving problems in the workplace, reducing or preventing waste from interfering with our work and patient care. Any of these methods should not be a one-time event; they should be part of an ongoing management system that helps sustain the methods and drives continuous improvement out of respect for patients and workers. Implementing these methods not only can reduce waste, but also can get employees engaged in improving the workplace instead of just complaining about problems.

Lean Lessons

■ Visual management helps expose problems and avoid miscommunications and waste.
■ 5S reduces waste through improved organization and visual methods.
■ 5S is not a one-time event—it is a plan to be sustained to maintain and improve workplace organization.
■ Supplies and items that are used most frequently should be kept closest to the point of use.
■ Hiding the mess behind cabinet doors does not fix the root cause of the disorganization problem.
■ *Kanban* can be implemented using cards, plastic bins, or electronic signals.
■ *Kanban* requires much less counting and time than par levels.
■ With materials, we need to view trade-offs between the cost of inventory and the cost of running out. Hospitals might need to err on the side of not running out.
■ When we have more variation in the system, we need more safety stock to protect us.

Points for Group Discussion

■ What is an example of an information deficit in our area? What waste does that cause? Can we use visual management to eliminate that waste?
■ How much time is wasted each day due to disorganization? What could we better use that time for?
■ How can we free up time to work on Lean methods?
■ What are some problems we face with our existing materials management systems? What drives people to hoard supplies?

Notes

1. Takahara, Akio, and Collin McLoughlin, *Clinical 5S For Healthcare* (Bellingham, WA: Enna, 2010), 1.
2. Leone, Gerard, and Richard D. Rahn, *Supplies Management in the OR* (Boulder, CO: Flow, 2011), 1.
3. Galsworth, Gwendolyn, *Visual Workplace, Visual Thinking* (Portland, OR: Visual-Lean Enterprise Press, 2005), 13.
4. Ibid., 15.
5. Liker, Jeffrey K., *The Toyota Way* (New York: McGraw-Hill, 2003), 159.
6. Hemmila, Donna, "Banding Together for Patient Safety," *NurseWeek*, http://nsweb.nursingspectrum.com/CFForms/GuestLecture/bandingtogether.cfm (accessed December 20, 2007).
7. Touissant, John, presentation, First Global Lean Healthcare Summit, June 25, 2007.
8. Takahara and McLoughlin, *Clinical 5S*, 11.
9. Yee, Chen May, "Hard Times Curtail Park Nicollet's Ambition," *StarTribune.com*, May 23, 2009, http://www.startribune.com/business/45871162.html?elr=KArks:DCiU1OiP:DiiUiD3aPc:_Yyc:aULPQL7PQLanchO7DiUr (accessed April 3, 2011).
10. Productivity Press Development Team, *5S for Operators* (New York: Productivity Press, 1996), 12.
11. Wellman, Joan, Howard Jeffries, and Pat Hagan, *Leading the Lean Healthcare Journey* (New York: Productivity Press, 2010), 88.
12. Productivity Press Development Team, *Kanban for the Shopfloor* (New York: Productivity Press, 2002), 1.

13. Lusky, Karen, "Laying Lean on the Line, One Change at a Time," *CAP Today*, July 2009, http://www.cap.org/apps/cap.portal?_nfpb=true&cntvwrPtlt_actionOverride=%2Fportlets%2FcontentVie wer%2Fshow&_windowLabel=cntvwrPtlt&cntvwrPtlt%7BactionForm.contentReference%7D=cap_today%2F0709%2F0709h_laying_lean.html&_state=maximized&_pageLabel=cntvwr (accessed April 3, 2011).

14. Brook, Andy, presentation at Park Nicollet Health Services, August 2010.

15. Wellman, *Leading the Lean*, 91.

16. Wellman, 91.

17. Wellman, 91.

18. Jones, Del, "Hospital CEOs Manage Staff Time, Inventory to Cut Costs," *USA Today*, September 10, 2009, http://www.usatoday.com/news/health/2009–09–09-saving-money-hospitals_N.htm (accessed April 8, 2011).

19. ValuMetrix Services, "Northampton General Hospital uses Lean to cut turnaround time by 40%, avoids £158,000/year in labour, storage, and inventory costs," website, http://www.excellence.eastmidlands.nhs.uk/EasySiteWeb/getresource.axd?AssetID=37152&type=full&servicetype=Attachment (accessed August 8, 2011).

20. ValuMetrix Services.

21. ValuMetrix Services.

22. ValuMetrix Services.

23. Liker, Jeffrey K., and Michael Hoseus, *Toyota Culture: The Heart and Soul of the Toyota Way* (New York: McGraw-Hill, 2008), 7.

Chapter 7

Proactive Root Cause Problem Solving

The Mary McClinton Story

The case of Mary McClinton's death at Virginia Mason Medical Center (VMMC) (Seattle, WA) is well known in patient safety circles. McClinton died in 2004 after being injected with chlorhexidine, an antiseptic solution, instead of a contrast dye. During her procedure, there were three clear liquids that were kept in stainless steels bowls on a tray: the antiseptic, the dye, and a saline solution. Anticipating the interventional radiologist's need, an experienced technician prelabeled an empty syringe as "contrast dye." However, he later allegedly filled the syringe with the antiseptic, not the dye.[1] A Lean thinker would recognize the potential for systemic error in a situation like this and would not be satisfied with well-trained people being careful. The error that caused McClinton's death was an accident waiting to happen.

Before the fateful day, the hospital had switched from a brown iodine solution to the clear antiseptic. Some versions of the story said the hospital had "recently" switched, but another report said the clear antiseptic had been in place for two years before McClinton's death.[2,3] It is hindsight, but one might ask how a risk like that could have gone ignored. The technician involved, Carl Dorsey, knew of the change and mentioned this "setup" for error to his supervisor two months before the incident. This error was not the result of an unforeseen risk. The technician knew, the supervisor knew—yet the risky situation persisted.

A 69-year-old social worker and her family suffered from this preventable error, but so did the technician. Dorsey had an "unblemished" 34-year career, with 17 of those years at VMMC. He was "fined by the state, accepted blame, and resigned from the hospital," although he was "not certain" whether he or the doctor actually filled the syringe.[4] As Dorsey reflected on what happened, he said, "Mistakes will happen, we are exceptionally human."

The Toyota philosophy was originally called the "respect for humanity" system. This means that we not only respect each individual, but also respect our own humanity—our human nature. Humans are not perfect. As much as we try to be careful, mistakes can happen. As Sir Liam Donaldson of the World Health Organization said, "Human error is inevitable. We can never eliminate it. We can eliminate problems in the system that make it more likely to happen."[5]

After McClinton's death, the antiseptic was replaced with a gel on a swab, eliminating the risk of mistaking chlorhexidine for the dye with future patients. We can only hope that this same systemic risk has been addressed at every other hospital.

Improving Quality and Patient Safety

As we saw in the house diagram in Chapter 5, quality is one of the two pillars of Lean. Of all the motivations for implementing Lean in healthcare, there is likely no higher purpose than that of improving the quality of care delivery and improving patient safety. Certainly, hospitals and advances in medical care are saving many lives, thanks to clinical excellence, but the complexity of modern hospitals makes processes and value streams hard to manage. While it is a testament to the extraordinary efforts of many healthcare workers that there are not more errors, hospital leaders must work to create an environment in which errors and harm can be significantly reduced.

How many patients are injured, suffer infections, or die as the result of preventable errors in hospitals? Statistics from various sources use different estimates and methodologies, all trying to determine numbers that cannot be known precisely. Some studies rely on the review of medical records, for which the true nature of errors may be underreported. While there are some mechanisms for voluntary reporting, it is hard to argue that all hospitals or people report all errors equally.[6] Many errors may go undiscovered since it is often difficult to tell if an error caused a death or just contributed to it, leading to further problems with the data.

There is, however, widespread agreement that the relative scale of this problem is unacceptable—whatever the numbers, too many patients are being harmed. This is a global problem, not isolated to certain countries or certain payer structures. We also have proof that Lean methods for quality improvement can reduce the number of preventable injuries, infections, and deaths, while also improving clinical outcomes even when harm is not an issue.

Lean is not a "silver bullet" approach that will instantly eliminate all errors, but the tools and the mindsets can help our hospitals and employees reduce preventable errors.

Cultural Obstacles to Quality Improvement

Hospitals have some long-standing cultural obstacles to overcome before Lean quality improvement methods can be effective. For one, we have to shift from "naming, blaming, and shaming" employees to an environment in which we learn from errors, using knowledge gained to prevent future errors.[7] Hospitals need to be more proactive in preventing errors, anticipating possible or likely errors or responding to near misses, rather than responding only after injury or death has occurred. Improving quality relies more on leadership, culture, and creative thinking than on any specific technology or tool.

McLeod Regional Medical Center (Florence, SC) changed its culture from one of blame to one of problem solving and prevention. While the national average for adverse drug events is two to eight per 1,000 doses, McLeod's rate was reduced to less than one per 1,000.[8]

Another obstacle is incorrect perceptions about medical errors, in the general public and the medical community. One study showed that patients and physicians thought published estimates of avoidable death numbers were "much too high."[9] This is despite the fact that some estimates are based on errors that were actually reported, which makes those conservative estimates, given underreporting. Surgeons and the general public often blame individual surgeons, rather than the system, for errors. This perception was confirmed in *To Err Is Human*, as the general public viewed medical mistakes as an "individual provider issue" instead of a systems failure.[10]

The tendency to blame individuals leads to responses that focus on punishing or removing bad people instead of improving the system. Look at almost any news report on high-profile medical errors, and you will likely see reports of individuals being punished, fired, or even jailed. Senior leaders often publicly criticize their own organizations, after the fact, for not following policies and procedures, saying that there is "no excuse" for such errors.[11] Instead of retrospective lambasting, we all need to work together as a team toward proactive prevention.

Why Do Errors Occur?

If adverse events are not always caused by individual negligence, why do errors occur? Where traditional management is quick to blame individuals for errors, the Lean mindset understands Dr. W. Edwards Deming's teaching that 94% of errors "belong to the system."[12] *To Err Is Human* concluded, "The majority of medical errors do not result from individual recklessness or the actions of a particular group—this is not a 'bad apple' problem. More commonly, errors are caused by faulty systems, processes, and conditions that lead people to make mistakes or fail to prevent them."[13]

Accountability and personal responsibility are important and cannot be minimized. One might say that responsible individuals are necessary, but not sufficient, to ensure quality in a highly complex system. The Lean philosophy does not encourage us to make excuses for individuals who knowingly do the wrong thing and take wild risks. Leading patient safety experts, including Dr. Robert Wachter, concurred that we must find the proper balance between "no blame" and "no accountability."[14] Arguably, prelabeling a syringe before it is filled is a risky practice and somebody's intentional choice, as seen in the McClinton case. There are some circumstances for which a physician is known to get upset about delays, such as waiting for a syringe to be filled, which might lead an individual to do something in advance to avoid that situation, although there are no indications that was the case with Dorsey.

Violations and Errors, Lapses, and Slips

Violations are intentional actions that go against accepted practices and are, by definition, avoidable; however, not all violations are motivated by bad intentions. A violation might be necessary and defendable in certain conditions for the sake of the patient. For example, an anesthesiologist might not take the time to keep all normal records for an emergency surgery.[15] Harmful and willful violations, such as an addicted anesthesiologist skimming some of the drugs intended for surgical patients, fall more squarely on individuals, making traditional punishment approaches more appropriate (although we could ask if the hospital had been previously aware of an ongoing problem without taking action, making it a systemic issue). One study concluded that only 27.6% of adverse events were caused by negligence, including willful violations of policies.[16] Prelabeling a syringe might be considered a violation.

Errors, on the other hand, include events when things go wrong even if every party involved had the best intentions and was performing properly. Errors can be further broken down into skill-based errors, for which an unintended action took place. These include *lapses* (mental errors, such as forgetting a step in a procedure) and *slips* (physical errors, such as turning the wrong knob on a piece of equipment).[17] Filling a syringe with the wrong clear liquid would be considered a slip. The fact that something is described as human error is not an excuse for tolerating the error or thinking it is inevitable.

Many errors can often be traced to a lack of training or awareness, a problem that is the responsibility of managers and the system. Lapses can be prevented through the use of checklists and standardized work, while slips can be prevented through error-proofing methods, as discussed in Chapter 8.

There are some simple questions that leaders can ask to help determine if a problem was the result of a systemic error or a willful violation.

- Was this an error that has happened before, in some other place, involving some other person?
- Would another caregiver or employee likely have done the same thing in the same situation?
- Should administration have anticipated that this type of error could have happened?

If an answer to any of these questions is yes, then we probably have a systemic error that cannot be prevented in the future by merely removing a particular "bad apple" from the process. Without Virginia Mason making the systemic change from a clear liquid antiseptic to a gel and swab, the same error might have occurred again with a different technician on a different day.

Examples of Quality Improvement

It is not all bad news in healthcare. Many hospitals are using Lean methods to improve quality and patient safety. ThedaCare (Wisconsin) is widely known as one of the leaders in applying Lean to healthcare.[18] Former chief executive officer (CEO) John Touissant, MD, set an ambitious goal of reducing defects by 50% each year.[19] This is not a case of cautious, incremental improvement goal setting—it is a very aggressive goal that seemed likely to drive serious action.

ThedaCare began measuring defects per million opportunities (DPMO) in 2005 and estimated that their processes had 100,000 DPMO in areas, including providing consistent protocol-driven care for Code STEMI (Segment Elevation Myocardial Infarction) patients. A defect might include an instance when a step in the protocol was not followed, introducing risk to the patient. This corresponded with a Six Sigma-style quality level of 2.78 sigma, where the goal of Six Sigma quality corresponds with 3.4 DPMO. In 2006 and 2007, ThedaCare estimated its defect rates had fallen to 60,000 DPMO (3.05 sigma) and 20,000 DPMO (3.55 sigma), respectively. Overall, they were ahead of the 50% annual goal and continue to improve, aiming for perfection instead of just being better than they were before.

In examples with more specific data, ThedaCare has also

- Reduced lab specimen collection errors from 941 DPMO to just 100[20]
- Improved pneumonia bundle compliance rates from 38% to 95%[21]
- Reduced "early-term" induced births from 35% to zero, shortening neonatal intensive care unit (ICU) length of stay from 30 days to 16[22,23]
- Reduced medical reconciliation errors on admission from 1.25 per chart to zero, when done by a pharmacist[24]

As a type of error, specimen collection errors are pretty straightforward. But, in the third example given, ThedaCare started viewing an early-term induction, often done for convenience, as a "defect," although it was considered normal beforehand. Medical evidence pointed them not to perform delivery before 39 weeks if at all possible.

Hospitals can take steps, including standardized work, to prevent hospital-acquired infections. Hospitals that have successfully cut infection rates have analyzed work methods to identify the best way to insert lines and catheters. Allegheny General Hospital (Pittsburgh, PA) first set zero infections as a goal, an important strategic direction. Second, a team of clinicians standardized the methods for determining the proper line placement location, as well as the methods and tools for inserting the line itself and methods for maintaining the line. Improved communication methods were also put in place when anybody needed help with lines. The results after the first year were dramatic. The rate of line infection was reduced from 1 in 22 to just 1 of every 185. They still had not reached the goal of zero infections, but they had made significant progress.[25] Similar results have been achieved throughout the world; in a World Health Organization study on the use of checklists, hospitals in Michigan nearly eliminated catheter-related bloodstream infections and reduced ICU mortality rates by 10%.[26]

Allegheny General also learned that quality improvement freed time for staff to solve problems, to utilize known infection control procedures, and to spend more time on direct patient care. Some hospitals now understand that reducing infections reduces the average length of stay, which essentially frees beds and creates additional capacity, doing so in a far less-expensive way than building a new patient tower. These central line-associated bloodstream infection reductions are clearly good for the patients, the employees, the physicians, and the hospital.

Finding Root Causes and Preventing Errors

Errors and near misses in hospitals need to be turned into learning opportunities with the goal of preventing future occurrences. When errors are discovered, the best response, in the Lean approach, is to ask two straightforward questions:

1. What allowed that error occur?
2. What can we do so the error never occurs again?

The Lean response is different from traditional responses to errors, which usually ask, "Whose fault is it?" Managers often look to assign blame and rely on punishment to show they are addressing the problem, asking those employees who remain to "be careful" as an attempt at prevention. Placing blame is often unfair to employees, resulting in frustration and resentment. Telling caregivers to be careful and hanging cautionary signs do not prevent errors from harming other patients.[27] On the contrary, Lean managers start with the assumption that people are trying to do a good job (Douglas McGregor's theory Y)[28] and ask the question "How could this have happened despite the best of intentions?"

Workarounds and the Need for Fixing Root Causes

Before Lean, we often find hospital employees inventing and using workarounds in their daily work. A workaround is a short-term response to an immediate problem that does nothing to prevent the problem from occurring again. For example, a thermometer is missing from an exam room, so the nurse runs to another room to take its thermometer—helping her patient, but creating a new problem for the next patient and nurse in that other room. Although they seem to help in the short term, workarounds ultimately harm both quality and productivity as they doom us to wasting more time in the future responding to that same problem or error.

Time pressures on employees often prevent us from doing deeper analysis and problem solving. At a hospital pharmacy that had not yet implemented Lean, pharmacists spent a good deal of time inspecting physician medication orders and patient charts, looking for errors or process defects. They often found a number of preventable process defects, including

- Orders that did not match what was written in the patient's chart
- Doses that were not appropriate for the patient's age, weight, or condition
- Medications that conflicted with recorded patient allergies

When an error was spotted, the pharmacist just corrected it. It was difficult for the pharmacist to give feedback to the person who might have been the original source of the error, be it a physician (who might have written an order incorrectly) or a unit clerk (who might have incorrectly recorded or entered a physician's verbal orders). Rather than blaming individuals (since many people may make the same errors), it could be the design of the computer system that makes it more likely for an error to occur. The pharmacist felt like he or she did not have the time to call, page, or track down the person who entered the order or want to be in the position of trying to give constructive feedback to a physician, fearing a negative response.

If people are unaware that errors are occurring that have an impact on others, they cannot begin a problem-solving process that could help prevent future errors. Pharmacists reported finding the same errors every day, causing frustration from the wasted time and the perceived inability to work with others to fix the root of the problem. When errors occur, people often assume that others do not care or that others are "bad employees." Instead of blaming individuals, we need to shift to a constructive problem-solving mindset. Table 7.1 shows some examples of errors and the reaction of workarounds and blaming versus the problem-solving reaction.

When an error is found, the immediate reaction should still include fixing the problem in the short term. In the case where a pharmacy technician finds a pill in the wrong bin, the pharmacy technician should still put the pill back in the correct bin. This might be called an immediate countermeasure or a containment of the problem. At that point, or at a convenient time soon after, problem-solving measures should be used to identify the root cause so we can prevent reoccurrence of that particular problem.

In some cases, employees take pride in their ability to work around common problems. Heroic measures are often rewarded as a sign of a can-do attitude or a willingness to go above and beyond job expectations. An employee may become known as an expert in working around problems and is often called on to work around problems for others. These employees, or those who define "my work" as including frequent workarounds, may feel a sense of loss as problems are prevented with Lean methods.

Adopting these mindsets can create a leadership challenge, as one hospital chief operating officer (COO) realized he puzzled his employees by talking about the newly discovered need to eliminate workarounds. The COO had worked his way up through the organization, starting as an entry-level nurse, and employees knew he had risen through the ranks by being "the best firefighter." His pronouncements were counter to his 30 years of demonstrated behaviors, which was difficult to overcome, even as he worked on changing his approach away from being a firefighting senior leader.

Table 7.1   Workarounds and Blaming versus Problem Solving Mindsets

Problem	Workaround	Blame Mindset	Problem-Solving Mindset
Medications are missing or not available in the cabinet.	Nurse walks to other cabinets or units to find the medications.	"The pharmacy doesn't help us."	"Why are meds often not available? How can we work together to fix this?"
Labels are crooked on laboratory tubes.	Technologist relabels the tube properly.	"That assistant never gets this right."	"Is the assistant aware of proper labeling practices and their impact on the process?"
Medical record does not have a diagnosis code that will get the system paid for a home nebulizer.	Billing clerk searches through the record to find a way to recode the diagnosis.	"The doctor's office doesn't know how to code properly."	"Why do multiple offices make the same error? What is the systemic cause?"
Medication is found in the wrong bin.	Pharmacy technician puts medication back in the right place.	"Other people aren't careful."	"Why could that pill fall into the adjacent bin?"

Asking Why Instead of Who

When errors occur, the Lean approach prompts us not to ask who, as in "Whose fault is it?" Again, this is the Deming influence in the Lean culture and management system. Recalling Sir Liam Donaldson's quote about needing to eliminate problems in the system, "Human error is inevitable, we can never eliminate it. We can eliminate problems in the system that make it more likely to happen."[28] Similar phrasing was used by Gary Convis, former Chairman of Toyota Motor Manufacturing Kentucky, who taught "You respect people … you don't blame them. Maybe the process was not set up so well, so it was easy to make a mistake."[29]

Many errors cannot be simply traced to a single individual. We often blame the person who was physically present when the error occurred, but many errors are caused by upstream departments or other processes. When a nurse administers an incorrect medication to a patient, we have to look beyond that nurse to the value stream and different points at which errors could have been introduced into the system. When a pharmacist does catch a medication error, we have to look upstream to the point at which the error was created (without simply blaming the pharmacy tech).

Our first line of questioning ("What could have allowed that to occur?") leads us to systemic root cause problem solving. A *root cause* is an underlying condition or an aspect of the system that led to the error. As the term implies, thinking of the roots of a tree, we have to look beyond the surface symptoms of the problem. If a problem we have "fixed" is reoccurring, it is a sign that we have not discovered or fixed the root cause. This is one reason Lean hospitals must use the plan-do-check-act (PDCA) cycle. Any time we put a countermeasure in place for a problem, we have to measure (through observation or metrics), or check, to see that the problem truly has been solved.

> Some behavioral experts caution people against asking employees questions that begin with the word *why,* as it can often cause defensiveness.[30] This might be especially true at the start of your Lean journey if a blame-and-shame culture still exists. Be sensitive about this and realize that understanding why a problem occurred can be understood using phrases such as "What allowed that wrong medication to reach the patient's bedside?" instead of "Why did you send the wrong medication?" Another approach would be to focus on the event instead of the person, is to ask "Why did the wrong medication arrive at the unit?"

Start at the *Gemba*

When an employee comes to report a problem to a manager, the first step for a Lean leader should be to take the discussion and problem solving to the place where the problem occurred, the *gemba.* Lean teaches that problems are more effectively solved at the *gemba* instead of in meeting rooms. Going to the *gemba* allows us to see with our own eyes and to talk with other people who are directly involved in that process. When we are at the *gemba,* we can start asking why in our attempt to discover what could have allowed that problem to occur.

> ### Summary of Lean Problem Solving
>
> Go to the *gemba.*
> Talk to the people working in the process or area in question.
> Go beyond surface problems to the root cause (use the five whys).
> Look across departmental boundaries, across the value stream.
> Improve processes before spending money on capital or expansion.

ThedaCare's Toussaint shared a story in his book, *On the Mend,* that illustrates these principles and mindsets.[31] While on a *gemba* walk, Toussaint asked a nurse in a unit about their remarkably low medication error rate. The nurse told Toussaint, bluntly, they were simply not recording the errors. This admission might be a fireable offense in some organizations.

Instead of yelling or telling the nurse to follow the process, the first question was "Why?" The nurse responded that there was not enough time, and that the reporting method in the computer system was too complex. The nurse showed Toussaint how she had to go through different screens in the computer system and it took almost four minutes to submit an error. In addition, there was fear that reporting an error would bring punishment instead of improvement.

The fact that the nurse felt comfortable raising the issue without fear of blame or punishment was a positive sign of a maturing Lean culture. Another positive sign was that Toussaint thanked the nurse for bringing up the issue so openly. Toussaint immediately contacted the information systems department and requested that they improve the system to make it easier to report medication errors, an excellent example of servant leadership.

Find Root Causes Using Simple Methods

One powerful, yet simple, method for getting to a root cause of a problem is the five whys method, developed at Toyota. In this method, we ask a sequential series of why questions until we get an answer that seems like a correctable root cause. There is no particular magic in the number five. Sometimes, the root cause is found after three whys, and sometimes it might take ten. The point is to get beyond more commonplace problem solving that might only ask why once, leading to a surface symptom instead of the root cause. The five whys method is particularly effective in a group setting, where people can build off each other's ideas and gain shared understanding across department boundaries. For this to work well, we need an open environment in which people are less defensive and less fearful about being honest.

The five whys can be used in response to a specific process defect, for example, "Why did that specimen arrive at the lab unlabeled?" or "Why did that nurse walk back to the station instead of using the portable computer?" The five whys can also be used to ask general questions, such as "Why are patients being boarded in the ED?" When we have multiple contributing causes, we can use other basic quality tools like a "fishbone" diagram, otherwise known as an Ishikawa diagram.[32] Some types of problems will require more analytical and statistical rigor, bringing us into the realm of Six Sigma methods.

A3 Problem Solving

An increasingly popular problem-solving methodology in the world's hospitals is the "A3." An A3 gets its name from the international paper size that is roughly 11 by 17 inches. The method began in the 1960s as part of the Japanese "quality circles" movement but evolved at Toyota to become their standard format for problem solving, planning, and status reports. More important than the size of paper or any given template is the structured problem analysis (left side of the A3) and PDCA (right side of the A3) thinking and scientific method that is embedded in the document.

A problem-solving A3 should be embedded with Lean thinking and practices. An example A3 is shown in Figure 7.1.[33] In writing the issue and background statements, authors of an A3 must take care not to jump to a solution. An A3 titled "Get All Patients to the O.R. Prep Room by 7:00 a.m." might be jumping to a solution for the broader problem of cases not starting on time. A better issue or title might be "First Case On-Time Starts."

The current condition combines fact-based data, as opposed to opinions that are gather by going to the *gemba* and observing the process in a detailed way. The emphasis in this early stage is to "grasp the situation."[34] The current condition might include a value stream map or other drawings and visuals.

Before moving to the right-hand side of the A3 to talk about possible "countermeasures" (the word *solution* sounds too definitive for continuous improvement), we have to make sure we understand the root cause or causes of the problem. To solve a problem, we must properly define and understand that problem.

ISSUE   *Patients complain that meals are not hot in the Rehab Unit.*

BACKGROUND

Patient satisfaction survey results are less than 80% for hot meals. Meals are on large carts and often travel to other floors before arriving at the Rehab Unit.

CURRENT CONDITION

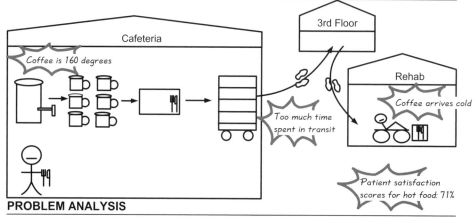

PROBLEM ANALYSIS

1. *Coffee arrives cool at the patients' bedside*
    Why? The coffee is not coming out of the coffee maker at the specified temperature (180 degrees)
        Why? The thermostat in the coffee maker is faulty
    Why? The coffee sits in cups for a long period of time while the trays are being assembled
        Why? Cups are poured in advance and arranged with other beverages to be added to the tray as prescribed
2. *Food spends too much time in transit*
    Why? Trays travel from kitchen to the 3rd floor before being delivered to Rehab
        Why? Delivery carts are large and trays for more than one unit are loaded together on one cart
            Why? Delivery carts are designed for more trays than there are patients in Rehab

Figure 7.1   An example of problem-solving A3. (From Jimmerson, Cindy, *A3 Problem Solving for Healthcare: A Practical Method for Eliminating Waste*. New York: Productivity Press, 2007. Used with permission.) (continued)

TARGET CONDITION   Title: Hot Food in Rehab Unit

TO	Tim
BY	Jane
DATE	March 5, 2007

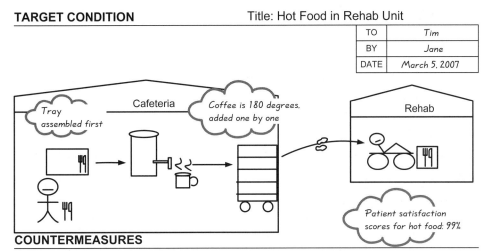

COUNTERMEASURES

1. Repair thermostat in coffee maker.
2. Rearrange order of filling coffee cups to fill one by one at the end of tray assembly.
3. Deliver trays to patients in order of assembly.

IMPLEMENTATION PLAN

What	Who	When	Outcome
Replace thermostat in coffee maker	Jane	March 12	Coffee will come out at 180 degrees
Re-order the assembly of trays so that coffee is poured and put on trays just before they leave the kitchen	Jane	March 20	Coffee will spend less time on the tray before arriving to patient
Use smaller transport carts so they carry only one unit's trays	Jane/ Tim	April 1	Less travel time from kitchen to Rehab
Educate staff re: delivering trays from top of cart to bottom to avoid 1st loaded tray spending most time on cart	Tim	April 5	Trays will all be warm when delivered

COST/BENEFIT

Cost	$$$
Thermostat for coffee maker	$8.50
Benefit	$$$
Patients are satisfied with the temperature of the food they recieve	Patient Satisfaction

FOLLOW UP

May 30, 2007 – Patient satisfaction scores for hot food: 100%

Figure 7.1 (continued) An example of problem-solving A3. (From Jimmerson, Cindy, *A3 Problem Solving for Healthcare: A Practical Method for Eliminating Waste*. New York: Productivity Press, 2007. Used with permission.)

John Shook says the three most common problems in problem solving involve not properly grasping the situation:

- Assuming you know what the problem is without seeing what is actually happening
- Assuming you know how to fix a problem without finding out what is causing it
- Assuming the action you have taken to fix a problem is working without checking to see if it is actually doing what you expected[35]

The target condition (similar to a future state map), the countermeasures (what we plan on trying) and the detailed implementation plan comprise the do of the PDCA cycle. An A3 also prompts us to plan for the check and the adjust, or act, phases. The author of an A3 anticipates which qualitative and quantitative factors will be used to evaluate success in the problem-solving process. In the PDCA mindset, we do not assume that our countermeasures will work. If our honest assessment shows that improvement did not occur, we can go back and try again in a blame-free manner.

Writing an A3 is not meant to be a solitary exercise. They are often written as part of a group improvement exercise, and even solo A3 authors do their best when coached by an experienced A3 mentor. As John Shook, the CEO of the Lean Enterprise Institute, said, "It takes two to A3."[36] The best A3s are iterative documents, continually refined and adjusted as the author better grasps the situation and root causes, frontline workers provide additional feedback, and the mentor asks challenging questions and provides constructive feedback.

A3s are also used to gather feedback and input from a larger group, laying the groundwork (*nemawashi* in Japanese) for consensus that ensures the root cause is understood, and that the team is in agreement regarding how to move forward. The A3, as presented to others, is the basis for discussions and further refinement of the ideas on the paper.[37] The Lean facilator at one hospital commented, "When I coach A3 authors, I always know they are on track when they have to rewrite something on either side when they share progress with people."

Effective use of the A3 methodology leads to people development in addition to tactical problem solving. John Toussaint, MD, said:

> A3 thinking was critical in my development as a Lean leader. It made me understand that getting the problem clearly defined is the most important aspect of improvement work. Thinking about it in a medical model, the hard part of what a doctor does is to make the diagnosis. This occurs when all backround information (history), the patients' current state (physicial examination) and core data (lab analysis) are completed. The treatment is fairly straightforward, once you understand the problem. This is basic scientific method thinking. It's simple but it changes the way you manage."[38]

Example of the Five Whys: Hand Hygiene

Hospitals often struggle with getting caregivers and employees to follow proper hand hygiene practices. It is common knowledge that unclean hands can spread germs that cause hospital-acquired infections (HAIs), harming patients, increasing length of stay, and increasing costs. Hospitals have policies that say, for example, that people must clean their hands on the way in and out of any patient room or patient encounter. Managers cannot audit this by following people 100% of the time. Employees often resent being spied on and fear being written up. They would likely prefer to have their leaders be partners in improvement instead of having them serve a policing role.

SIGNS DO NOT WORK

Hospitals have to find better ways to respond instead of hanging up more clever signs (or wearing buttons) that admonish or encourage people to wash. One hospital had a yellowed hand-washing sign with a 1984 copyright, hanging along other signs that featured cute kittens, cartoon organisms, or a warning that struck fear in parents. If signs worked, hand hygiene compliance would have been solved decades ago. Our problems are often more complex, so we need an approach that involves more than the print shop. Organizations are well intended, using signs because they are assumed to be effective. Instead, we can apply PDCA thinking to these signs: Do they really work, and if not, can we find a better way?

THE FIVE WHYS

Solving this problem should start with the question "Why?" The focus must be on eliminating barriers to hand hygiene—not making excuses for people, but finding legitimate problems that can be solved.

One hospital had a team of nurses and other employees go through a five whys exercise. Their first attempt at answers can be seen in Figure 7.2. You can see there was not a single answer to the question, and that the team probed certain responses more deeply—this initial brainstorming could have also been done in a tool called a fishbone diagram.

Kevin Frieswick, a director of organizational improvement at Vanguard Health Systems, built a creative and low-cost error-proofing device to help ensure hand hygiene is done before a person enters or departs the room. Using materials bought at a local store, Kevin connected a thin bar and a motor into the hands-free hand sanitizer dispenser. When a person activates the dispenser, the bar raises up and out of the person's way, using a light sensor to ensure the bar does not go down until it has been cleared. Care was taken to ensure that the bar would break away if personnel had to enter the room in an emergency. This device does not absolutely prevent somebody from entering a room without using the dispenser, but it provides a visual cue that makes it harder to forget to clean your hands.[39]

Many of the root causes focused on training, resources, and senior leadership, rather than blaming the individual employees. The group found a few practical changes that could be made to further encourage hand hygiene, such as making carts more readily available. More training could educate people about using only hand gel instead of alternating between gel and soap and water. Gel dispensers had already been placed in every patient room and many other locations, but putting them on the portable computers was another small step that could be taken. Doing more to make carts available was another action, utilizing the 5S method to properly locate and organize carts.

The question of time and general overwork was also raised as a barrier to hand hygiene. Employees and physicians complained that they were too busy or that they had too many patients to see in a short time. This is an instance when, instead of taking this overwork as a given, waste reduction can free time that can be used for proper hygiene. If there truly are situations for which overwork exists, the *heijunka* and standardized work methods can be used to make sure that workloads are properly balanced and that staff members are not pressured into cutting corners to get their work done.

Many of the practical items, as well as the more difficult cultural issues, can be traced to the responsibility of top leadership. We are more likely to find effective solutions when we quit blaming or assuming that problems are the fault of individuals. Blaming others is often a hard habit to break, as this is deeply engrained behavior in humans from early childhood through our experience working in organizations.

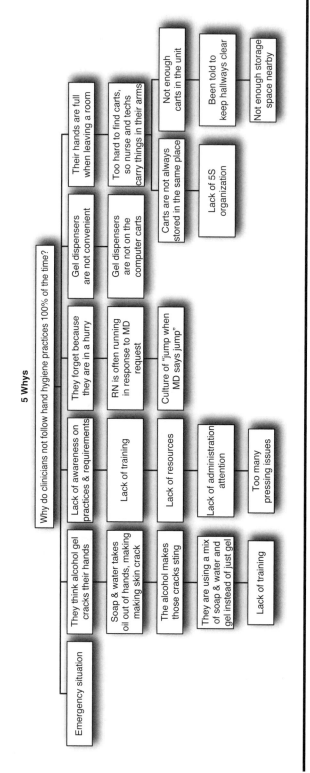

Figure 7.2 An illustration of a five whys problem-solving method showing multiple branches and root causes.

Was this five whys exercise a cure-all? No, but it helped shift the mindset from one of thinking nothing could be done about the problem to a belief that actions could be taken that would help increase hand hygiene compliance.

If you look at the problem slightly differently, one could ask, "Why do we have to wash our hands?" One answer might be, "Because we touch the patients." Some have suggested that one real root cause solution would be to avoid touching patients unless absolutely necessary.[40] A more complete solution to hand hygiene would include training and a leadership committment to responding appropriately when unsafe behaviors are seen.

At one Pittsburgh veterans' hospital, an effort was made to solve problems that prevented employees from washing properly, issues raised in response to the why question. Supplies and tools (such as stethoscopes) were properly located in each room. The unit started testing all patients for methicillin-resistant *Staphylococcus aureus* (MRSA) to properly isolate carriers. With the new methods, MRSA infection rates fell 90% in a short time. The approach, unfortunately, spread to only one other unit in the hospital and fell apart when the main driver of the program left to work on another project. That illustrates the need for having a true management-led standardized work system, as opposed to relying on a single change agent.[41]

Example of the Five Whys: Lost Specimens

A few years into their Lean journey, a hospital lab realized that they were still fighting their predominant shame-and-blame culture, even with the local improvements they had made in methods and departmental culture.

On a single day, the histology lab lost three separate patient specimens. This meant delayed testing and results and that two of the patients had to undergo a second biopsy—adding pain for the patient and consuming additional time and resources, increasing cost due to the waste. Because this was a serious sentinel event, the quality department at the hospital did what they called a root cause analysis, with the conclusion being that the histology technologist simply needed to be retrained.

The lab director realized that the analysis was flawed. A truly actionable root cause had not been identified. So, he started his own analysis—going to the *gemba* and talking to all of the histology techs to understand what had happened. The five whys analysis looked like this:

- Why were the specimens lost?
  The one technologist was overworked that morning.
- Why?
  Because one technologist was sick, and one was late due to traffic.
- Why was the technologist rushing and trying to do the work of three people?
  He was trying to hit the "first slides by 8 a.m." deadline.
- Why?
  He wanted to please the pathologist.
- Why?
  That is the traditional hospital culture.

This view led the director to see the problem as the local management system, not as "that technologist." The team agreed that "first slides by 8 a.m." was more of a general goal than a quota that had to be hit no matter what. It was good that nobody was under extreme pressure to hit that deadline, but the team members had placed pressure on themselves, as they wanted to do a good job. In talking with the pathologists who receive slides from histology, nobody had ever yelled at the lab for being late or being slow (a fact confirmed by the technologists). Part of the director's response was to emphasize that nobody should ever cut corners to hit that, or any, target.

The director also realized that there had been no standardized work for how to respond when one or two people were off. With one technologist, or even with two, work would obviously be done more slowly than when all three technologists were working. The team, unfortunately, did not have standardized work for situations when they were less than fully staffed; this was something the team could follow up. In addition, there had been no communication plan for letting the pathologists know that slides would be late and why. The pathologists, sharing everybody's concern for quality and patient safety (not wanting mixed-up specimens), were happy to have communication in place of rushing and cutting corners.

So, what had started with an exercise in blaming the individual turned, instead, into an exercise in improving standardized work, communication, and the management system. The lab director, managers, pathologists, and team members looked deeply into their problems, finding proactive ways to prevent reoccurrence of the same situation and errors.

Be Proactive and Use Failure Modes and Effects Analysis

A methodology called failure modes and effects analysis (FMEA) is a helpful tool for identifying and prioritizing errors that could occur in a process, rather than just reacting after an incident has occurred. FMEA was originally developed by the U.S. military in 1949 to proactively anticipate potential failures and became more widely used in the automotive industry in the 1970s. FMEA already tends to be used in hospital transfusion medicine and pharmacy settings but can be used to improve any process.[42]

An FMEA document is typically built in a spreadsheet and is based on team brainstorming about what could go wrong in their process. As with standardized work and *kaizen*, FMEA is most effectively done by the people who actually work in the process, although the FMEA process could be facilitated by someone experienced with that methodology. An FMEA could have helped anticipate the error that caused the death of Mary McClinton, along with other risks in the interventional radiology setting.

To create an FMEA, we brainstorm all of the different errors that could occur in an area or a process. For each failure mode, the team ranks each of three categories:

- What is the severity of the error when it occurs?
- What is the likelihood of occurrence?
- How difficult is it to detect the error?

Each category gets a score on a 1–10 scale (low to high), and the scores are multiplied together to give a risk priority number (RPN) for each failure mode. To help prioritize our improvements (assuming we cannot fix everything at once), we sort the failure modes by their RPN score. The failure modes with the highest scores should receive our initial attention. If a failure mode is very likely to occur (score of 10), is very hard to detect (score of 10), and would cause a patient death (score of 10), the RPN score would be 1,000.

Using an FMEA is in keeping with the Lean concept that we have to be open in talking about problems (and potential problems) in our workplace. FMEA is just a tool. Leadership must take the responsibility for creating an environment of openness in the name of patient safety and error prevention.

Proactive Resolution of Near-Miss Problems

In addition to FMEA brainstorming, hospitals must react appropriately to near misses, turning each problem into an opportunity to drive process improvements that prevent that same error from happening again.

One foreseeable hospital process defect is administering an incorrect intravenous drip to a patient. Potential risks include giving the wrong dose or the wrong medication. One study estimated an error was made in 49% of intravenous preparations and administrations.[43] While there are numerous checks and rechecks of intravenous bags during the intravenous production process in the pharmacy, errors still get through to the point at which a nurse is poised potentially to administer the wrong drug. The fact that all errors are not caught in the pharmacy is evidence of how 100% inspection is not 100% effective, even with multiple successive inspections.

Think about a case in which a nurse properly inspects the medication and finds an error at that last stage of the value stream of the intravenous bag through the hospital. In a perfectly error-proofed process, this should never happen. The nurse's reaction—and the reaction of the organization—to such a near miss is crucial. A non-Lean organization might consider the nurse catching the error by the pharmacy as proof that the system worked. People might ask, "What is the problem? The patient was not harmed." Catching the error before the patient was harmed is certainly a positive event, but it should be considered the sign of a weak process that allowed the error to get as far as it did. The next time, the nurse might not catch the error in time.

A common workaround would be for the nurse to correct the immediate problem, for example, by going and getting the right dose. The real problem is not solved, however, as the error is likely to be repeated if the root cause of the underlying error is not solved. The nurse might say, "We were lucky. Let's hope that doesn't happen again." There might be a temptation not to report the problem or to cover up the near miss. Employees, including the nurse, might not have the time to follow up properly or conduct root cause problem-solving analysis because of overwork and the need to move on to caring for other patients. The error will certainly happen again, at some point, because of the same systemic cause.

In the McClinton case, let us assume that the syringe was being filled with the wrong solution, but another person in the room saw the error and called it out. This would-be "near miss" would have been as much of an opportunity to improve the process and to prevent any harm to patients.

In a Lean culture, we need a number of conditions to ensure that the root cause is solved, including

- An environment in which employees are encouraged to stop and solve problems when they are found (or as soon as possible)
- Available time for root cause problem solving (freed up through earlier waste reduction)
- A blame-free environment in which employees are not punished for raising problems to the surface for root cause problem solving
- Managers who take the time to help resolve issues with or for employees as they are raised
- Cross-functional cooperation to work together on problems that are generated upstream but create waste for a downstream function or department

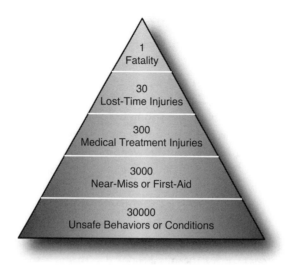

Figure 7.3 The Alcoa safety pyramid. (Adapted from Woletz and Alcoa.)

The Safety Pyramid

The Alcoa Corporation has built an impressive track record for improving employee safety in what was traditionally considered a dangerous industry. Rather than being resigned to employee injuries and deaths, the company, under the leadership of CEO Paul O'Neill, who later advocated these same ideas through the Institute for Healthcare Improvement, set out on a quest to become the safest company to work for in the world. Although many in the company felt it was unrealistic, O'Neill set a goal of zero lost workdays as the only acceptable goal, a goal that was set to break the complacency and the idea that accidents were bound to happen. The company reduced its lost work per day rate from 1.87 in 1987 to 0.42 in 1997.[44]

A key to the safety improvement at Alcoa was the use of the safety pyramid, as shown in Figure 7.3. Rather than only reacting to employee fatalities or severe injuries, O'Neill and Alcoa management focused on near misses, minor injuries, and unsafe behaviors. Unsafe behaviors might include rushing through one's work, acceptance that risk is part of the job, being distracted, or being fatigued.[45]

The safety pyramid illustrates that for every fatality caused by an unsafe condition, there are many more instances for which that same condition causes a less-severe outcome. This same idea can apply to hospitals, for both patient care and employee safety. For example, it is estimated that for every drug mistake there are 100 near misses.[46]

For every case for which a patient died because a central line was flushed with insulin instead of heparin, there are many more instances when insulin and heparin vials are sitting next to each other in bins at a nurse's station. For every intravenous administration error, there might have been many instances when intravenous solutions, stored next to each other in overflow bins, fell into the wrong location. Each time a wrong-site brain surgery was performed, there may have been many cases when the "time-out" process was not followed. Reacting with root cause problem solving and prevention when unsafe conditions are found can help avoid patient harm and catastrophic situations.

In a Lean culture, leaders have to create an environment in which employees are encouraged or obligated to speak up when they identify unsafe conditions or see a near miss. We must change the culture of workarounds that leads employees to "fix" problems without telling anybody, a culture in which we consider fixing problems as part of our job instead of viewing the problems as waste or process defects that must be prevented.

Conclusion

Improving quality, through Lean methods, is more about the philosophy and mindset than it is about specific tools, like fishbone diagrams and FMEAs. It can take time for individual leaders, or an entire organization, to unlearn old habits of blaming individuals, hiding problems, and employing workarounds. Leadership can set expectations, such as a goal of zero infections, that emphasize that patient safety incidents should not be considered a given or necessary part of providing care. Beyond just setting goals, however, leaders also have a responsibility to set an example for the daily behaviors that will lead to quality improvement. Training in tools can help, but establishing a culture of safety, quality, and root cause problem solving is critical.

Lean Lessons

- Hospitals need to shift from naming, blaming, and shaming to a more productive systemic improvement method.
- Most errors are caused by the system rather than by individual negligence.
- Look at the process rather than blaming individuals.
- Start your problem solving by going to the *gemba*.
- Keep asking why to identify the root cause of a problem.
- Use proactive methods for identifying problems before they occur.
- Use near misses as opportunities to prevent future problems that would cause harm.

Points for Group Discussion

- What are the lessons from the Mary McClinton case? Is it fair that Carl Dorsey lost his job?
- Why do we tend to blame individuals when errors occur?
- If workarounds prevent identification of root causes, why are they so tempting?
- Is leadership taking responsibility for creating an environment of openness in the name of patient safety and error prevention?
- What can we do to encourage people to report errors, near misses, and unsafe conditions?
- How can we free time for proper root cause problem solving?
- How do you turn errors into learning opportunities?
- How do we find a balance between blaming the system and making excuses for people?
- What prevents hospitals, employees, or physicians from being open about problems, errors, or near misses?

Notes

1. Kenney, Charles, *Transforming Healthcare: Virginia Mason Medical Center's Pursuit of the Perfect Patient Experience* (New York: Productivity Press, 2010), 58.
2. Ibid., 59.
3. Nalder, Eric, and Cathleen Crowley, "When Few Hospitals Report, Honest Ones Look Bad," *Hearst Newspapers*, July 30, 2009, http://www.chron.com/disp/story.mpl/deadbymistake/wa/6555174.html (accessed April 7, 2011).
4. Ibid.
5. Szabo, Liz, "Global goal: Reduce medical errors," *USA Today*, August 23, 2005, http://usatoday.com/news/health/2005-08-23-medical-errors_x.htm (accessed July 4, 2011).
6. Woolcock, Nicola, and Mark Henderson, "Blundering Hospitals 'Kill 40,000 a Year,'" *The Times Online*, August 13, 2004, http://www.timesonline.co.uk/tol/news/uk/health/article469178.ece (accessed April 10, 2011).
7. Black, Nick, "Management Mistakes in Healthcare: Identification, Correction and Prevention," *Journal of the Royal Society of Medicine,* 2005, 98: 432–33.
8. Bodinson, Glenn W., "Change Healthcare Organizations from Good to Great," *Quality Progress*, November 2005, 22–29.
9. "Testimony on Patient Safety: Supporting a Culture of Continuous Quality Improvement Hospitals and Other Health Care Organizations, testimony of Carolyn M. Clancy, MD, before the Senate Permanent Subcommittee on Investigations Committee on Governmental Affairs," June 11, 2003, Agency for Healthcare Research and Quality, Rockville, MD, http://www.ahrq.gov/news/tst61103.htm (accessed April 10, 2011).
10. Committee on Quality of Healthcare in America and Institute of Medicine, *To Err Is Human* (Washington, DC: National Academies Press, 2000), 43.
11. Breuer, Howard, "Dennis Quaid's Newborn Twins Hospitalized," *People*, November 20, 2007, http://www.people.com/people/article/0,,20161769,00.html (accessed April 3, 2011).
12. Deming, W. Edwards, *The New Economics*, 2nd ed. (Cambridge, MA: MIT CAES, 1994), 33.
13. Committee on Quality, *To Err Is Human*, 19.
14. Wachter, Robert, and Peter Pronovost, "Balancing 'No Blame' with Accountability in Patient Safety," *New England Journal of Medicine*, 2009, 361: 1401–6.
15. Committee on Quality, *To Err Is Human*, 110.
16. Merry, Allan, and Alexander McCall Smith, *Errors, Medicine, and the Law* (Cambridge: Cambridge University Press, 2001), 32.
17. Committee on Quality, *To Err Is Human*, 54–55.
18. Mamberto, Carola, "What Factory Managers Can Teach Hospital Wards," *Wall Street Journal*, June 25, 2007, p. B3.
19. Touissant, John, presentation, First Global Lean Healthcare Summit, June 25, 2007.
20. Toussaint, John, and Roger Gerard, *On the Mend: Revolutionizing Healthcare to Save Lives and Transform the Industry* (Cambridge, MA: Lean Enterprise Institute, 2010), 69.
21. Ibid., 29.
22. Toussaint, John, "Writing the New Playbook for U.S. Health Care: Lessons from Wisconsin," *Health Affairs,* September 2009, 28, no. 5: 1347.
23. Toussaint and Gerard, *On the Mend*, 106.
24. Ibid., 24.
25. Hollenbeak, Christopher S., "Dispelling the Myths: The True Cost of Healthcare-Associated Infections," *Healthcare Financial Management*, March 2007, http://findarticles.com/p/articles/mi_m3257/is_3_61/ai_n18764839/ (accessed April 10, 2011).
26. Pronovost, Peter, et al., "Sustaining Reductions in Catheter Related Bloodstream Infections in Michigan Intensive Care Units: Observational Study," *British Medical Journal*, 2010, 340: c309, http://www.bmj.com/content/340/bmj.c309.full (accessed April 4, 2011).
27. Agnew, Judy, and Aubrey Daniels, *Safe by Accident?* (Atlanta: Performance Management Publications, 2010), 57.

28. Kopelman, Richard E., David J. Prottas, and Anne L. Davis, "Douglas McGregor's Theory X and Y: Toward a Construct-Valid Measure," *Journal of Managerial Issues*, June 22, 2008, http://www.all business.com/science-technology/behavior-cognition/11414872-1.html (accessed April 3, 2011).

29. Rode, Jenny, "Breaking the Rice Ceiling," *Battle Creek Enquirer*, February 12, 2006, http://www.lean sigmainstitute.com/news/lean/2006/02/breaking-rice-ceiling.html (accessed January 2, 2008).

30. McSween, Terry E., *The Values-Based Safety Process: Improving Your Safety Culture with Behavior-Based Safety* (New York: Wiley, 2003), 90.

31. Toussaint and Gerard, *On the Mend*, 115.

32. Ishikawa, Kaoru, *Introduction to Quality Control* (New York: Productivity Press, 1990), 448.

33. Jimmerson, Cindy, *A3 Problem Solving for Healthcare.* (New York: Productivity Press, 2007), 102.

34. Shook, John, *Managing to Learn* (Cambridge, MA: Lean Enterprise Institute, 2008), 13.

35. Shook, John, "Managing to Learn" workshop, January 19, 2010.

36. Shook, *Managing to Learn*, 113.

37. Sobek, Durward K., II, and Art Smalley, *Understanding A3 Thinking: A Critical Component of Toyota's PDCA Management System* (New York: Productivity Press, 2008), 82.

38. Toussaint, John, Personal correspondence, April 7, 2011.

39. Graban, Mark, "LeanBlog Video Podcast 2—Kevin Frieswick, Error Proofing Handwashing," April 28, 2009, http://leanblog.org/v2, (accessed April 8, 2011).

40. Gawande, Atul, *Better* (New York: Metropolitan Books, 2007), 21.

41. Ibid., 24.

42. Institute for Healthcare Improvement, "All FMEA Tools," http://www.ihi.org/ihi/workspace/tools/fmea/AllTools.aspx (accessed April 3, 2011).

43. Taxis, K., and N. Barber, "Ethnographic Study of Incidence and Severity of Intravenous Drug Errors," *British Medical Journal,* 2003, 326: 684.

44. "Testimony on Patient Safety."

45. Woletz, Todd, "Behavioral Safety Observation Program Presentation," March 15, 2007, http://www.conney.com/expo2007/expo07_presentations/ToddWoletz_BSOP_Safety%20Day.ppt (accessed December 22, 2007).

46. Bates, D. W., D. L. Boyle, M. B. Vander Vilet, J. Schneider, and L. Leape, "Relationship between Medication Errors and Adverse Drug Events," *Journal of General Internal Medicine,* 1995, 10: 199–205.

Chapter 8

Preventing Errors and Harm

A Problem That Is Not Going Away

For all of the attention placed on patient safety and medical harm since 1999, a study released in 2010 suggested that "harm to patients was common and the number of incidents did not decrease over time," contrary to the figures in the landmark 1999 Institute of Medicine (IOM) study that said medical mistakes cause as many as 98,000 deaths a year in the United States.[1] In the more recent study, roughly 18% of patients were harmed, and more than 60% of those injuries were considered preventable. Data in a 2011 study in the journal *Health Affairs* showed that medical errors and adverse events occur in one of three admissions, and that errors may occur 10 times more frequently than the IOM study indicated.[2]

Moving Beyond Blaming Individuals

In recent years, a number of high-profile medical errors have made the news, in addition to the untold suffering that occurs on a daily basis. Josie King, an 18-month-old girl, died at Johns Hopkins after being given an additional dose of morphine by a visiting nurse after a physician had already changed her orders. The error worsened her dehydration as she should have been on the path to recovery.[3] Josie's tragedy has inspired her mother and clinical leaders such as Dr. Peter Pronovost to work tirelessly to educate healthcare professionals and patients about the need to improve processes, systems, and communication in healthcare.[4]

The twin babies of the actor Dennis Quaid were harmed after multiple nurses mistakenly gave them adult doses of the blood thinner heparin while in the care of the neonatal intensive care unit (NICU) at Cedars-Sinai Hospital in California. This was the result of a number of process errors that should not have occurred.[5] Nurses did not think to check for an adult dose, as the pharmacy should have never delivered an adult dose to a neonatal unit. Even if nurses had been on guard for that mixup, the packaging of heparin and Hep-Lock were too similar, two shades of light blue that could be hard to distinguish in the proverbial dark room at 2 a.m. Sadly, Cedars-Sinai could not prevent this medical harm after the same set of circumstances had led to the deaths of three babies at an Indianapolis, Indiana, hospital.[6]

The Darrie Eason Case

In another case that was featured prominently in the news, Darrie Eason, a woman from New York, was the victim of an unnecessary radical double mastectomy after another patient's laboratory specimen was mislabeled with her information.[7] Not only was Eason misdiagnosed with cancer, but also another patient had her cancer diagnosis delayed because of the mixup. As is common in such cases, news reports included quotations that blamed an individual, as the chief executive officer (CEO) of the private pathology lab that handled her case said, "The technician responsible for the mix-up also no longer works there."

Another news report contained the detail that the "technician who handled Eason's test admitted to his supervisors that he 'occasionally cut corners by batching,' or handling more than one tissue specimen at a time, and did not always verify patients' initials when labeling them."[8]

One could ask if "occasionally" cutting corners was actually a common practice in the lab. Given that working on more than one specimen at a time greatly increases the risk for errors, why would this take place, especially given that there is minimal time savings from labeling multiple patients' slides at once? Lean thinkers might suspect that the technicians had too great a workload or they were pressured, explicitly or implicitly, into working faster than they should have been.

If supervisors knew that corners were being cut, what is their responsibility in this case? The supervisors should have been ensuring that standardized work (one specimen at a time) was followed, and that the environment and workload allowed people to work at the correct pace for high quality. The CEO said the technician no longer worked there, but what about the supervisors? What about the CEO's responsibility? As Dr. W. Edwards Deming wrote, quality starts with top management. In the Quaid case, the chief medical officer (CMO) of Cedars-Sinai said, "This was a preventable error, involving a failure to follow our standard policies and procedures, and there is no excuse for that to occur at Cedars-Sinai."[9] Yes, these were indeed preventable errors, but whose responsibility is it to ensure that policies and procedures are followed?

I have seen the practice of "batching" histology specimens in a number of hospital laboratories, as shown in Figure 8.1. The three stacks of slides are all sitting in the field of work, each having been labeled for a different patient. When the laboratory manager was asked about this opportunity for error (thinking in terms of failure modes and effects analysis [FMEA], as described in Chapter 7), the manager said, "It's OK. My people are very careful." Careful people are a good starting point, but that is, unfortunately, not enough to ensure perfect quality and patient safety. To ensure the best quality, we need Lean methods, such as error proofing, and Lean mindsets, such as looking at systems instead of blaming individuals.

Creating Quality at the Source through Error Proofing

Preventing errors at the source (the Japanese word *jidoka*) is one of the pillars of the Toyota Production System. The history of *jidoka* dates to the time before the company (then called Toyoda) built cars, with the invention of a weaving loom that automatically stopped when the thread broke; this invention saved time, increased productivity, and reduced waste.[10] The automatic weaving loom has served as an inspiration for quality throughout Toyota and among adopters of the Lean approach.

Thinking back to the Quaid case, even if we have not had a death at our own hospital from a mixup of heparin doses, the opportunity for error, the unsafe conditions might be there. Preventing that same error from occurring in our own hospital is good for the patients (protecting their safety), good for the employees (preventing the risk that they will participate in a

Figure 8.1   Photo of three stacks of slides representing three different patients in the field of work.

systemic error), and good for the hospital (avoiding lawsuits and protecting our reputation as a high-quality facility).

Being Careful Is Not Enough

When managers blame individuals for errors, there is an underlying—but unrealistic—assumption that errors could be prevented if people would just be more careful. Errors are often viewed as the result of careless or inattentive employees. Warning, caution, or "be careful" signs throughout our hospitals are evidence of this mindset. If signs or memos were enough, we would have already solved the problems of quality and safety, not only in hospitals but also in the world around us.

A good exercise is to go on a *"gemba* walk" through a department looking for signs that remind or tell employees to be careful. Each sign is an indicator of a process problem and evidence that the root cause of the problem has not been properly addressed through error proofing. A good metric for the "Leanness" of a hospital might be the number of warning signs—fewer warning signs indicate that problems have been solved and prevented, eliminating the need for less-effective signs and warnings.

For example, we might see a sign in the pharmacy that reads: "Please remember fridge items for cart delivery." This suggests that this process error was made at least once. We need to ask why it was possible to forget the refrigerated items. Does the department not have a standard checklist that is used before going out to make a delivery? Is the refrigerator in an inconvenient location, making it easy to forget about when employees are in a rush?

Nurses' stations might be full of signs, such as "Avoid overtightening syringes in microbore tubing." In this case, a new type of tubing was being purchased by the hospital, tubing for which the connector had "wings" that made it too easy for nurses to get too much leverage into the twisting motion. Instead of asking nurses to be careful, a root cause might point more to the design of the tubing or the purchasing decision of the hospital. Too many signs can, in and of themselves, present a safety hazard. If each bears a truly important admonition, the worker can develop what pilots call "alarm fatigue," with too much confusing dialogue going on around them.

Of course, we would not want just to go around taking down signs without first preventing the problem. Signs may be, at best, a short-term response that can eventually be replaced with a root cause fix.

Why 100% Inspection Is Not 100% Effective

Healthcare organizations tend to rely on inspection and double checks, for which the focus is on finding problems before they reach the patient. Error prevention is preferable to inspection for a number of reasons. First, if we rely on people to inspect their own work or work done by others, we introduce the risk of human error into the process. At the end of a long day, a person might forget to do a particular inspection or check, a problem that we could address by rotating jobs frequently to keep people mentally alert. Or, we can rely on checklists, similar to what an airline pilot uses before every flight, as mentioned in Chapter 5.

Adding extra inspections is not guaranteed to prevent surgical errors, as evidenced by Rhode Island Hospital, which was in the news for having performed four wrong-site brain surgeries over 6 years.[11] After an incident in July 2007, the hospital was ordered to add a second physician to review the proper site before surgery (a form of inspection). Even so, another wrong-site surgery occurred in August 2007, leading to yet another review. The hospital is now requiring an attending physician be present for brain surgery procedures since the last error was committed by a resident. The hospital appears to be blaming residents, saying they are incapable of working unsupervised. The added attending physician is serving partly as an inspector of the resident's work. It is possible that this inspection may also suffer from the same sort of human error that failed to prevent previous errors that occurred when the first extra inspection was in place. Residents may very well be capable on their own, without errors, if better error-proofing methods and standardized work were in place. Lean thinkers would ask why those errors occurred, looking for the systemic problem that allowed the same error to occur so many times.

Eric Cropp, a pharmacist in Ohio, was convicted and jailed in 2009 for his role in a medication error that killed a two-year-old girl, Emily Jerry.[12] Cropp was blamed for not finding an error created upstream by a pharmacy technician. Michael Cohen for the Institution of Safe Medication Practices was among those who spoke out and called Cropp an easy target, saying that healthcare quality and patient safety are better served by focusing on process issues that allow tragedies like this to occur.[13]

When multiple people, in parallel or sequentially, have responsibility for inspecting for a defect, a normal human reaction is to get complacent, to think that the other person will catch an error if you miss it. At one health system's billing department, up to five different employees inspected charts to make sure details, such as the ordering physician's name, were correct. When employees are busy, it can be tempting to save time by not checking for certain problems, knowing that someone else down the line is supposed to look for the same problem. In this case, even with all of the inspections, errors were frequently found at the final inspection step and sometimes got out as erroneous payment submissions.

Types of Error Proofing

Error proofing can be defined as the creation of devices or methods that either prevent defects or inexpensively and automatically inspect the outcomes of a process each and every time to determine if quality is acceptable or defective. Error proofing is not a specific technology. Rather, it is a mindset and an approach that requires creativity among those who design equipment, design processes, or manage processes.

Make It Impossible to Create the Error

Ideally, error proofing should be 100% effective in physically preventing an error from occurring. In everyday life, think about gasoline pump nozzles. Diesel nozzles are larger and do not fit into an unleaded gas vehicle. It is impossible to make that error. The error proofing is more effective than if we only relied on signs or warning labels that said: "Be careful; do not use diesel fuel in this vehicle." This error-proofing method does not, however, prevent the opposite error of using unleaded fuel in a diesel vehicle (an error, while harmful to a diesel engine, that is less likely to occur).

In a hospital, we can find examples of 100% error proofing. One possible hospital error, similar to the gas pumps, is connecting a gas line to the wrong connector on the wall. Many regulators and gas lines have pins and indexing that prevent a user from connecting to the wrong line, medical air instead of oxygen, as shown in Figure 8.2. The connectors will not fit and there is no way to circumvent the system to make them fit.[14]

One type of preventable error is the injection of the wrong solution into the wrong IV line, an error that has been reported at least 1,200 times in the past five years, meaning it has likely occurred far more that that, given the common under-reporting of errors.[15] Instead of telling clinicians just to be careful, some hospitals have switched to IV tubing that physically cannot be connected to feeding syringes—a strong form of error proofing, similar to the gas line error proofing.

In 2006, a Wisconsin nurse, Julie Thao, was convicted and imprisoned after mistakenly injecting an epidural, instead of an antibiotic, into the bloodstream of a 16-year-old expectant mother. The patient's death "might have been avoided if containers, tubing and connectors for epidural medications were vastly different from intravenous medications," said a newsletter from the Institute for Safe Medication Practices. In fact, the Joint Commission had put out a bulletin in early 2006 warning of such line risks, yet a patient died, and an experienced nurse ended up in jail.[16]

Make It Harder to Create the Error

It is not always possible to fully error proof a process, so we can also aim to make it harder for errors to occur. Think about the software we use every day to create word-processing documents

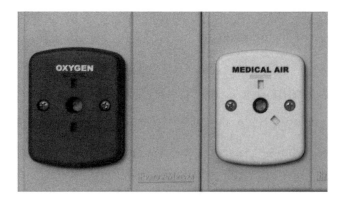

Figure 8.2 Photo of error-proofed connectors for medical gases.

(or e-mail). One possible error is that the user accidentally clicks on the "close" button, which would lose the work. Most software requires a confirmation step, a box that pops up and asks, "Are you sure?" It is still possible for a user to accidentally click "yes," but the error is less likely to occur. A better, more complete error proofing is software that continuously saves your work as a draft, preventing or severely minimizing data loss.

In hospitals, a certain type of infusion pump has a known issue that makes it too easy for a data entry error to occur—it even has its own name, the double-key bounce. The keypad often mistakenly registers a double digit, so if a nurse enters 36, it might be taken as 366 and could lead to an overdose.[17] Some hospitals have posted signs asking employees to be careful. A better approach might be a change to the software that asks "Are you sure?" and requires an active response when double numbers are found or when a dose above a certain value is inadvertantly entered. This approach would still not be as effective as a redesign or an approach that absolutely prevents that error from occurring.

Hospitals already work to error proof medication administration, as medication errors are a common cause of harm to patients; estimates put this at 1.5 million injuries or deaths in the United States alone each year.[18] Automated storage cabinets are one error-proofing method that many hospitals have implemented to help ensure that nurses take the correct medications for their patients. With these cabinets, nurses must scan a bar code or enter a code to indicate the patient for whom they are taking medications. The computer-controlled cabinet opens just the drawer (and sometimes just the individual bin) that contains the correct medication. This makes it harder to take the wrong drug, but there are still errors that can occur:

■ The nurse can reach into the wrong bin in the correct drawer (with some systems).
■ The pharmacy tech might have loaded the wrong medication into the bin.
■ The wrong medication might be in the correct package that the pharmacy tech loaded into the correct bin.
■ The correct medication might still be given to the wrong patient after being taken from the cabinet.

When error proofing, we have to take care that we do not create complacency and overreliance on a particular device. To properly error proof the entire process requires wider analysis and error-proofing methods at each step along the way.

Figure 8.3 Simple error-proofing device that protects against accidental bumping of the centrifuge knob.

Often, the workplace can be retrofitted with simple, inexpensive error-proofing devices if we have the mindset of prevention. One laboratory implemented two simple error-proofing devices in a short time. In one area, a centrifuge had knobs that controlled timing and speed, knobs that were too easily bumped by a person walking by the machine. Instead of hanging a "be careful" sign, a technologist took a piece of clear plastic packaging material that would have otherwise been thrown away and put it over the knobs, as shown in Figure 8.3. The prevention method cost nothing and was probably faster than making a sign. The mindset was in place to figure out how that error could be prevented.

In the microbiology area, visitors dropped off specimens on a counter and were often tempted to reach across the counter rather than walking to the end, where the official drop-off spot was located. The problem with reaching across the counter is that a person, unfamiliar with the area, could have easily burned himself or herself on a small incinerator that sat on the counter, without an indication that it was hot. Instead of posting warning signs, a manager had maintenance install a flexiglass shield that prevented people from reaching across the bench, as shown in Figure 8.4. It was a small investment but helped prevent injury better than a sign.

Pharmacies often have signs warning personnel about high-risk medications, for which similar names or different doses can cause harm to patients. Many pharmacies are rethinking the practice of placing medications in alphabetical order on shelves in an effort to prevent some errors. In one case, UPMC St. Margaret reduced re-admission rates for chronic obstructive pulmonary disease (COPD) by 48% by moving different doses of a drug that is commonly used with these patients. Instead of the 0.63- and 1.25-milligram doses being side by side, they were placed in different drawers with distinctive labels.[19]

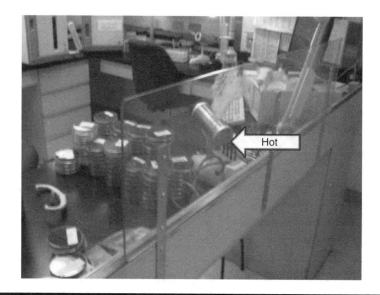

Figure 8.4 Simple error-proofing device that prevents burns and specimens from being dropped off in the wrong location.

Make It Obvious the Error Has Occurred

Another error-proofing approach is setting up the process so it is obvious when errors have occurred, through automated checks or simple inspection steps.

One possible error in instrument sterilization is that equipment malfunctions or misuse result in an instrument pack not being properly sterilized. There might be multiple methods for error proofing the equipment or its use, but common practice also uses special tape wraps or inserts that change colors or form black stripes to indicate proper sterilization. The absence of these visual indicators makes it obvious an error has occurred, helping protect the patient.

In a hospital setting, there is a risk that intubation tubes are inserted into the esophagus instead of the trachea, which would cause harm by preventing air from getting to the patient's lungs. A 1998 study indicated this happens in 5.4% of intubations.[20] Warning signs posted on the device or in the emergency department would not be an effective error-proofing strategy. If we cannot engineer the device to ensure the tube goes into the airway, we can perform a simple test after each insertion. Plastic aspiration bulbs can be provided so the caregiver can see if air from the patient's lungs will reinflate a squeezed bulb within five seconds.[21] If not, we can suspect that the tube is in the esophagus, looking to correct the error before the patient is harmed. This form of error proofing is not 100% reliable because it relies on people to adhere to the standardized work that they should check for proper placement.

Other error proofing might include monitors and sensors that can automatically detect and signal the anesthesiologist that the patient was intubated incorrectly, although there are limitations to the effectiveness of monitoring oxygen saturation levels as an inspection step for this error. A chest X-ray might also be used as an inspection method, but studies showed that is an ineffective method.[22] "Commonly used" clinical inspection methods in this case are often inaccurate, so medical evidence should drive the standardized work for how clinicians check for intubation errors.

Make the System Robust So It Tolerates the Error

At gas stations, there is a risk that a customer could drive away without detaching the pump nozzle from the car. They have been able to error proof this not by physically preventing the error or by hanging signs; instead, gas stations have anticipated that the error could occur and designed the system to allow for this. If a driver does drive off, the pump has a quick-release valve that snaps away and cuts off the flow of gasoline, preventing a spill or possible explosion (although you might look silly driving down the road with the nozzle and hose dragging from your vehicle).

In a laboratory, one hospital found a test instrument that was not designed to these error-proofing standards as the instrument was not robust against spills of patient specimens. The lab had responded by posting two separate signs on the instrument that told employees: "Do Not Spill; Wipe Spills Immediately." The signs did nothing to prevent the error as employees generally tried not spilling patient specimens. The root cause of the situation was that a circuit board in the instrument was exposed underneath the place where specimens were loaded. A different hospital, using that same equipment, posted a memo notifying staff that they had "blown three electronic boards in just a few weeks," costing $1,000 each. The memo emphasized that people should not pour off specimens or handle liquids above the equipment as part of their standardized work. As a better root cause preventive measure, the designer of the instrument should have anticipated that patient specimen spills were likely to occur at some point in the instrument's use and taken steps to protect the sensitive board.

One lesson for hospitals is to consider design and error proofing, even going through an FMEA exercise, when buying new equipment. Hospitals can pressure manufacturers and suppliers to build error-proofing devices into equipment, using their market power to reward suppliers who make equipment that is more robust against foreseeable errors.

Error Proofing, Not Dummy Proofing

Error proofing has a Japanese equivalent term, *poka yoke*, which is sometimes used in Lean circles. With this phrase, the focus is on the error itself, and our problem-solving response is to understand and prevent the error. The phrase *mistake proofing* is sometimes used interchangeably with *error proofing*, but that phrase seems to steer focus toward who made the mistake and blame. Errors occur, often as the result of a system, in which a *mistake* is defined as "a wrong action attributable to bad judgment or ignorance or inattention."[23] Not all errors are necessarily caused by bad judgment, ignorance, or inattention.

Everyday use of the English language features phrases such as "idiot proofing" or "dummy proofing." Terminology like this should not be used, as it does not demonstrate respect for people. Errors, particularly in hospital settings, are not caused because people are stupid. Errors are caused by smart people who mean well but are forced to work in complex and often-broken systems.

There is another Japanese phrase, *baka yoke*, which translates to "fool proofing." Shingo told a story about using the *baka yoke* phrase in a factory in 1963. Shingo wrote, "One of the company's part-time employees burst into tears when the department head explained that a 'foolproofing' mechanism had been installed because workers sometimes mixed up left- and right-hand parts. 'Have I really been such a fool?' the employee sobbed."[24]

As much as some of us might not want to admit it, we are all human, even in a medical environment, and we are prone to committing errors and mistakes. Systems need to be designed and error proofed accordingly.

Examples of Error Proofing in Hospitals

There are many examples of error-proofing methods that already exist in hospitals, with varying degrees of effectiveness. Many of the examples we see are error proofing through standardized work, a method that is more likely to reduce errors than to prevent them altogether.

Banned Abbreviations as Error Proofing

Many hospitals have implemented lists of banned abbreviations that have the potential to be confusing or misinterpreted. Rather than telling doctors and employees to be careful, hospitals have recognized there is a risk from using the old abbreviations.

For example, micrograms and milligrams can be confused when micrograms is written by hand and abbreviated with the Greek letter for *micro*, leading to an incorrect dose being given to a patient. Rather than telling doctors and employees to be careful, hospitals have recognized there is a risk from using the old abbreviations. The preferred abbreviation is to designate micrograms as "mcg," which is much harder to confuse with milligrams ("mg") when written by hand. In addition, the use of the letter U for units can be mistaken for a zero, leading to a dosing error.

The challenge with this form of error proofing is that we are relying on individuals to follow the new standardized work. It is not enough to say, "We have a policy in place, so the problem is solved." Leaders must check constantly for adherence to the standardized work and need to encourage employees to monitor each other for, in this case, the proper use of abbreviations.

In a Lean hospital, when the old abbreviation is found, we cannot just work around the problem by fixing the abbreviation (as might be done by a nurse or a unit clerk). Employees must feel obligated to address the process defect (somebody using the banned abbreviation) with the physician, or report the practice to managers, using something like the "patient safety alert" process at Virginia Mason Medical Center (Seattle, WA).[25] Unfortunately, a survey by the American Association of Critical-Care Nurses showed that fewer than 10% of physicians, nurses, and other critical care providers directly confronted their colleagues, and 20% of physicians had seen patient harm as a result. Leaders have to create an environment in which raising a patient safety concern does not lead to punishment or retribution, which is one reason caregivers would avoid confronting each other. Hospitals might also want to consider providing training in constructive confrontation and communication skills to help employees work together more effectively. Teaching healthcare workers the most effective way to speak up is one aspect of the increasingly popular "crew resource management" (CRM) training that brings aviation and cockpit safety practices into healthcare.[26]

In the CRM approach, workers are not "encouraged" or "empowered" to speak up: They are expected to speak up. At Allegheny General Hospital in Pennsylvania, where central line insertion and care were being 100% standardized, the chief of medicine, Dr. Richard Shannon, instructed the nurses to stop a nonstandard procedure. Until this time, this was not part of the hospital culture. Ultimately, the nurses did stop procedures that were being done incorrectly, and Dr. Shannon backed them up. The result was a change in culture, more respect for nurses as team members, and drastically reduced central-line infections.[27]

Leaders must follow up with physicians and remind them of the importance of using the approved abbreviations, emphasizing the impact on patient safety (focusing on the customer) and, secondarily, the risk to the hospital if an error were to occur. It can be a difficult dynamic when we are reliant on keeping physicians happy to drive new patient revenue to the hospital. In cases like this, hospitals in a community should reach common agreements that they are going to hold all physicians accountable, equally, to standardized work and patient safety guidelines, reducing the risk that a physician takes his or her patients to a competing hospital.

Computer Systems as Error Proofing

One technological method for reducing handwriting errors, for pharmacy prescriptions, laboratory test orders, or other communications, is electronic systems, such as computerized physician order entry (CPOE) or other electronic medical record (EMR) systems. The Leapfrog Group estimated that if CPOE were implemented at all urban hospitals in the United States, almost 1 million serious medication errors could be avoided each year. CPOE adoption is still far from universal, as a 2005 study estimated that only 4% of U.S. hospitals had such systems.[28] By 2010, only 14% of hospitals had at least 10% CPOE use, the minimum required for so-called meaningful use standards.[29]

Even at hospitals with CPOE, physician resistance is often high, particularly when systems are not designed effectively around physician workflow. As with nurses not wanting to use mobile computer carts, physicians might resist using CPOE or EMR systems if the technology slows them down. The situation is complicated by dynamics between physicians and hospitals, where most physicians are not direct employees. This eliminates the ability of management to mandate use of the system through traditional supervisor control. Of course, as discussed in Chapter 5, the Lean management style relies more on explaining why and convincing people of the benefits of a tool or method instead of relying on formal positional authority. When physicians, or others, resist standardized work or new tools, we should first ask why.

The former Toyota executive Gary Convis is often quoted as being told by Japanese Toyota leaders to "lead the organization as if I had no power."[30] Although Convis had much formal power (with thousands of employees reporting to him), relying on mandates was a last resort, after first using coaching, setting an example, and understanding others to help them achieve their goals. This leadership style should be particularly transferable to a hospital environment in which senior leaders have little or no formal control over physicians.

In a further connection between quality and efficiency, CPOE and other hospital information systems provide automated checks of pharmacy prescriptions, inspecting for interactions and patient allergies, among other process defects. This reduces the amount of time required of pharmacists for manual order review and inspection, freeing them to serve more of a clinical advisory role to physicians and patients.

Preventing Surgery Errors through Error Proofing

Wrong-site surgeries, while not the most frequently occurring medical mistake, can have a severe impact on patients, creating high-profile cases in the news. One study estimated that a typical large hospital would have a serious surgical incident every 5–10 years.[31] Mistakes like these can be error proofed through standardized work (including checklists) and visual management methods, as they are often caused by poor communication, time pressures, and organizational dynamics that prevent people from speaking up.

In July 2003, the Joint Commission released its "Universal Protocol for Preventing Wrong Site, Wrong Procedure, and Wrong Person Surgery," aimed at putting standardized work methods in place for accredited hospitals. The three major components of the protocol are

■ A formal process for presurgical verification
■ Marking the operative site
■ A time-out process done immediately before the procedure

Since this is a standardized work approach to error proofing, the success of the method mainly depends on consistently following the standard. The Joint Commission stated that time-out compliance is only at 78–80%,[32] a slight increase from the 2007 report of 74.2%.[33] Nurses and other employees are often afraid to speak up with certain surgeons, so leaders have an important role in creating an environment in which fear does not prevent the time-out from taking place.

Guidelines include the person performing the procedure marking the site in an unambiguous way (such as "YES") and making sure the mark remains visible after skin prep. An "X" (a commonly used mark) might be interpreted as "cut here" or "wrong spot," an ambiguity that could lead to an error. Compliance with this protocol is higher, at 93.4%. Leaders need to ensure that surgeons are not just following the letter of the law, as one news account suggested some surgeons make what one surgical chief called "passive-aggressive marks," tiny marks that cannot be seen and cannot be helpful.[34]

As with any example of standardized work, leaders have an obligation to look for signs that methods like the universal protocol are not being followed. We need to do so proactively, rather than assuming the standardized work is being followed and just reacting after an error occurs. Leaders can also continually emphasize the importance of taking time for quality when employees are concerned about moving patients through operating rooms as quickly as possible.

Stopping the Line (*Andon*)

A method frequently associated with Toyota is the *andon* cord, cords that hang down over the assembly line to be pulled when any worker sees a problem. The line will stop if additional time is needed to solve the problem before the car moves on to the next station. In more than 99% of cases, the problem is solved quickly, often with a team leader's help, without stopping production.[35] Problems are fixed at the source (the concept of *jidoka*) instead of being passed along to be fixed at the end of the line.

In a hospital setting, we can teach the *andon* concept, the idea that any process should be stopped at the sign of a problem (or problems should be solved immediately if possible). The time-out process is one example, but one hospital took the idea of stopping the line even further, in the name of patient safety.

As told by the CEO of the hospital, the facility had gone nine years without a wrong-site surgery before one occurred. More surprisingly, they soon had three more, for a total of four errors in eight weeks. The hospital president decided that the operating rooms would be shut down until the root cause of the problem had been found—stopping "the line." Their error, the CEO explained, was that they had not stopped the line immediately after the first error, taking time to find the root cause right then. With more investigation, it was discovered that surgical teams had stopped doing the time-out procedure, another warning that we cannot let success (good results) lead to complacency (falling back to bad processes). As a temporary fix, the hospital added an independent auditor to be present at each presurgical time-out, with random audits taking place long term.

Understanding Lean is one thing; implementing it in the face of an existing culture can be another story altogether. For example, Ford Motor Company's new truck plant (Dearborn, MI) copied a tool, installing *andon* cords. Workers, though, were afraid to pull them, expecting a negative response from their supervisors instead of a supportive or helpful one.

Why do Toyota employees pull the cord 2,000 times per week, while Ford employees only do so twice a week at this one plant?[36] It is not because Toyota has 1,000 times the problems. Toyota has created a culture in which it is acceptable, even encouraged, to report problems instead of covering them up. At the Ford plant, the infrequent use of the *andon* cords was attributed to "the legacy of generations of mistrust between shop-floor workers and managers."[37]

The equivalent of *andon* cord pulls or line stoppages in a hospital setting should be immediate and direct communications. At some hospitals, the mechanisms for identifying problems include an e-mail account and a phone line (that sometimes might go to voice mail). While it is good to have avenues for employees to report safety concerns, a true *andon* system requires people to stop and address the problem (or at least ask a question) immediately, so that patient harm can be prevented. Again, leaders have a responsibility for building a culture in which employees are not afraid to speak up without retribution from colleagues.

Virginia Mason Medical Center has been a leader in the use of this philosophy, what they call "patient safety alerts," or PSAs.[38] PSAs are categorized as

- Red: Life-threatening situations, a "never event," or anything that could pose serious harm to a patient
- Orange: Less-severe situations
- Yellow: Slips or latent errors (situations that carry the potential for patient harm)

Beyond the mechanisms for reporting problems, the leadership team at Virginia Mason has emphasized that they have "got your back" if you are a staff member who raises a concern, reducing the fear of retribution. By 2004, an estimated one-third of employees had reported a PSA, and the hospital has tallied more than 15,000 alerts since 2002. The hospital attributed staff acceptance of this system to the fast response that people received when calling an alert and the cultural changes that have surrounded this system. At Virginia Mason, problems, falls, and near misses lead to systemic improvement, not punishment.

As a result of their safety improvement efforts, the professional liability costs at Virginia Mason fell by 26% from 2007 to 2008, and they declined another 12% the next year.[39] As a result of their quality and safety improvement, Virginia Mason was named one of two "Hospitals of the Decade" by the Leapfrog Group.[40]

Error Proofing the Error Proofing

When implementing error-proofing methods, we have to take care that employees do not have easy ways of working around the new system. One example of this, from outside the hospital, was shared by an employee who had observed a neighbor who used an electric lawn mower with an error-proofing device. The user had to press a lever together to keep the engine running. As a safety measure, releasing that lever stopped the mower engine and blade. But, in an effort to save motion, the neighbor had circumvented the protection by wrapping the electric cord around the lever so it would stay engaged without having to hold the lever, creating a safety problem and risk of injury.

We should keep that example in mind when looking at error-proofing methods, particularly when the method creates extra work for employees. If employees are overburdened and already have too much other waste in their day, they may resist having the extra work or look for ways to cut corners to save time. We need to anticipate how employees might circumvent the error proofing by applying the same thought process that went into the original error proofing itself:

- How can we prevent the circumvention of the error proofing?
- Why do people feel the need to circumvent error proofing?
- How can we make it harder to circumvent the error proofing?
- How can we make it obvious or apparent that the error proofing has been circumvented?

Leaders need to watch for the proper use of error-proofing methods and must hold people accountable for following the correct standardized work. At the same time, we should first ask why, as in "Why would that employee want to circumvent the error proofing?" We have to look for the root cause of why that person might do so, either because there is not enough time in his or her day (a need to reduce waste) or because the error-proofing method is too hard to use.

In some hospitals, nurses are required to scan bar codes on patient wristbands to ensure the proper match of patient to medication. If nurses call in sick and a unit is understaffed, the nurses on duty might feel pressured to cut corners to save time. Nurses sometimes create surrogate patient wristband labels to scan all of the medications at once (in a batch) instead of doing it at the bedside. This corner cutting is a workaround to the problem of being understaffed. Lean hospitals would hold nurses accountable but would also look to solve the root cause of the problem—the pressure and the need to cut corners. A five whys analysis could be performed to identify weaknesses in staffing policies and reaction plans for when nurses call in sick.

Conclusion

Hospitals are full of smart, conscientious employees, yet errors and patient harm still occur. If telling people to be careful were effective, we would have already eliminated quality and patient safety problems in our hospitals. Error proofing is a mindset that we have to adopt, always asking why an error could have occurred and what we can do to prevent that error from occurring the next time. In keeping with the principle of respect for people, Lean thinkers assume that people want to do safe, high-quality work; we just have to design systems and processes that allow that to happen.

Lean Lessons

- Being careful and hanging warning signs is not enough to prevent errors.
- A 100% inspection is not 100% effective.
- Adding more inspection steps will not ensure quality outcomes.
- Error proofing (*poka yoke*) physically prevents errors from occurring or makes them less likely to occur.
- Avoid phrases like "dummy proofing" to keep with the principle of respect for people.
- Do not forget to error proof the error proofing.

Points for Group Discussion

- Are the caution and warning signs in your hospital anything more than a short-term response to quality problems?
- Can you find a sign that can be replaced with better standardized work or with error proofing?
- How would you evaluate your equipment and tools differently, keeping error proofing in mind?
- What are frequently occurring errors and mistakes in our area?
- What ideas for simple error proofing do our team members have?
- How do we ensure that methods like banned abbreviations are followed all of the time?
- How can hospitals better learn from mistakes made at other facilities?
- In what circumstances would it be appropriate for society to jail individuals who are involved in errors that harm patients?

Notes

1. Grady, Denise, "Study Finds No Progress in Safety at Hospitals," *New York Times*, November 24, 2010, http://www.nytimes.com/2010/11/25/health/research/25patient.html (accessed April 8, 2011).
2. Classen, David C., Roger Resar, et al., "'Global Trigger Tool' Shows that Adverse Events in Hospitals May Be Ten Times Greater than Previously Measured," *Health Affairs*, April 2011, 30, no. 4: 581–89.
3. Josie King Foundation, "What Happened," http://www.josieking.org/page.cfm?pageID=10 (accessed April 3, 2011).
4. Pronovost, Peter J., *Safe Patients, Smart Hospitals: How One Doctor's Checklist Can Help Us Change Health Care from the Inside Out* (New York: Hudson Street Press, 2010), 1.

5. Kroft, Steve, "Dennis Quaid Recounts Twins' Drug Ordeal," *60 Minutes*, March 16, 2008, http://www.cbsnews.com/stories/2008/03/13/60minutes/main3936412.shtml (accessed April 3, 2011).

6. Davies, Tom, "Fatal Drug Mix-Up Exposes Hospital Flaws," *Washington Post*, September 22, 2006, http://www.washingtonpost.com/wp-dyn/content/article/2006/09/22/AR2006092200815.html?nav=hcmodule (accessed April 3, 2011).

7. Celizic, Mike, "I Don't Want This to Happen to Anyone Else," *Today*, October 4, 2007, http://today.msnbc.msn.com/id/21127917/ns/today-today_health/ (accessed April 3, 2011).

8. Epstein, Reid J., "Medical Blunder," *Newsday*, October 2, 2007, http://www.newsday.com/news/medical-blunder-1.664691 (accessed April 4, 2011).

9. *Mail Online,* "Dennis Quaid's Newborn Twins Rushed to Intensive Care After Accidental Drug Overdose," http://www.dailymail.co.uk/tvshowbiz/article-495359/Dennis-Quaids-newborn-twins-rushed-intensive-care-accidental-drug-overdose.html (accessed April 4, 2011).

10. Toyota Motor Corporation, "Toyota Production System," http://www.toyota-global.com/company/vision_philosophy/toyota_production_system/ (accessed April 10, 2011).

11. Kowalczyk, Liz, "R.I. Raps Hospital for Errors in Surgery," *Boston Globe*, November 27, 2007, http://www.boston.com/news/local/articles/2007/11/27/ri_raps_hospital_for_errors_in_surgery/ (accessed April 10, 2011).

12. Atassi, Leila, "Former Pharmacist Eric Cropp Gets 6 Months in Jail in Emily Jerry's Death from Wrong Chemotherapy Solution," http://www.cleveland.com/news/plaindealer/index.ssf?/base/cuyahoga/1250325193310800.xml&coll=2 (accessed April 4, 2011).

13. Blitzer, Wolf, "The Situation Room," http://transcripts.cnn.com/TRANSCRIPTS/1002/15/sitroom.02.html (accessed April 4, 2011).

14. Grout, John, *Mistake-Proofing the Design of Healthcare Care Processes*, AHRQ Publication 07-0020 (Rockville, MD: Agency for Healthcare Research and Quality, 2007), 41, 76.

15. Wahlberg, David, "Day 1: Medical Tubing Mistakes Can Be Deadly," *Wisconsin State Journal*, http://host.madison.com/news/local/health_med_fit/article_bc888491-1f7d-5008-be21-31009a4b253a.html (accessed April 4, 2011).

16. Joint Commission, "Tubing Misconnections—A Persistent and Potentially Deadly Occurrence," http://www.jointcommission.org/assets/1/18/SEA_36.PDF (accessed April 4, 2011).

17. "Double Key Bounce and Double Keying Errors," Institute for Safe Medication Practices, January 12, 2006, http://www.ismp.org/Newsletters/acutecare/articles/20060112.asp?ptr=y (accessed April 10, 2011).

18. Kaufman, Marc, "Medication Errors Harming Millions, Report Says," *The Washington Post*, July 21, 2006, http://www.washingtonpost.com/wp-dyn/content/article/2006/07/20/AR2006072000754.html (accessed April 4, 2011).

19. California Healthcare Advocates, "Creative Interventions Reduce Hospital Readmissions for Medicare Beneficiaries," October 7, 2010, http://www.cahealthadvocates.org/news/basics/2010/creative.html (accessed April 9, 2011).

20. Sakles, J. C., Laurin, E. G., Rantapaa, A. A., and Panacek, E., "Airway Management in the Emergency Department: A One-Year Study of 610 Tracheal Intubations," *Annals of Emergency Medicine,* 1998, 31:325–32.

21. Grout, *Mistake-Proofing*, 78.

22. Dittrich, Kenneth C., MD, "Delayed Recognition of Esophageal Intubation," *CJEM Canadian Journal of Emergency Medical Care,* 2002, 4, no. 1: 41–44. http://www.cjem-online.ca/v4/n1/p41 (accessed April 9, 2011).

23. WordNet Search 3.0, http://wordnet.princeton.edu/perl/webwn?s=mistake (accessed December 20, 2007).

24. Shingo, Shigeo, *Zero Quality Control: Source Inspection and the Poka-Yoke System* (New York: Productivity Press, 1986), 45.

25. Kenney, Charles, *Transforming Healthcare: Virginia Mason Medical Center's Pursuit of the Perfect Patient Experience* (New York: Productivity Press, 2010), 50.

26. Gaffney, F. Andrew, Stephen W. Harden, and Rhea Seddon, *Crew Resource Management: The Flight Plan for Lasting Change in Patient Safety* (Marblehead, MA: HCPro, 2005), 1.

27. Grunden, Naida, *The Pittsburgh Way to Efficient Healthcare: Improving Patient Care Using Toyota Based Methods* (New York: Productivity Press, 2007), 53.

28. Pedersen, Craig A., Philip J. Schneider, and Douglas J. Scheckelhoff, "ASHP National Survey of Pharmacy Practice in Hospital Settings: Prescribing and Transcribing—2004," *American Journal of Health-System Pharmacy,* 2005, 62: 378–90.

29. Monegain, Bernie, "CPOE: Stumbling Block on Way to Meaningful Use," *Healthcare IT News,* June 17, 2010, http://www.healthcareitnews.com/news/cpoe-stumbling-block-way-meaningful-use (accessed April 4, 2011).

30. Convis, Gary, "Role of Management in a Lean Manufacturing Environment," Society of Automotive Engineers, http://www.sae.org/manufacturing/lean/column/leanjul01.htm (accessed April 10, 2011).

31. Kwann, Mary, David Studdert, Michael J. Zinner, and Atul A. Gawande, "Incidence, Patterns, and Prevention of Wrong-Site Surgery," *Archives of Surgery,* 2006, 141: 353–58.

32. Burger, Maureen, "Time Out for Patient Safety at the Bedside," Joint Commission Resources, http://www.jcrinc.com/Time-Out-for-Patient-Safety/ (accessed April 4, 2011).

33. Joint Commission, "Improving America's Hospitals the Joint Commission's Annual Report on Quality and Safety—2007," http://www.jointcommission.org/assets/1/18/2007_Annual_Report.pdf (accessed March 13, 2011).

34. Davis, Robert, "'Wrong Site' Surgeries on the Rise," *USA Today,* April 17, 2006, http://www.usatoday.com/news/health/2006–04–17-wrong-surgery_x.htm (accessed April 4, 2011).

35. Meier, David, personal interview, January 2, 2008.

36. Schifferes, Steve, "The Triumph of Lean Production," *BBC News Online,* February 27, 2007, http://news.bbc.co.uk/2/hi/business/6346315.stm (accessed April 10, 2011).

37. Ibid.

38. Kenney, *Transforming Healthcare,* 52.

39. Ibid., 65.

40. The Leapfrog Group, "The Leapfrog Group Announces Top Hospitals of the Decade," November 30, 2010, http://www.leapfroggroup.org/news/leapfrog_news/4784721 (accessed April 4, 2011).

Chapter 9

Improving Flow

Waiting: A Worldwide Problem

Around the world, patients often wait far too long for their medical care. In Ontario, Canada, the government maintains a Web site that shows the expected delay for different types of surgery. As of April 2011, patients near Toronto could expect to wait up to 118 days for cataract surgery and 114 days for magnetic resonance imaging (MRI), much longer than their target of 28 days.[1] In England, the National Health Service (NHS) goal is 126 days (18 weeks) between referral and the start of treatment.[2] Care delays are typically caused by a lack of capacity or budget constraints. In the United States, getting access to certain specialists can be difficult, as the average waiting time for a routine skin cancer screening appointment with a dermatologist in a given city ranged from 10 to 50 days, with the longest provider waiting times in a given city averaging 100 days, depending on the location.[3] Lean methods are proving helpful in reducing the amount of time spent waiting for an appointment, as ThedaCare (Appleton, WI), for example, has reduced the waiting time between referral to the first CyberKnife cancer treatment from 26 days to just 6 days.[4]

Once patients have arrived for care, waiting times for emergency and acute care are often longer than they need to be due to poor flow. In the United States, the average emergency department (E.D.) length of stay is 4.1 hours, while patients in Alberta, Canada, have a median wait time of 4.6 hours.[5,6] Lean success stories are becoming more common with emergency care around the world, including Mary Washington Hospital (Virginia), which reduced length of stay from 4 hours to 3, reducing "left without being seen" rates from over 6% to 2%, while seeing a 25% higher patient volume.[7] Hôtel Dieu Grace Hospital (Windsor, Ontario) reduced the average length of stay for discharged patients from 3.6 to 2.8 hours, also reducing the number of patients who left without being seen from 7.1% to 4.3%.[8]

In outpatient settings, one survey showed that excessive waiting room time was the primary complaint of 72% of U.S. dental patients.[9] Sami Bahri, DDS, is an example of a dentist who has used Lean to eliminate waiting room time for patients while increasing patient volumes. Traditionally, patients who required care beyond a basic cleaning would be diagnosed and then scheduled for a follow-up appointment. The Bahri Dental Group rethought this and changed their flow to be able to treat most patients in a single visit if the patient wishes. The time required for a complex patient's complete treatment fell from 99 days in 2005 to 10 days in 2008.[10]

Traditionally, access and cost are seen as trade-offs. The oft-proposed solutions for reducing delays typically mean spending money to increase capacity, meaning constructing or expanding new facilities, purchasing new equipment, and hiring additional staff. Lean is helping organizations improve patient flow in far less expensive ways. One major children's hospital reduced waiting times for outpatient MRIs from over 12 weeks to a sustained 2.5 weeks through setup reduction, waste elimination, and a change in anesthesiologist staffing patterns. MRI utilization levels during working hours were increased from 40% to about 65% through Lean methods, a far more cost-effective approach than buying another MRI machine.

Focusing on Flow

Traditional organizations often focus more on cost and the efficiency of individuals or departments. One way in which Lean is different from traditional thinking is the focus on flow. Instead of asking people to work faster, Lean organizations focus on reducing delays and systemic barriers to flow. By focusing on flow, we can often increase capacity (which often leads to revenue increases) and reduce costs as an end result of these improvements.

It is often said that there are seven types of flow in healthcare, as shown in Table 9.1. These seven flows are taken into space and process design exercises called "3P" or the production preparation process. ThedaCare and Park Nicollet (St. Louis Park, MN) have been among the leaders in the use of this approach.[11] Seattle Children's Hospital is among those using 3P as part of an "integrated project delivery" design and construction approach.[12]

Value Streams Should Flow Like a River

Along with quality, flow is the other pillar of the Lean house. Smooth, steady flow through a value stream should be the primary goal of a hospital. That might mean the smooth flow of support products (such as test specimens, medications, or surgical instruments), or it might mean the

Table 9.1 The Seven Flows of Healthcare

Type of Flow	Example
Patients	Movement of patients through acute care; high-level care process, including handoff from primary to specialty care
Clinicians and staff	Physical movement within or between departments
Medications	Physical flow from pharmacy to floor stock or patient rooms
Supplies	Processes, movement, and storage of consumables
Equipment	Processes, movement, and storage of pumps, beds, wheelchairs, etc.
Information	Discharge information passing from clinician to clinician
Process engineering	Flow of equipment through the biomed department or the repair process

smooth flow of patients through the hospital and their continuum of care. There are many causes of delays in hospitals—some that just occur, while others are imposed on by our own decisions and policies. Flow improvements do not come from doing the value-adding work faster; improvements generally come from reducing and eliminating waiting, interruptions, and delays from the value stream.

Lean terminology often includes references to the phrases "one-piece flow" or "single-piece flow." In a perfect flow environment, the product (or patient) would move in batches of one, as this minimizes delays. Think of an escalator, which allows people to move between floors in continuous single-piece flow, as opposed to an elevator, which accomplishes the same thing by batching passengers. One-piece flow is more of a directional goal than an absolute, as we might not be able to move to batches of one immediately due to short-term constraints in the system. We must work to reduce these constraints, rather than letting the barriers become an easy excuse for not having good flow.

Lean instructors often use visualization from Toyota, viewing flow as a river or stream. In a river, rocks stick up through the surface of the water, impeding the smooth flow of water or boats. In the analogy, we view those rocks as problems that need to be solved so flow can be improved (as opposed to speeding up the stream in some artificial way).

In making improvements, we should first identify the "rocks," asking why we cannot have predictable schedules that are followed like clockwork. Rocks in the surgery department system might include the following:

- Patients sometimes show up late.
- Lab results are not always back in time for the surgery.
- Order sets were not completed properly.
- Supplies, blood, or instruments needed to start surgery are missing.
- Surgery lengths are unpredictable.

We may be able to find effective countermeasures for some of those problems. Improvements in the laboratory could reduce turnaround times, preventing some surgery delays. We can also ask why patients are late, viewing the process through their experience. One reason could be a confusing hospital layout and a lack of clear signage to direct first-time visitors or a proper reminder call not being placed. One hospital had an ongoing problem with patients showing up at the wrong building. After years of blaming the patients, a team realized that paperwork sent to the patients was confusing, leading someone to arrive at the outpatient services building instead of the main hospital or vice versa.

In some hospitals, surgery patients wait for hours because they are all instructed to arrive first thing in the morning. This is typically done because there is uncertainty (real or perceived) about how long procedures might actually take, and surgical teams set up the system to ensure that they are never waiting, maximizing their own utilization. The trade-off in this approach is long patient waiting times. Some hospitals are starting to give patients actual surgery times throughout the day, a more patient-centered approach. Initially, patients are asked to arrive 90 or 120 minutes before their case, but we might gradually reduce the patients' early arrival time from 90 to 60 minutes as we make improvements.

Uneven Workloads as a Barrier to Flow

Many delays, for patients and products, are caused by uneven workloads. As introduced in Chapter 5, *heijunka* is one of the three foundations of the Toyota house. Having level demand for processes leads to lower resource requirements, in both staffing and equipment. Some unevenness in our demand occurs naturally, but a large amount is due to our own policies and choices. Lean teaches us to identify sources of *mura* (uneven workloads) so we can work on leveling the load instead of taking the unevenness for granted.

Naturally Occurring Unevenness

Hospitals have many examples of workloads that are not level. This unevenness is often beyond our immediate control, such as when patient volumes increase during the winter months because certain illnesses are more prevalent. The heavier seasonal illness volume leads to increased costs for the hospital, as emergency departments (EDs), the number of inpatient rooms, and support departments must be sized to account for the busy periods. Otherwise, patients will suffer longer delays when demand is high. Even though we can often vary staffing levels by hiring seasonal employees, physical resources go to waste when volumes are lower. Hospitals cannot control all of the seasonality, even with improved preventive care and community safety initiatives.

Lean hospitals might view slow periods during the year as opportunities to more actively market elective procedures in an attempt to level out the overall load on the hospital and its resources, shifting cross-trained personnel between the ED and the operating room (OR) as demand shifts. Slow periods can also be used as opportunities for staff training and process improvement efforts, as Toyota does during slow sales periods.[13] This training and improvement activity has a cost, but it is considered an investment that will pay off for the long-term good of the organization.

Mura *Caused by Morning Rounds*

The traditional practice of morning rounds by physicians leads to *mura* for support departments, such as the laboratory. Since physicians want daily lab results on patients' charts before their morning rounds, laboratories have to get a large volume of work done by 7 a.m. In one very typical lab, 34% of the daily volume arrived in a three-hour timeframe from 3 to 6 a.m. Figure 9.1 shows the hourly test volumes for that typical clinical laboratory.

Since we cannot schedule medical technologists (or other lab employees) for short shifts just to cover the busy time, we end up with excess staffing and equipment during the slower periods that follow the morning spike. To meet this demand, hospitals typically send out large numbers of phlebotomists to draw patients' blood early in the morning, resources we continue to pay for after the rush is over.

Morning physician rounds also lead to a spike in inpatient discharge activity. This bolus of discharge orders passes through the system, creating *mura* in support roles ranging from social work (preparing to get patients discharged into nursing homes) to patient transport (trying to move many patients at the same time) to housekeeping (trying to clean many empty rooms at the same time).

In hospitals where physicians are not employed, it might not seem practical to level-load physician rounds, even with the benefits for patients and some departments. On the other hand, some hospitals with employed physicians have some afternoon rounds, including Saint Göran Hospital (Stockholm,

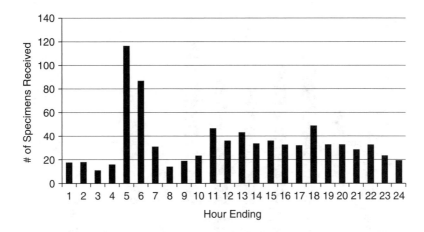

Figure 9.1   Clinical laboratory: number of specimens received each hour during an average day.

Sweden). The physicians must initiate or agree to changes like this rather than having this forced on them, not that Lean thinkers should make a habit of forcing new processes on anyone.

Mura *Caused by Suboptimizing Courier Routes*

In many situations, uneven workloads are caused by decisions made by a single department looking to minimize its own cost, often at the expense of the overall system. Labs that receive specimens from outside sources, such as off-site clinics or private physician offices, often find that courier deliveries are not level loaded throughout the day.

Kaiser Permanente of the Mid-Atlantic States (Rockville, Maryland) made changes in its regional laboratory to level the flow of specimens to test instruments. Before Lean, specimens arrived infrequently, said laboratory operations manager Jane Price Lewis. "At three in the afternoon, we would get a giant 'fish cooler' full of specimens from all 29 medical centers," said Lewis. "At 7:30 P.M. we received another one, and then at 10:30, and then again at 1 A.M. Each time we had a huge spurt of activity while the staff struggled with this bolus of work." The lab had wasted and unused capacity during the late morning and early afternoon, so the lab arranged for the courier service to deliver smaller batches of orders starting in the morning. While this added courier expense, the lab was able to reduce overtime within the lab, as work was more easily completed during the afternoon shift. Similar effects are often seen inside the hospital, where adding additional phlebotomists (one of the lower pay rates in the hospital) can help reduce overall laboratory costs or costs for the entire hospital.

Leveling also improved service. When Kaiser's couriers delivered the fish coolers at 10:30 P.M., the large batches often contained samples from the morning or early afternoon. "Many times, doctors would be waiting for follow-ups on highly abnormal results," said Lewis. "But we might not call them until three or four o'clock in the morning." After adopting an approach that calls for smaller, more frequent batches, the lab now calls with those results by 5 or 6 P.M. "The doctor can get the patient back into the medical center for additional testing or get them on therapy more quickly," said Lewis. "We're actually having an impact on our patients by providing more timely results to our providers."[14]

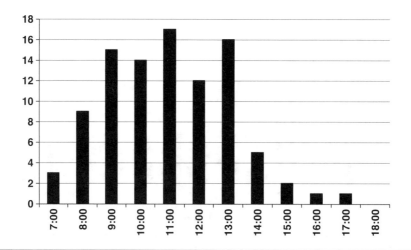

Figure 9.2 Outpatient chemotherapy treatment center: number of patients scheduled each hour.

At one large reference laboratory, trained Lean team members went to the *gemba* and rode along with couriers on their routes. In many instances, couriers drove right past the entrance to the lab as their route brought them to additional offices to pick up specimens. When asked why they did this, the couriers responded that they were measured on the number of specimens they collected each hour—stopping to drop off specimens they had already collected would hurt this measure. The lab realized that this suboptimization (caused by their own policies) was to the detriment of overall lab flow and unnecessarily delayed patient care.

Mura *Created by Clinic Scheduling*

In another example of self-imposed *mura*, an outpatient chemotherapy center struggled with a midday peak of patients, with a typical daily schedule shown in Figure 9.2. This led to delays, as more patients arrived than could be seated for treatment, as chair or nurse availability became a constraint. Before looking at the problem with a Lean perspective, the treatment center, looking only within its own silo, was convinced it needed more people and more space.

After some initial training, the department started looking at the entire value stream from the patient's perspective. The typical patient pathway included an appointment with an oncologist at one of the clinics in another part of the building before walking to receive chemotherapy. While observing in the oncology clinic, the treatment center discovered that the oncologists built their schedules so that chemotherapy patients were clustered together (or batched) first thing in the morning. This left other patients, such as those receiving a consultation or radiation therapy, for later in the day.

When the treatment center asked the oncologists why they created this kind of schedule, the oncologists replied they thought the schedule helped the patients. From the limited visibility oncologists had within their department silo, they thought that scheduling the chemotherapy patients first thing in the morning helped get them through treatment so they could get home earlier. This would have been true for a single patient but was not true for the full patient schedule. Clustering chemotherapy patients caused the artificially high number of patients who arrived for treatment in the middle of the day. This, ironically, led to longer patient delays and increased stress for the staff.

The clinic and the treatment center put together a plan for leveling the load of chemotherapy patients throughout the day (taking care to schedule those with longer, five-hour chemotherapy treatment early enough in the day). Changing the schedule did not have an impact on the oncologists, but leveling the workload made a big difference for the chemotherapy center, as the department had less of a busy time in the middle of the day. The chemotherapy center was able to increase its capacity while shortening patient delays, eliminating the need to expand the physical space or increase staffing.

Mura *in the Patient Discharge Process*

A common impediment to patient flow is the discharge process. Delayed discharges can hamper the flow of patients through the ED and postanesthesia recovery units, as patients cannot be admitted or moved to inpatient rooms until discharges have occurred. In extreme cases, these delays can lead to EDs going on diversion or canceled surgical procedures.

When a hospital has a high percentage of Medicare or Medicaid patients, this delay and increased length of stay have a direct impact on the bottom line for the hospital, as costs increase without additional revenue coming in. One hospital estimated that, in the course of analyzing its existing discharge process, a length of stay reduction of just half a day, created by reducing discharge delays, would represent a $6 million savings.

There can be, of course, *muda* or waste in the discharge process itself once it is initiated. The University of Michigan Medical Center was able to reduce the elapsed time in the discharge process by 54%, from 195 minutes to 89. Process improvements included doing more discharge work in parallel, instead of serially from physician to clerk to nurse. Improving the discharge process had a positive impact on the emergency care value stream, as patients could be admitted more promptly.[15] This illustrates a case for which the discharge process maybe a bottleneck to overall patient flow.

Discharge delays also cause frustration for patients and their families when an expectation has been set that a patient will be discharged soon, yet process problems or miscommunications prevent that from happening. Even if the patient gets out that same day, a family member might have been waiting many hours at the hospital to transport that patient home.

Discharge processes are complex, involving many different functions, roles, and departments. Multiple handoffs increase the risk of miscommunications that can push a planned discharge into the next day. A value stream map (VSM) of a discharge process tends to be complex, with process steps and communication taking place among more than a dozen different roles. At one hospital, not a single person could accurately describe the entire discharge process; each only knew his or her own work and, in some cases, the work of a few people with whom he or she directly interacted. The VSM activity created greater awareness and understanding of the interactions between roles and highlighted some opportunities to improve coordination and reduce waste.

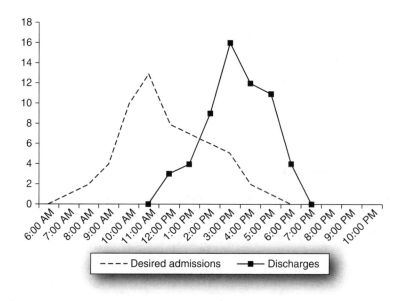

Figure 9.3   Actual pattern of discharges and admissions during the day, showing how beds are needed (admission) earlier than discharges are occurring; neither is leveled over the day.

It is common for hospitals to discharge the bulk of their patients in the afternoon hours. That timing often does not match with the need for beds, particularly planned admissions and postoperative admissions. Figure 9.3 illustrates how that mismatch between bed demand (admissions) and bed supply (discharges) might appear during the day.

Since discharges are time consuming for nurses and other inpatient unit staff, the spike in workload might overburden and distract them from other patient care needs. The hospital might also find a conflict between a desire to get patients discharged by the end of the day and the end of nurses' shifts. When nurses change shifts at 5 p.m., they might avoid or delay discharges in an attempt to get home.

When the hospital has a spike of discharge activity in just a few afternoon hours, it creates an artificially high load on other hospital resources, including housekeeping, patient transport, and the laboratory. Goals for improvements would include matching bed supply with demand, as well as applying *heijunka*, as shown in Figure 9.4.

A just-in-time discharge would occur right before the bed is needed by the next patient (allowing time for proper room cleaning and changeover activities). A Lean discharge process would also bring a fast resolution to the discharge order once written. At one hospital, improvement efforts for the entire discharge process were initiated after it was found that while 46% of discharge orders were written before 11 a.m., only 5% of patients left before 11 a.m.[16]

Discharges are also often not levelly loaded throughout the week. In many cases, significantly fewer discharges are done on weekends, which can be due to physicians not having rounds, social workers not working on weekends, or nursing homes not accepting new patients on weekends. This increases length of stay and leads to another spike of discharge activity on Mondays. A Lean approach would look for ways to increase weekend discharges, finding the root causes of what prevents them from happening.

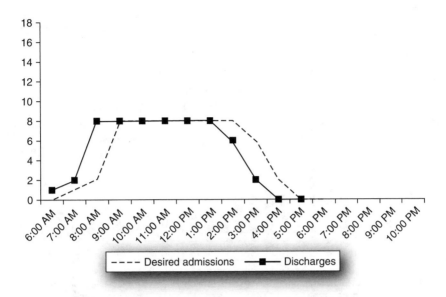

Figure 9.4 Improved pattern of discharges and admissions: Discharges occur just before an admission; both are leveled out over the day.

Addressing *Mura* by Matching Staffing to Workloads

If workloads cannot be leveled, the next-best alternative is to make sure staffing levels vary with demand. As basic as it might seem, staffing levels and workloads are not always synchronized. Staffing levels might be based on historical guidelines, benchmarks, or arbitrary financial targets more so than the workload.

Figure 9.5 shows a lab's staffing and hourly testing volume, before Lean; phlebotomist and technologist staffing increased after the morning run period.

By analyzing workloads, the lab was able to bring phlebotomists in earlier and reduce afternoon overstaffing. New staffing levels are shown in Figure 9.6.

The adjusted staffing schedules, combined with waste reduction and productivity improvements, allowed the lab to reduce total phlebotomy staffing (through attrition) by 21% and technologist staffing by 14%.

Looking again at the chemotherapy example, typical nurse staffing for a day is shown in Figure 9.7. As the scheduled workload increased in the middle of the day, staffing levels decreased due to scheduled lunch breaks. This disparity between workloads and staffing caused a number of problems, including longer patient waiting times or nurses feeling pressured into not taking lunch breaks. With Lean, the level-loaded schedule helped solve the midday spike, but the nurses also had to reconsider when they took their lunch breaks and how many could go at the same time to ensure there were no interruptions in patient care.

EDs often complain that their workloads are unpredictable because they do not know who is going to arrive and when. Data consistently show that patient arrival patterns are actually quite consistent and predictable on given days of the week and given hours, as shown in Figure 9.8.[17] Looking at a pattern like this can help a department determine when to increase capacity, either

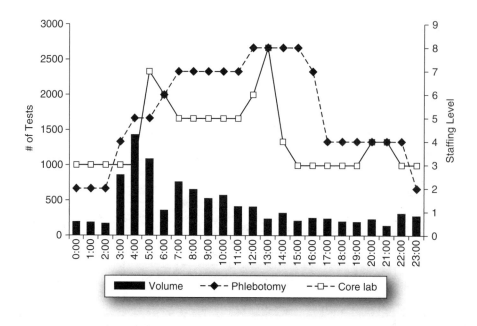

Figure 9.5 Clinical laboratory hourly test volumes, shown with phlebotomy and core lab technologist staffing, before Lean implementation.

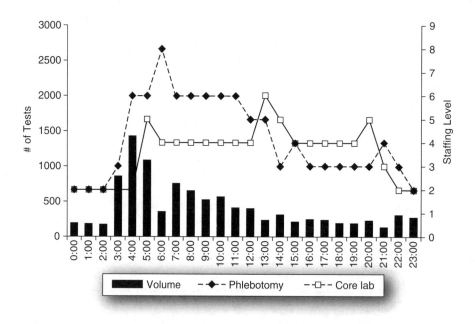

Figure 9.6 Clinical laboratory hourly test volumes, shown with phlebotomy and core lab technologist staffing, after Lean implementation.

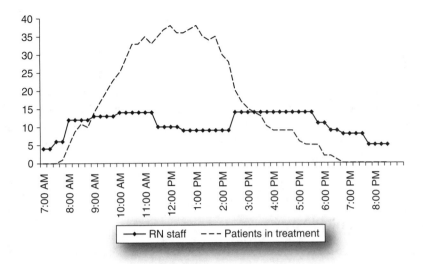

Figure 9.7 Number of chemotherapy treatment center patients in chairs or beds plotted with nurse staffing levels; one-day snapshot prior to Lean efforts.

by opening more groups of rooms in the department or by adding additional staff. An old staffing pattern of 12-hour shifts all running from 7 to 7 might not best match demand. More EDs are moving to staggered scheduling; physicians and staff start at varying times of day to create the right total staffing levels.

The idea of matching staff to workloads sometimes gets interpreted, unfortunately, as meaning that a hospital needs to send staff home any time patient census drops, a practice

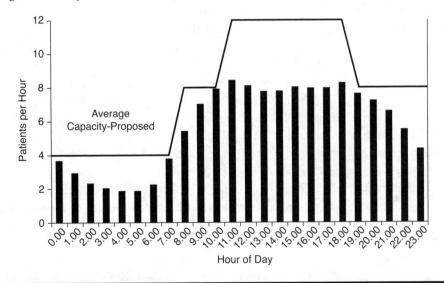

Figure 9.8 Expected emergency department patient volume by hour with a staffing pattern to match. (From Crane, Jody and Chuck Noon, *The Definitive Guide to Emergency Department Operational Improvement: Employing Lean Principles with Current ED Best Practices to Create the "No Wait" Department.* **New York: Productivity Press, 2011. Used with permission).**

sometimes called "flexing." While it makes financial sense not to be habitually overstaffed, sending nurses home early with a few hours left in their shift is a personal loss and disruption that might not rank highly in the scale of "respect for people." This practice is a known dissatisfier for nurses, as one nursing journal reported that some nurses left their hospital because flexing made them feel not valued.[18] When census is low and there are a few hours left in the day, alternatives to sending nurses home early include training and education or following Toyota's lead by participating in process and quality improvement efforts. A visual idea board, as discussed in Chapter 10, provides a ready queue of small projects for nurses and other staff to work on when time is avaiable.

Improving Patient Flow

Problems with patient flow are a major issue that hospitals can address using Lean concepts and methods. In this section, a few examples are shown to demonstrate some of the problems that interfere with flow, including that in the ED and an outpatient cancer treatment center. Hospitals are using Lean to improve patient flow in other areas, including outpatient surgery, radiology, and physician clinics.

Improving Patient Flow in the Emergency Department

When EDs become congested, a number of problems have an impact on patients and employees. The congestion and stress have an impact on ED employees, as they face patient complaints and often feel powerless to fix the system. Headlines often incorrectly point blame at the ED, when the root of the problem is often found in other parts of the value stream.

Patients who arrive at an ED may have many different waits, between different steps in the value stream, before being admitted or being able to go home. The U.S. average waiting time before being seen has increased by 25 minutes since 2006.[19] Patients also might wait for admission in the ED hallways, which creates physical congestion and mental stress as the hallway is not a very private or dignified place to wait. Waiting for an inpatient room is such a common problem that it has its own name—*boarding*. One study showed that 200 U.S. emergency room physicians said they knew of a patient who died because of boarding in their hospital.[20]

The Lean approach challenges us to rethink the way things have always been done, including in emergency care. Some hospitals are now doing a "miniregistration" prior to triage that includes just the most basic registration information, helping to reduce the "door-to-doc" time. The department then uses what would otherwise be time spent waiting for test results (or some other natural delay) as an opportunity to do the full registration.

In addition, it is becoming more common for hospitals to question the value and effectiveness of traditional triage processes and sequential care, realizing that triage often leads to the patient telling his or her story to multiple people, a cause of complaints. While triage was intended to expedite treatment for highest-acuity patients, more experts are taking the view that triage can actually delay treatment in the acutely ill.[21] Newly rethought triage models often involve a physician or a team consisting of a physician, nurse, and paramedic performing that initial triage.[22]

The Penn State Hershey Medical Center used Lean concepts to help design what they call a "no-wait ED." The physical layout and the care model both changed, as triage is now done by a physician.[23] As a result of their changes, the average length of stay was reduced 23%, rates of those who left without being seen fell from 5.6% to 0.4%, door-to-physician time was reduced to an average of just 18 minutes, and patient satisfaction increased from the 17th to the 75th percentile.[24]

Hospital leaders may also turn to a common practice of putting the hospital "on diversion"; a hospital requests that ambulances take patients to other hospitals unless the patient would be harmed by a delay or additional transportation. Notice two of the types of waste in that example, waiting and transportation. Being on diversion might negatively impact patients and their care, and it also has an impact on the hospital in terms of lost revenue, since that diverted patient is likely to be admitted to the hospital to which they are ultimately taken.[25] Most would probably recognize that the practice of diversion is hardly fixing the root cause of ED overcrowding. It is, at best, a stopgap measure.

EDs have incredible demands placed on them, as the number of ED beds has declined while visits have increased. For many patients, the ED is their best or only option for routine primary care, causing further congestion. Between 1995 and 2005, ED visits increased by 20%, while the number of beds decreased by 38%.[26] ED visits increased another 8% between 2004 and 2006 alone.[27] EDs face some serious systemic challenges that cannot be fixed by asking people to work faster. The good news is that hospitals are using Lean methods to improve their processes, improving flow in the face of enormous challenges.

When directly observing patient flow, hospitals find waiting times that can be eliminated through process improvements. At Avera McKennan (Sioux Falls, SD), a team observed ED patients, looking for value-added time (the times they were being examined) and waiting time. While the average length of stay was 140 minutes, two-thirds of that time was spent waiting. Part of this delay was caused by lab tests not being ordered until 45 minutes into the patient visit. The department reconfigured its triage process, ensuring each patient would be initially seen within 20 minutes of arrival. If that does not happen, protocols are triggered (a form of standardized work), which include the automatic ordering of lab tests, reducing testing and patient delays. As mentioned in Chapter 1, Avera McKennan was able to use flow improvements to reduce a planned ED expansion from 24 rooms to just 20, saving $1.25 million in construction costs.

If a hospital does not get to the root causes of poor ED flow, it risks spending large amounts of money on mere symptoms of the problem. Many solutions to ED overcrowding focus on expanding the ED itself, spending millions to add rooms and bays to the physical space, often not reducing length of stay. We can use a five whys exercise for this problem:

- Why are we having to divert ambulances?
  We don't have any open ED rooms.

- Why don't we have any open ED rooms?
    We can't get patients admitted into inpatient beds fast enough.
- Why can't we get patients into beds faster?
    Patients are physically out of the rooms but do not show as discharged in the system.
- Why are they not discharged in the system?
    The nurse did not notify the unit clerk to enter the discharge into the system.
- Why is the process dependent on the nurse notifying the unit clerk?
    It has always worked that way.

Instead of only looking at expensive capital spending, we now have a root cause (and other root causes) that can be fixed through other improvement efforts, illustrating that it is a value stream problem, not a departmental one.

Reducing "Door-to-Balloon" Time

Patients arriving at the ED with chest pain could be suffering from a type of heart attack called a STEMI. A core measure of flow is often referred to as "door-to-balloon time," measuring the time that elapses from the patient's arrival to the point when their heart blockage is cleared in the cath lab. As in many cases, improving flow by reducing delays leads to better patient outcomes since less damage occurs to the heart if the arterial blockage is cleared more quickly.

Over a number of years, ThedaCare used Lean methods to reduce its average door-to-balloon time from 92 minutes to 37 minutes, leading to measurably better care. As they say, "time is muscle" since mortality increases when the time exceeds 90 minutes.[28] When ThedaCare first looked at this value stream in 2006, they were hitting the national 120-minute target 70% of the time.[29] Benchmarks aside, there was a clear opportunity for improvement.

ThedaCare made a number of changes over the next few years, decreasing the average time for each of the next three years, as shown in Figure 9.9. Clinicians standardized the process for evaluating patients, hanging a sign in each ED bay reminding everyone of the standardized work sequence that best minimized time to obtain an electrocardiogram (EKG) completed most quickly. Cardiologists ceded control of reading the EKGs to emergency physicians, ensuring everybody was properly trained to do the highest-quality work. This change eliminated a possible delay that would occur when cardiologists would be called at home during the middle of the night. With the new process, there were only two "false-alarm" diagnoses in the first 2,000 patients with heart attack.[30]

Even now, ThedaCare strives to further reduce variation and the average door-to-balloon time. Any time an individual patient exceeds 90 minutes, which happens rarely, the team takes the opportunity to investigate, looking for a root cause and process changes that can be implemented to prevent delays for future patients. In keeping with the Lean thinking mindset of always pursuing perfection, ThedaCare would now like to have ambulance drivers performing the EKG, transmitting the readout electronically to be read before the patient even arrives at the hospital.[31]

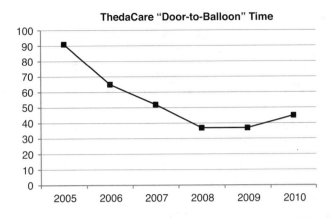

Figure 9.9   Chart showing reduction of "door-to-balloon" time at Appleton Medical Center.

Improving Patient Flow in Outpatient Cancer Treatment

Back to the case of the cancer center, the scheduling of appointments and physician schedules created many of the patient delays in the oncology clinics. One general challenge with patient scheduling is that it is not known exactly how long different appointments will take. Physicians value their time—and it is indeed valuable time—so everyone has an incentive to avoid the waste of waiting for physicians; however, many of the steps taken to avoid this physician waiting impose significant waiting time on the patients.

As discovered during the direct observation of patient flow, many morning patients saw their oncologist 30–60 minutes late, even the first patient of the morning. One particular oncologist arrived 40 minutes late during the observation, and the nurse assistant commented, "That doctor is always 45 minutes late." By purposely creating a backlog of three patients to start the day, the oncologist was helping ensure there was no waiting time in case some appointments went faster than expected. A different oncologist was said to always schedule a two-hour block of patient appointments when he was scheduled for rounds at the hospital. A third oncologist intentionally scheduled 14 patients in a single hour, knowing this was unrealistic. The nurse assistant commented, "The 9 o'clock patient probably won't be seen until 10:30." This behavior created patient backlogs and waiting, but again, it ensured that the oncologist would have a steady stream of patients to see.

A Lean process would do more to balance the objectives of preventing physician and patient waiting times. Some amount of patient waiting time might have to be tolerated, but a hospital should decide which scheduling policies are acceptable for consistency and to avoid upsetting patients. Getting physicians to cooperate with scheduling changes might be difficult, as they might justify their methods as ensuring the effective use of their time. Attempts to change these practices should involve the physicians, with leadership helping to establish the case for minimizing patient delays, asking physicians to help come up with solutions.

If the delays to see the oncologist were long, patients might have already missed their treatment appointment at the chemotherapy center. Treatment appointment slots were scheduled based on the expected time for getting through the oncologist appointment, but these times were not perfectly predictable. Disrupted chemotherapy schedules created additional rework and motion for the charge nurse, who had to prioritize patients, constantly juggling and readjusting the schedule throughout the day.

Once they were ready for the chemotherapy session, patients often waited due to defects in the process. This included the physician's office not properly sending the treatment order, a problem that consistently occurred 20% of the time. This created more rework for employees, more adjustments to the schedule, and more delays for the patients. When that process defect occurred, the chemotherapy staff fixed the short-term problem—they called or faxed the physician's office to get the orders, and the problem was considered solved. Certain offices were known to frequently create the same process defects, but the chemotherapy center had neither the time nor the political pull to give feedback to the physician's office in an attempt to solve the root cause. This lack of root cause problem solving made it unlikely that the defects would be prevented in the future.

Even getting a treatment chair did not guarantee that the patient's waiting time was over. For treatment to begin, many factors had to line up. Missing any one of these would cause a delay in treatment:

- Treatment chair
- Nurse
- Lab results
- Chemotherapy intravenous bag

One of the required factors was often missing. A patient might get seated in a chair, only to be delayed because the nurses were busy with other patients. The treatment center had standard patient-to-nurse ratios, but if too many patients were starting or finishing treatment at the same time, there was a short-term spike in the workload that could not be handled without causing treatment delays. The lab results were often delayed, sometimes because the wrong orders had been sent, leading to more rework and delays. The chemotherapy intravenous bag was often delayed because there had been a question with the order, and they were waiting for the physician to call back. In other cases, the intravenous bags had been sent to the treatment center but were misplaced because of poor organization. This led to the nurse walking and searching for the bag, which delayed that patient and other patients who were waiting for that chair.

The hospital realized that to reduce or minimize patient delays, it had to make a number of systemic improvements. It started with first identifying the root causes of process errors and defects over which it had control, including ensuring that nurse schedules lined up with patient demand and that charge nurses had standardized methods for prioritizing and rescheduling patients. After fixing problems in its control, the treatment center planned on working with the oncology clinics to help prevent delays due to errors that were created there, related to orders for chemotherapy, the lab, and the pharmacy.

Improving Flow for Ancillary Support Departments

Beyond patient flow, hospitals have successfully used Lean methods to improve the flow in many ancillary or support functions, including laboratories, pharmacies, perioperative services, and nutritional services. In these settings, the product is not the patient, but an item that is required for decision making or continued care.

Improving Flow in Clinical Laboratories

Many hospitals have applied Lean methods to multiple areas of the laboratory, including the clinical lab, transfusion services (or blood bank), microbiology, and anatomic pathology. Many Lean efforts begin in the clinical lab area because testing volumes are highest, and the turn-around time expectations are often the fastest and most critical. Clinical lab specimens may be delayed in multiple stages of the value stream: during specimen collection, specimen receiving, or testing areas.

Reducing Delays in Specimen Collection

To understand the causes of long delays that keep specimens from getting to the lab, we need to observe the process to identify waste and delays in the complete testing value stream. During initial assessment activities, labs often find that up to 90% of the total turnaround time from specimen collection to lab result is spent waiting. To improve turnaround times, labs should reduce those delays instead of getting faster equipment or asking employees to work faster.

In this chapter, we discussed that labs typically have a busy morning spike due to physician rounds. In many cases, the lab might not start receiving specimens until 4 a.m., even though phlebotomy draws started at 3 a.m. This delay is due to intentional batching, either directed by managers or initiated by the phlebotomists themselves.

What might seem inefficient from the perspective of the lab, or the patient, is completely rational and efficient for the phlebotomist. The individual phlebotomist is maximizing productivity, which is often measured in terms of patient draws per hour. To minimize the waste of motion, the phlebotomist reduces the number of walking trips to the lab or to the tube system station. Tube systems that automate the transportation of specimens to the lab are often located in nurses' stations, which are sometimes inconveniently located at the end of long hallways.

In the Lean philosophy, we have to understand the root cause of the batching. Just mandating that phlebotomists send smaller batches to the lab might lead to unfortunate corner cutting, such as rushing through their work. If phlebotomists are pressured, they might take a single larger batch from their cart, dividing it up and sending small batches in succession to the lab. That workaround, creating the appearance of small batches, is not a true system improvement, as individual turnaround times would still be as slow as before.

By defining standardized work for phlebotomists and understanding the trade-offs with smaller batches, laboratory managers can make a decision that helps optimize the entire value stream. The exact balance point will vary based on the physical layout of the department and the inpatient units, but moving phlebotomy toward single-piece flow often means that phlebotomists make trips to the tube station after every two or three patients, a planned and consistent delay of 10–15 minutes, which is better than longer and less-consistent delays. If the layout allows, phlebotomists might travel to the tube station after each and every individual patient, minimizing delays.

Managers must take care that phlebotomists are treated fairly in this process, that they are not given an unfair faster standard to which they are held accountable. Standardized work will help employees and managers understand how long the work takes to complete—drawing specimens and transporting them to the lab in a timely manner. Some hospitals have even taken the step of increasing the number of phlebotomists, recognizing that the trade-off between adding phlebotomist labor (which is relatively inexpensive) and time and reducing turnaround time is worthwhile. The trade-offs between larger and smaller batches are summarized in Table 9.2.

Table 9.2   Batch Size Trade-Offs

Larger Batches	Smaller Batches
Less phlebotomist walking	More phlebotomist walking
Longer turnaround time	Faster turnaround time
Fewer phlebotomists required	More phlebotomists required

Reducing Delays in the Receiving Areas of the Lab

When observing the flow of specimens through the laboratory, we are likely to see more batching and more delays, including those in the preanalytical phase of the process.

Typically, specimens first arrive at a dedicated receiving area. This area might be further divided into an accessioning area (where specimens are received into the computer system by an assistant) and a processing area (where specimens are centrifuged or receive further preparation for testing). In many labs, the processing department is located out of the main flow, as specimens go into a separate room and then backtrack to testing. The physical separation of the processing area leads to poor communication and teamwork between assistants and medical technologists in the main laboratory testing area.

The distance and separation also lead to another understandable result—more batching. When the preanalytical work is further divided across two separate subdepartments, two different employees do the work with a handoff in between, as shown in Figure 9.10. When faced with the prospect of carrying a tube of blood 20 feet to the processing area, the assistant who did the accessioning work will naturally want to accumulate a batch (a tray or a bin) before moving specimens. Again, to be locally efficient, the assistant (like the phlebotomist) figures it is better to wait and carry 10 specimens instead of just 1.

Children's Medical Center (Dallas, TX) took the step of combining its accessioning and processing departments into a single area. Flow benches were created that had all of the tools required for accessioning and then immediately processing or centrifuging each specimen, without batching or delay. Employees were cross-trained and responsibilities were reconfigured into the single area, as illustrated in Figure 9.11. Specimens that previously took up to 30 minutes to get through accessioning and processing flowed through in 5 to 10 minutes. Employees were not working faster; instead, the underlying system and layout had been improved. The new layout made the

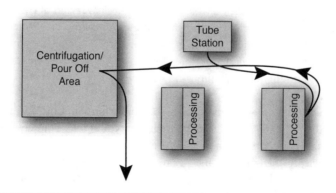

Figure 9.10   Functional silo layout encouraged batching and delay.

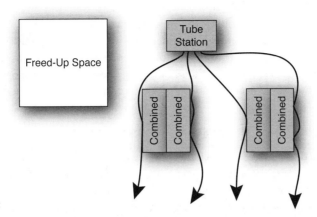

Figure 9.11 Combined flow benches allowed specimens to flow without batch delays.

waste of walking (transportation for the specimen and motion for the assistant) that had been "required" under the old process unnecessary. Reconfiguring the benches in the lab was quick and inexpensive. The biggest expense was purchasing a few centrifuges for a few hundred dollars each, well worth the improvement of testing turnaround time.

Improving Flow Also Improves Quality and Teamwork

Other benefits of changing the layout and improving the flow include improved quality and teamwork. When batches are created, it is possible that the same process defect is created for each and every specimen. With single-piece flow, a defect can be caught immediately, preventing the accumulation of defects. Before Lean improvements, one lab director explained, "We would have 12 patient labels curled in a strip on the floor. So the first order didn't get processed until all 12 had been labeled. When you took all 12 of those over to the analyzer, you could only do four at a time. Think of the possibilities for error when you label 12 orders at a time."

By moving to single-piece flow, a lab can reduce the opportunities for mislabeled specimens. As the lab director explained, "Switching to single-piece flow reduced the risk of errors due to mislabeling. You have one set of orders in front of you, and you have one set of labels in front of you. It's almost impossible to mislabel somebody else's blood." The number of mislabeled specimens, as tracked by the lab, decreased from an average of eight per month to an average of four per month, leaving some opportunity for additional root cause problem solving.

Poor layouts can also hamper communication, teamwork, and problem solving. In one hospital lab, the old layout had receiving separated from the testing area. A new bench was created where specimens were processed and centrifuged by a lab assistant, who then handed specimens directly across a shared workbench to a technologist. Working directly across from each other improves communication and allows for immediate feedback and quick corrective actions.

If a new lab assistant is not placing labels on the specimen tubes just right, the labels might be misread by the instruments, leading to delayed test results. With the new layout, the technologist could provide immediate coaching and feedback. Before, the technologist would typically just fix the label (a workaround) instead of communicating with the person who created the process defect. In a Lean environment, having the opportunity to give direct feedback often ends up proving the assistant meant to do a good job but had not been fully trained properly.

Part of the principle of respect for people is that we assume people want to do a good job, and it is fair to them to give feedback about their errors so they can do quality work the next time.

This new layout also helped improve specimen flow by building flexibility into the standardized work. Since the centrifuges were in the middle of the workbench, they were accessible by both the technologist and the assistant. While it was ideal for the assistant to unload the centrifuge for the technologist, the technologist could also unload specimens if time allowed.

Reducing Delays Inside the Testing Areas of the Lab

Clinical laboratories tend to have very departmentalized, fragmented layouts that hamper efficient specimen flow in the testing areas. This is partially due to history, where testing specialties, such as chemistry and hematology, were their own academic departments. When hospitals created unified labs, the habit of maintaining separate subdepartments, often separated by walls or tall cabinets, remained. The overly functional layout does not correspond with the skills of medical technologists, who are often cross-trained and could do different types of testing work without harming the quality of results.

On night shifts, when volumes and staffing are low, a traditional lab might have just one medical technologist assigned to hematology and urinalysis, with work areas that might be more than 100 feet apart. Given that distance, the technologist is not likely to constantly walk back and forth between departments. Specimens tend to accumulate (or "batch up") in hematology when the technologist is in the urinalysis area and vice versa. One lab observed employees and measured that one night shift technologist walked more than four miles per shift between the distant urinalysis and microbiology departments. This added up to more than 1 hour per day of walking waste. This distance and walking slows turnaround since many overnight test requests need to be done quickly for the sake of patient care. Employees feel pressured to be in two places at once, which is not realistic or fair to them, especially given the poor layout.

In some labs, this departmentalization might translate into higher staffing levels than would be needed in an improved layout. Before Lean, medical technologists are stationed in each area for the work that comes into the subdepartment. "We had several people who worked one instrument only," said a director in one hospital. "So someone might be sitting in microbiology, waiting for work, while people in hematology or urinalysis were flooded with orders." With long distances between departments, we cannot easily take advantage of efficiencies that would come from having a combined department that has all of the high-volume test instruments located close together.

Instead of two people each in the four subdepartments, we might be able to get the same amount of work done with just six people in a combined department. This conclusion would come from a detailed study of the work content and workloads in both subdepartments, not from a gut feel. Labs might reassign any extra employees to test development work, do more cross-training with the freed time, or dedicate time to further improvements. When an employee leaves voluntarily, we might choose not to fill that position again. But, the remaining employees will not be overworked, stressed out, or fear future head count reductions.

Improving Flow in Anatomic Pathology

Before Lean was introduced at St. Paul's Hospital (Vancouver, British Columbia), part of Providence Health Care, the anatomic pathology lab's turnaround times for pathology reports were slower than desired. Less than 7% of reports were completed within 1 day, and only about 33% were completed within 2 days. Another challenge the lab faced was an increasing workload in a time of technologist shortages and fiscal constraints. After analyzing the existing process, the lab realized there were opportunities for improving turnaround times and handling the increasing work volume without pressuring employees to work faster or sacrificing quality. The lab rearranged the physical layout, created standardized work methods and schedules (as discussed in Chapter 5), and made other systemic changes that improved flow and reduced delays.

After improvements were made, the average turnaround time was reduced by 1 day, from 4 days to 3, meaning that physicians had information earlier, allowing them to make key decisions about patient care, including those who had cancer, in a more timely manner. With a Lean process in place, the lab was now completing more than 30% of reports in 1 day and almost 60% in 2 days. The average turnaround times include all pathology reports, even highly complex cases that require in-depth analysis and therefore inherently longer testing and analysis times.

Lean improvements helped the patients through the faster turnaround time. The changes also helped improve the workflow for pathologists who review slides and dictate reports that are sent on to the patient's physician. Before Lean, work was done in large batches, resulting in slides not being delivered to the pathologists for reading until 11 a.m. This created a spike of work and increased pressure to finish reports quickly before the end of the day, to avoid extending the work-day into the evening. As the lab improved its flow by reducing batching and other forms of delay, slides began arriving to the pathologists earlier in the morning, spreading out their workload and increasing their satisfaction.

Improvements to the layout and the overall design of the laboratory also reduced wasted time and motion for the employees. Reduced batching helped minimize the risk for errors and misla-beled specimens, reducing some stress on the employees (who feared making errors) and improving quality for the patients. After the pathologists examined slides, transcriptionists received dictated tapes from the pathologists that contained single cases, instead of lengthy tapes with multiple cases. This smoothed out the workload for the transcriptionists and further reduced waiting time for the final reports to be sent to the ordering physicians.

Employee satisfaction surveys, taken before and after the improvements, show how Lean did not lead anyone to sacrifice quality or employee morale in the name of productivity. When asked if "quality is a top priority in my area," the average score was 4.5 on a 5.0 scale after Lean was started (where 5.0 indicated employees agreed strongly), compared to a 3.5 score pre-Lean. Employees also agreed they were "satisfied with the department as a place to work," with a 4.0 score compared to an average score of 3.5 before Lean. These results and attitudes are common in effective Lean implementations.

All of the above benefits are good for the hospital: improved patient outcomes through faster turnaround time and improved quality, improved physician satisfaction, and improved employee satisfaction. Additionally, the hospital recognized direct financial savings from the Lean efforts. The department was able to phase out $60,000 worth of pathology equipment that was no longer needed as a result of improved flow. More importantly, the technologists were able to safely absorb a 9% increase in workload with existing staff.

Jane Crosby, the laboratory services director, commented, "St. Paul's Laboratory has always had a reputation for high quality. Sometimes this made our processes very complex as we tried to cover every possible contingency. With Lean we were able to further improve quality while simplifying our processes, and it has been very rewarding for the staff who feel less stressed while handling a higher work volume."

Improving Flow in Pharmacies

Unlike the lab, where faster results are better (unless results sit and wait before being read by the ordering physician), pharmacies have a different set of time and flow requirements. Speed in response time is important for some medication orders. In many cases, though, one of the general objectives is not delivering medications too early since medications delivered early are more likely to be returned to the pharmacy, creating more work for nurses and pharmacy employees.

Medication orders (such as first doses or missing medications) that do need a fast response might be delayed for a number of reasons before reaching the pharmacy. The flow of the order from the physician's thought of "I need to prescribe this medication" until the pharmacy receives the order could have delays due to miscommunication or bad processes. Unit clerks or nurses might literally not see an order due to disorganization or being busy with other tasks. Physician order entry can help reduce these missed handoffs and delays.

Inside the pharmacy, medication orders might be delayed in numerous ways. One delay may come from an overall mismatch in workloads and pharmacy staffing. If the overall workload is not level loaded, delays may occur at certain peak periods. At one pharmacy, before Lean, there was one "cart fill" run per day, when medications were gathered in the pharmacy to be sent to the inpatient units, and a single large daily batch of work was done for all units. Unfortunately, this cart fill was done during the morning, when doctors wrote new prescriptions (first doses) that had to be filled as soon as possible. This lack of *heijunka* led to delayed medications and frustrated employees, as one pharmacist recounted, "Somebody in here was crying just about every day because of the stress." With a Lean implementation, the pharmacy started doing four cart fills per day, which spread out the workload more evenly and avoided the morning conflict.

The response time of the pharmacy may also suffer from badly designed physical layouts and processes. Technicians might be walking many miles per day because the tools they use (such as label printers, computers, and the tube system station) are not located near each other. High-use medications may be scattered throughout the lab, which increases technician walking and delays medications. Poor layouts may, again, encourage employees to batch up work to suboptimize their own walking at the expense of medication flow.

Once medications have been picked, the layout and process may cause delays and batching of the pharmacist verifications. If pharmacists sit in their own area, outside the flow and separated from the pharmacy technicians, a single-piece flow verification might not be possible, meaning verifications will be batched. If technicians drop off medications to be verified, there might be a delay before the technician comes back to pick up verified medications, further delaying transportation to the patient.

Other medications are not sent individually. Many medications are stored, as general non-patient-specific inventory, in the ED or inpatient units, so nurses can easily take them from a cabinet, as needed, although these are usually not made available until a pharmacist has reviewed the order and released the medication. Medications are also stored in units to allow the batching of replenishment from the pharmacy. Instead of sending commonly used medications one at a time all day long (which requires additional labor, packaging materials, and delivery time), larger quantities are restocked in a batched trip.

Before Lean, this is often done just once a day or a few times per week. As with many situations, there are trade-offs that need to be considered. Delivering every other day minimizes the walking involved in technicians delivering medications throughout the hospital. On the other hand, more frequent replenishment, while requiring more walking, leads to higher availability of medications in the units and fewer instances of unplanned (when meds are not available) "as needed" orders coming down to the pharmacy throughout the day. It may seem unintuitive to pharmacy employees at the start of their Lean journey, but delivering more frequently (hourly or every few hours) can reduce the total workload as the reactive trips to the inpatient units are reduced.

For medications that are stored in the nursing unit for a patient, the goal for the pharmacy is just-in-time delivery. If a physician writes a prescription for a medication to be given three times every eight hours, it is not in the best interest of the pharmacy to deliver three doses at once. Delivering a large batch would reduce walking, but it increases the chances that some of those doses will not be needed because of a change in the orders or the patient being moved or discharged. Often, when a patient is moved, meds are sent down to the pharmacy to be reissued to the new unit instead of being moved with the patient (creating the waste of transportation and the waste of motion).

Memorial Health (Savannah, GA) is one example of a hospital pharmacy that has implemented Lean. A team of department employees started by analyzing their own process, directly observing and measuring waste in the value stream and wasted motion by employees. The team made a number of systemic improvements over a 17-week period that reduced waste and improved response times and the availability of medications where they were needed.

The layout of the pharmacy was redesigned, reducing walking times and distances for the technicians by more than 50%. This led to faster response time for the typical first-dose order. In the new layout, one pharmacist was incorporated into the flow, as technicians could hand medications to the pharmacist for verification in a single-piece flow manner. This redesign impacted not only the layout but also the standardized work for the pharmacists. Before Lean, all three pharmacists did everything and anything. The overlap in responsibilities often led to confusion and delays when medications were waiting to be verified. Each pharmacist might have thought another was going to review a particular medication, or more often, all three of the pharmacists were busy with phone calls or other consultative duties. The standardized work dedicated each pharmacist to one of three roles (fills, ordering checking, and phone consultations), although they could help each other out if time allowed and it did not hamper the flow in their area of responsibility.

At the end of the Memorial Health project, the pharmacy was providing better service for the patients and nurses. In an internal survey, nurses agreed with the following statements (as measured on a scale for which "strongly agree" scores a 1 and "strongly disagree" scores a 5):

- Medications seem to be more available when they are needed than they were six months ago. (Score = 2.04)
- I am pleased with the main pharmacy's improvements and attempt to provide better service to the floors and the patients. (Score = 1.75)

At Memorial, and other hospitals, improvements to pharmacy processes have helped make sure the right medications in the right doses are available in the right places as needed at the right time. This improves patient care while making work easier for the employees and reducing costs for the hospital. Lean also moves the emphasis away from process problems, such as missing doses and the resulting phone calls that come in, to letting the pharmacists focus on their true role of optimizing a patient's medication use.[32]

Conclusion

Many of the root causes of poor flow illustrated here can be seen in other departments, such as poor layouts, a lack of *heijunka*, and poorly designed value streams. If you work in a department not mentioned in this chapter, try to see how the general concepts fit your processes. If you do work for a department mentioned here, you still should not try to copy what others have done. Make sure the Lean principles are being used to solve your particular problems. To improve flow, go to the *gemba* and observe the process firsthand. Look for value-added and non-value-added time and identify the root causes of delays. Rather than accepting delays or the causes of delays as given, go and make changes that will improve flow.

Lean Lessons

- Make improvements that remove rocks instead of covering the problems with more water (workarounds or waiting queues).
- Single-piece flow is a direction more than an absolute mandate.
- Flow improvements apply to patients, both waiting for appointments and waiting for care on arrival; similar ideas can apply to the flow of any material or information.
- Unevenness in flow can be the result of natural occurrences or our own policies.
- Lean teaches us to not accept *mura* as a given.
- When flow is interrupted, ask why and fix the systemic causes of batching or other delays.
- Improving flow often improves quality and teamwork and reduces cost.
- Faster is not always better, depending on the customer needs.

Points for Group Discussion

- How would hospital processes or your department be different if physician rounds were level loaded?
- How can you better balance staff levels with workloads?
- Why might nurses feel disrespected or not valued by being sent home early when census is low?
- What improvements would the hospital see if we could discharge patients evenly across all 7 days of the week? Is this possible?
- How might the hospital level load elective surgeries throughout the year? What departments or functions might need to get involved?
- How might improved flow help improve the quality of care for patients?
- What are the longest waiting times for appointments or care that we might want to address with Lean?
- What is the proper balance between patient waiting time and physician waiting time?

Notes

1. Ontario Ministry of Health and Long-Term Care, "Ontario Wait Times," http://www.health.gov.on.ca/en/public/programs/waittimes/surgery/default.aspx (accessed April 6, 2011).

2. Department of Health, "NHS Referral to Treatment waiting time statistics, January 2011," http://www.dh.gov.uk/en/Publicationsandstatistics/Publications/PublicationsStatistics/DH_125005 (accessed April 6, 2011).
3. Merritt Hawkins & Associates, "2009 Survey of Physician Appointment Wait Times," http://www.merritthawkins.com/pdf/mha2009waittimesurvey.pdf (accessed April 6, 2011).
4. Toussaint, John, and Roger Gerard, *On the Mend: Revolutionizing Healthcare to Save Lives and Transform the Industry* (Cambridge, MA: Lean Enterprise Institute, 2010), 95.
5. UPI, "Average U.S. ER Wait Time 4-Plus Hours," July 26, 2010, http://www.upi.com/Health_News/2010/07/26/Average-US-ER-wait-time-4-plus-hours/UPI-76891280122494/ (accessed April 6, 2011).
6. Alberta Health Services, "What's the Length of Stay for Patients in Our Busiest Emergency Departments?" http://www.albertahealthservices.ca/764.asp (accessed April 9, 2011).
7. Crane, Jody, and Chuck Noon, *The Definitive Guide to Emergency Department Operational Improvement: Employing Lean Principles with Current ED Best Practices to Create the "No Wait" Department* (New York: Productivity Press, 2011), 195.
8. Ng, David, Gord Vail, et al., "Applying the Lean Principles of the Toyota Production System to Reduce Wait Times in the Emergency Department," *CJEM Canadian Journal of Emergency Medical Care,* 2010, 12, No. 1: 50–57.
9. NPress, "NPress Reveals Patient Pet Peeves Survey Results," February 13, 2010, http://texasprnews.com/texas_articles/2010/02/npress-reveals-patient-pet-peeves-survey-results-137109.htm (accessed April 9, 2011).
10. Bahri, Sami, *Follow the Learner* (Cambridge, MA: Lean Enterprise Institute, 2009), 29.
11. "Ellerbe Becket Minneapolis, MN: Park Nicollet Melrose Institute St. Louis Park, MN," *Healthcare Design,* September 2009, 9, no. 9: 260–61.
12. Wellman, Joan, Howard Jeffries, and Pat Hagan, *Leading the Lean Healthcare Journey* (New York: Productivity Press, 2010), 216.
13. Graban, Mark, "Toyota's Commitment to People," LeanBlog.org, September 1, 2008, http://www.leanblog.org/2008/09/toyotas-committment-to-people/ (accessed April 9, 2011).
14. ValuMetrix Services, Kaiser Permanenete Case Study, http://www.valumetrix_services.com/sites/default/files/client_results_pdf/cs_KaierEast_Lab_OC10113.pdf (accessed July 1, 2011).
15. Berczuk, Carol, "The Lean Hospital," *The Hospitalist,* June 2008, http://www.the-hospitalist.org/details/article/186537/The_Lean_Hospital.html (accessed April 9, 2011).
16. Korner, Kimberly T., and Nicole M. Hartman, "Lean Tools and Concepts Reduce Waste, Improve Efficiency," *American Nurse Today,* March 2011, http://www.americannursetoday.com/Article.aspx?id=7600&fid=7364 (accessed April 9, 2011).
17. Crane and Noon, *Definitive Guide,* 133.
18. Nelson, Roxanne, and Maureen Shawn Kennedy, "The Other Side of Mandatory Overtime," *American Journal of Nursing,* April 2008, 108, no. 4: 23–24.
19. Costello, Tom, "Hospitals Work to Improve ER Wait Times," MSNBC.com, November 20, 2006, http://www.msnbc.msn.com/id/15817906/ (accessed April 10, 2011).
20. American College of Emergency Physicians, "Emergency Department Waiting Times," http://www.acep.org/content.aspx?id=25908 (accessed April 6, 2011).
21. Otto, M. Alexander, "ED Triage May Delay Treatment in Acutely Ill," *ACEP News,* http://www.acep.org/Content.aspx?id=49469 (accessed April 9, 2011).
22. AHRQ Innovations Exchange, "Team Triage Reduces Emergency Department Walkouts, Improves Patient Care," http://www.innovations.ahrq.gov/content.aspx?id=1735&tab=1#a3 (accessed April 9, 2011).
23. Hafen, Mark, "A Case for Getting Rid of Waiting Rooms," *Veterinary Hospital Design,* January 4, 2011, http://veterinaryhospitaldesign.dvm360.com/vethospitaldesign/article/articleDetail.jsp?id=701835&pageID=3 (Accessed April 9, 2011).

24. Przybylowski, Ted, Jr., and Mary Frazier, "No Waiting," *Healthcare Design*, November 2010, http://www.healthcaredesignmagazine.com/article/no-waiting (accessed July 4, 2011).
25. McConnell, K. J., et al., "Ambulance Diversion and Lost Hospital Revenues," *Annals of Emergency Medicine,* 2006, 48: 702–10.
26. Ibid.
27. American College of Emergency Physicians, "Emergency Department."
28. Toussaint and Gerard, *On the Mend*, 34.
29. Toussaint, John, "Writing the New Playbook for U.S. Health Care: Lessons from Wisconsin," *Health Affairs,* September 2009, 28, no. 5: 1343–50.
30. Ibid.
31. Toussaint, John, Presentation to Healthcare Value Network, March 2011.
32. ValuMetrix Services, Pharmacy at Memorial Health University Medical Center Case Study, http://www.valumetrixservices.com/sites/default/files/client_results_pdf/CS_MemorialHealth_Savannah_Pharmacy_OC10134.pdf (accessed July 4, 2011).

Chapter 10

Engaging and Leading Employees

Changing How We Manage

Lean is not just about tools. It is also a distinct management method that guides what we do as managers and how we lead our employees. Convis wrote, "Management has no more critical role than motivating and engaging large numbers of people to work together toward a common goal. Defining and explaining what that goal is, sharing a path to achieving it, motivating people to take the journey with you, and assisting them by removing obstacles—these are management's reason for being."[1]

The challenge is not just about getting through an initial Lean project. Once that phase is over, we still have people and processes to manage on an ongoing basis. That is why Lean is a never-ending journey—we have to guard against slipping back into old methods, and we have to push for continuous improvement. An engaged workforce, in which everybody is participating in the improvement, is the best way to achieve long-term success.

The traditional management mindset looks at a set of standard operating procedures and thinks, "We put a lot of thought into these processes, and they must be perfect." Assuming otherwise might be considered a sign of failure or incompetence. Lean thinkers, on the other hand, assume that a process can always be improved, even if it seems to work fine today. The adage "If it's not broke, don't fix it" does not apply in a Lean setting. Lean leaders accept that they are not perfect. Not being perfect is acceptable as long as the team is working toward perfection through continuous improvement efforts. Lean thinkers might say, "It's not broke, but it's not perfect, so let's make it better!"

People often attribute this quotation to a senior Toyota executive, comparing themselves to their Detroit competitors: "Brilliant process management is our strategy. We get brilliant results from average people managing brilliant processes. We observe that our competitors often get average (or worse) results from brilliant people managing broken processes."[2] Hospitals typically have brilliant people. Imagine how much better things could be with brilliant processes. They are not mutually exclusive.

Before Lean, managers might not be aware of what is broken. With the best of intentions, employees might hide problems by working around them. It might look like people are busy, but they are busy dealing with waste. By learning to recognize waste, by getting out of our offices, and by encouraging people to speak up, we can finally start to see what is broken in the details of our processes.

It is not enough to tell our employees they have to find and eliminate waste in their own work. We also have to commit to managing differently. Many supervisors and managers cannot make the transition to managing in the Lean workplace. Just as employees might fear layoffs, supervisors often fear losing their power or becoming irrelevant in a culture of employee engagement. Some managers will have to be replaced, but most can be taught and coached in the Lean approach. David Mann said, "What makes Lean difficult is not that it is so complicated but that it is so different from what we've learned."[3]

Traditionally, organizations tend to be very hierarchical and top down in their approach, many hospitals included. One hospital director said, "We struggle with this. We still have a very command and control middle management workforce who are extremely protective of their departments and their problems." Managers in a Lean environment do not make all the decisions or solve all the problems. Lean managers avoid giving directives to their employees. Many managers do not know how to operate in any other way.

John Toussaint, MD, former chief executive officer (CEO) of ThedaCare, humbly talked about his efforts to shift his own personal leadership style to set an example for the rest of the organization. Table 10.1 shows his comparison of Lean leadership styles to what he calls

Table 10.1 A Comparison of Leadership Styles

"White Coat Leadership"	"Improvement Leadership"
All knowing	Patient
In charge	Knowledgeable
Autocratic	Facilitator
The buck stops here	Teacher
Impatient	Student
Blaming	Helper
Controlling	Communicator

traditional "white coat" leadership.[4] The white coat, not limited to physicians, signifies formal position-based authority. The attributes of white coat leadership tend to stifle open communication and quality improvement.

One U.S. hospital was a few years into its Lean journey, yet the CEO still made many top-down decisions. Patient surveys showed that late-night noise was the biggest cause of complaints. Inpatient unit managers were, needless to say, surprised when workers arrived to install carpet in the hallways. Unfortunately, the new carpet made it physically harder for nurses to push computer carts down those hallways, so they spent more time at the nurses' station. One executive mandate (use technology to get out from the station) ran into conflict with the other mandate (carpeted hallways). Instead of following a plan-do-check-act (PDCA) cycle, the carpet was introduced to other floors before the impact on the first unit was fully determined. Noise complaint data ironically showed that complaints dropped starting the month before the carpet was installed, as nurses had taken initiative to close doors and turn TV volumes down at night. So, as nurses were learning Lean principles and their executives said they supported that effort, the senior leaders were not yet thinking Lean themselves.

What Is a Manager's Role?

What, then, is the role of a manager in a Lean culture? Managers have a responsibility to set direction and lead the way, making sure their employees understand customer needs, organizational priorities, and how the pieces fit together. Shook described the role of a manager at Toyota as having two objectives:

1. Get each person to take initiative to solve problems and improve his or her job.
2. Ensure each person's job is aligned to provide value for the customer (or patient) and prosperity for the company (or hospital).[5]

How do we get people to take initiative? It is hard to accomplish that through direct orders and formal, positional authority. Managers, especially in hospital departments that do not have direct patient contact, need to ensure that their people are oriented around providing value-added activity for the customer, our patients.

Managers often have difficulty empowering their employees to come up with solutions and answers of their own. Many managers define their value by their own firefighting or problem-solving abilities; after all, they were made for the boss for a reason. This dynamic tends to become stronger as you move up the organizational chart. It can be more effective, in the long run, to challenge your people to come up with solutions, even if it initially takes longer or they stumble along the way through the PDCA process.

One hospital chief operating officer (COO) lamented that his new pronounce-ments that "firefighting is bad" ran in conflict with how people knew him from his 30-year career in that organization. While he knew, logically, that everybody needed to focus on improving systems and preventing fire, he said that people knew he rose through the ranks to COO because he "was always the best at fighting fires and figuring out how to get things done through workarounds." This is an understandable leadership challenge.

Lean managers are neither dictatorial nor extreme delegators who are hands-off leaders. As Shook said, Lean managers are not the "modern, enlightened leader" of the 1980s empowerment or total quality management styles. Lean managers do not say, "I don't care how you do it, as long as you get results."[6]

Setting objectives and boundaries is something a manager can do, but objectives are not a "make-the-number-or-else" target. Lean managers say, "Follow me. Let's figure this out together."[7] In a Lean organization, goals, objectives, and strategy tend to flow top down. Ideas and solutions should flow from the bottom up, with the assumption that frontline (or "value-adding") employ-ees are closest to the process. Lean organizations have frequent feedback loops between the levels, as information flows in both directions. As upper managers set direction and vision, they ask employees to confirm that it seems correct. As ideas flow up, managers may question and challenge ideas, testing the thought process involved in the solutions. This is illustrated in Figure 10.1.

Strategy Deployment

A growing number of healthcare organizations, including Virginia Mason Medical Center (Seattle, WA), ThedaCare (Appleton, WI), Group Health (Seattle, WA), and St. Boniface General Hospital

• Executive/Senior Leaders

• VPs and Directors

• First-Level Managers

• Frontline Supervisors

• Charge/Senior Staff & Clinicians

• Value Adding Staff & Clinicians

Figure 10.1 Illustration of how goals and ideas flow up and down in a Lean organization.

(Winnipeg, Manitoba), are using a Lean management methodology called "strategy deployment," also known as "policy deployment" or *hoshin kanri* in Japanese. Following the top-down and bottom-up model, strategy deployment aims to create alignment at all levels of the organization. Seniors at an organization help define four or five "true north" objectives that cascade all the way to first-level supervisors and their staff.

For example, the four true north objectives at ThedaCare came from the question, "What are the most important problems and opportunities?" They are as follows:[8]

■ Safety and quality (preventable mortality and medication errors)
■ People (workplace injuries, employee engagement index, and wellness scores)
■ Customer satisfaction (access, turnaround time, quality of time)
■ Financial stewardship (operating margin and productivity)

The senior leadership team maintains high-level metrics and helps ensure that each level in the organization has local metrics that are aligned with true north. For example, a medical/surgical unit might track patient falls as a safety-and-quality metric, while an outpatient clinic might measure employee strains and sprains. Frontline managers in a mature strategy deployment setting can readily explain how their local metrics are important to their patients and how they contribute to the overall goals of the organization.

Going beyond measurement, strategy deployment also ensures that improvement ideas and projects are initiated primarily by lower-level employees, rather than being top-down mandates. Staff and managers help determine what to do (the how) to meet the goals of the organization (the what). The "catch ball" process ensures that top-down goals are adjusted based on feedback from employees, and improvement ideas from employees also receive feedback and input from their leaders. This collaboration distinguishes strategy deployment from older "management-by-objectives" methods that were only top down. As ThedaCare discovered, it is important to "break the cycle of hierarchy."[9]

Strategy deployment also creates focus by forcing an organization to prioritize key improvement initiatives instead of trying to do everything all at once. ThedaCare's senior leadership "visual room" has walls displaying Rapid Improvement Events and ongoing strategic initiatives, but they also have a process for formally "deselecting" initiatives that are not part of that year's priorities, leaving those ideas on the wall so they can be reconsidered in the future rather than being forgotten.

Toussaint said, "Strategy deployment is forcing a continuous improvement look at the world, whereas the traditional way is just a batch, which is a project." Previously, ThedaCare's annual planning process was "a big batch where we'd have a board retreat for four or five hours." By the time the plan was completed, it was "out of date," said Toussaint. ThedaCare now has a planning cycle that can be continuously revisited, following the PDCA mindset.[10]

Common Management Problems

We can find common management problems across most hospitals. Hospitals often take their best, most successful, or most personable nurse, for example, and make that person a supervisor overnight. People are often thrown into supervisory roles without formal training, forcing them to learn on the fly rather than being taught to follow a management model that is consistently applied throughout the hospital. This informal approach leads to some employees struggling and removing themselves from the management chain forever (another example of the waste of talent).

Many individuals who are promoted based on success in their individual contributor role lack certain skills and experiences that are necessary for success as a supervisor. For example, we may promote a supervisor who is uncomfortable having tough, necessary conversations with employees. Rather than confronting them constructively or holding them accountable, supervisors often look the other way. Or, they are so busy in meetings or reviewing reports and paperwork in their office that they do not have a chance to see waste at all. We cannot assume all managers have basic supervisory skills, such as knowing how to effectively train an employee in a task. By comparison, Lean and its foundational Training Within Industry methodology offers time-tested methods for teaching supervisors how to effectively train employees, as mentioned in Chapter 5. New methods combined with new Lean cultural mindsets can make management more appealing to our most talented people, setting them up to be more successful as leaders.

This is not to say that all hospital supervisors, managers, and leaders are ineffective. Hospital supervisors have many positive traits that can help them become even better managers. Unlike other industries, supervisors and other leaders in hospitals tend to be promoted into their roles, usually within the same organization. While this can create some challenges, such as how to effectively manage former peers, the big systemic advantage is that the supervisors are more likely to understand the daily value-added work. This advantage, however, may degrade over time, as the supervisor is away from the daily work longer and tools and technology change.

Much as we try not to blame individual employees for process problems, Lean thinkers avoid blaming individual managers for their past practices. Adopting a Lean management approach requires us to admit there are problems with the old system (or lack thereof). Without pointing blame about how we got this way, we should focus on improving our management system for the sake of patients, employees, and the hospital.

Lean as a Management System and Philosophy

As the 1990s ended, Toyota leaders wanted to document more detail about their management system. An internal document called "The Toyota Way" led to the publication of a book by the same name. *The Toyota Way* spells out 4 major principles and 14 additional principles, as shown in Table 10.2.[11]

A Daily Lean Management System

Successful hospitals and departments implement a management system to maintain improvements as well as drive *kaizen*. This management system consists of methods that include

- Process audits, or rounding
- Performance measures
- Daily stand-up team meetings
- *Kaizen* and suggestion management

Table 10.2   Principles from *The Toyota Way*

I. Long-Term Philosophy
1. Base your management decisions on a long-term philosophy, even at the expense of short-term financial goals.
II. The Right Process Will Produce the Right Results
2. Create continuous process flow to bring problems to the surface
3. Use "pull" systems to avoid overproduction
4. Level out the workload (*Heijunka*)
5. Build a culture of stopping to fix problems to get quality right the first time
6. Standardized tasks are the foundation for continuous improvement and employee empowerment
7. Use visual control so no problems are hidden
8. Use only reliable, thoroughly tested technology that serves your people and processes
III. Add Value to the Organization by Developing Your People and Partners
9. Grow leaders who thoroughly understand the work, live the philosophy, and teach it to others
10. Develop exceptional people and teams who follow your company's philosophy
11. Respect your extended network of partners and suppliers by challenging them and helping them improve
IV. Continuously Solving Root Problems Drives Organizational Learning
12. Go and see for yourself to thoroughly understand the situation (*genchi genbutsu*)
13. Make decisions slowly by consensus, thoroughly considering all options; implement decisions rapidly (*nemawashi*)
14. Become a learning organization through relentless reflection (*hansei*) and continuous improvement (*kaizen*)

This approach has been successfully implemented in many hospitals as they begin their journeys, or it has been adopted after struggling with the aftermath of a tools-driven approach to Lean. Group Health (Seattle, WA) has been at the forefront of developing a formal "daily management system" that is taught and practiced consistently at all levels of management throughout the organization.[12]

Process Audits or Rounding

As discussed in Chapter 5, process audits are necessary to ensure that standardized work is being followed. It is also necessary to observe the process to see what opportunities for continuous improvement exist. In some hospitals, the term *audit* has negative connotations, so the terms *rounding* or *daily checks* might be used instead. Supervisors and managers do not audit the process to catch employees doing something wrong, like a policing function.

Standardized Audits of the Standardized Work

Lean hospitals implement a hierarchy of audits and standardized work checks; the frontline charge, supervisor, or team leader is the primary auditor. Standardized work for conducting the audits includes a checklist that is carried around the department. The checklist identifies standard questions that should be asked, a list that can be customized to the needs of a particular area. ThedaCare leaders develop their own "standardized work for leaders" that vice presidents, directors, and managers will carry to the *gemba*.[13]

The list might include items related to the following:

◾ Are there any observed or reported safety risks or problems?
◾ Were equipment maintenance and other key tasks done according to schedule?
◾ Are there any patient complaints or concerns?
◾ Is standardized work being followed?
◾ Are metrics current and posted?
◾ Are 5S practices being followed?

The completed audit sheets are posted on a wall for all to see. This helps communicate what problems are found and creates some accountability to leaders to follow their own standardized work. If we intend for an audit to happen once each shift or once each day, leaders have to follow that standard to set a good example for their employees. The audits can help emphasize that standardized work is not just for frontline employees.

Audits should not be done just to "check the box." Audits are meant to be a primary input into the problem-solving process. It does no good to identify the same problems every day, continually writing them down on the audit sheet. Problems that are identified should be fixed right away, if possible. Or, the sheets can be discussed with employees during team meetings. If a problem is not being solved immediately, the planned action can be recorded on the audit sheet for communication and visibility purposes.

In some hospital or department cultures, people are afraid to write down problems. Often, there is a feeling that it is unacceptable to admit having problems. Leaders have to ensure that their supervisors are not overlooking problems in an attempt to make their audit sheets look good. Likewise, leaders have a responsibility to react to problems in a constructive manner, focused on solving problems and removing barriers to getting things fixed.

A Hierarchy of Rounding

In some areas, a senior technologist or charge nurse might be the one to audit the department each shift. The manager of the frontline auditor then audits the audits and so forth up the organization, as shown in Table 10.3. Ultimately, the responsibility for standardized work rests with the hospital CEO and other top leadership. It is not an acceptable excuse for senior leaders to say, after a patient safety incident, that their employees did not follow policies or procedures, especially if not following policies was a common occurrence. In the National Health Service (NHS) Releasing Time to Care program, the hospital CEO visits each ward, the *gemba*, on a monthly basis to see firsthand

Table 10.3   Auditing Hierarchy

Level/Role	Frequency of Audit	Frequency to Audit the Audits
Frontline supervisor	Shift or day	N/A
Manager	Week	Day
Director	Month	Week
Vice president	Quarter	Month
C-level	Quarter	Month

how things are working and to provide assistance, signing his or her name on a board to indicate the visit and that the CEO is checking that lower-level leaders have completed their checks.

Second-level leaders serve a dual purpose: to audit the audits and to conduct audits of their own, albeit less frequently than frontline leaders. A department manager who has multiple supervisors is responsible to do a daily check to see if the supervisors have completed their audits. Hanging all of the audits for an area on a single display board can make it easier for the manager to do a quick daily review while walking through the department.

The manager also should do a firsthand audit, with or without the frontline supervisor, of each area once per week. Doing audits with frontline supervisors provides opportunities for the manager to ask questions and to be available to the staff. Discussions about problems and possible improvements can be held during the audit, right in the *gemba*.

Going to *gemba* to do rounding cannot be an opportunity for leaders just to put a new name on old practices and behaviors. Blaming individuals, yelling at them for not following the process, looking the other way when core safety methods are not practiced, or chastising people for not reaching goals are behaviors that have no place in a Lean culture.

As we move up in the organization, these audits should still occur. They provide a way of forcing leaders to the *gemba*, to be out of their offices or the executive suite, to be out where the value-added work is being done. Having upper-level executives conduct audits can be helpful. For one, it gives them an accurate picture of what is happening day to day in different departments. Second, it makes them visible to the employees and provides accessibility for people to ask questions or make suggestions; many frontline employees rarely, if ever, see their vice president or C-level executives in their own workplace. Third, it sends a powerful message to the employees to see that higher-level managers are asking questions about standardized work and Lean methods. An upper-level manager should not be directive, as asking questions sends a powerful message about what is important.

Leaders who are new to the Lean process will often resist the need to oversee their employees' standardized work. They might argue that they have good employees or they should be trusted. Other times, managers might resist because they do not have time (time should be freed) or because they do not like conflict. These managers should be given training and skills for constructive interactions with their employees, as well as coaching from their leaders.

Performance Measures

The ability to measure performance effectively is necessary for continuous improvement. Employees often do not know how their department is performing in a quantitative way. It may be that performance measures (or metrics) are not tracked or that metrics are not shared by managers. Some managers want to shield their employees from the pressure that performance measures might bring. In a Lean environment, respect for people means we are honest with people about how the department is performing.

Before Lean, there are common dysfunctions with existing metrics. First, metrics are typically tracked using monthly averages, which hampers improvement efforts. Second, metrics are often focused on financial or accounting measures, such as work units or labor cost. Third, information is often posted in hallways outside the department, where it goes unseen.

A Lean culture must ensure that goals do not become inflexible targets that people must make at all costs. The National Health Service in the United Kingdom had a target for Accident and Emergency (A&E) Room waiting time, capped at four hours per patient. Hospitals were placed under a great deal of pressure to hit this target. When you have more pressure than process improvement, people often find it easier to game the system.[14] For example, news reports highlighted how ambulances were often forced to keep the patient in the vehicle so that the A&E clock did not start ticking against the four-hour target.[15] Of course, this kept the ambulances from hitting their own targets for responding to life-threatening situations within eight minutes, leading to their own gaming of the system. The NHS pledged in 2010 to scrap these targets due to the multiple dysfunctions and problems that were created.

Timely Measures Drive Timely Improvement

Timely measures give us much more helpful information than infrequent averages. How useful would the speedometer on your car be if it only displayed your average speed when you arrived at your destination? We need more continuous feedback to make sure we are not driving too fast at any given time.

Likewise, viewing process performance measures as monthly averages makes it difficult to drive process improvement. For one, averages tend to mask the detail of what happened on given days during the month. In the middle of a month (when the metrics are often tabulated as a batch and posted), lab staff might look and ask, "Why was turnaround time poor last month?" At that point, memories might be fuzzy regarding specific reasons, making it difficult to do anything beyond trying harder and hoping for better results. The average might have been skewed by a few bad days. If the monthly average is just slightly worse, it does not necessarily mean the underlying process is any worse than before, in a statistically significant way.

It is better to measure performance on a daily basis, once a shift, or more frequently (through ongoing visual management). This immediate feedback facilitates root cause problem solving and the prevention of problems. When we can ask the team a timely, specific question such as, "Why was our chemistry turnaround time much worse than usual yesterday?" we are more likely to get accurate reasons and root causes.

It is important that metrics are used to identify improvements in a blame-free environment. Performance measures can be used, unfortunately, in a context and method that does not show respect for people. If managers were to use the metrics as a way of merely pressuring employees to do better without a means for improvement, this would be unfair and might give Lean a "mean" reputation.

A Balanced Scorecard Focuses on All Stakeholders

Lean metrics focus on more than just accounting measures. For example, before implementing Lean, the managers at one lab focused on an accounting-driven productivity metric of hours worked per tested specimen. This was the primary measure for the department, viewed monthly. Through the Lean process, the lab instituted daily measures for turnaround time and started viewing the productivity metric daily, instituting more frequent improvement activity. Although the primary objective was turnaround time, labor efficiency and productivity also improved by 10%.

In addition to viewing averages, many departments start looking at the variation in their service levels. For example, a lab might measure the percentage of turnaround times that exceed certain thresholds. What most internal customers remember is not the average, but the worst or the best. Measuring the time under which 90% of your orders are filled might more accurately reflect what your customers are feeling.

In a Lean environment, we focus on more than just cost. The mantra is SQDCM—safety, quality, delivery, cost, and morale. This balanced approach, often reflected in the strategy deployment true north goals, emphasizes that cost is not the primary motivation for improvement. If safety, quality, and delivery (as seen in the turnaround time performance of a lab) are improved, then cost tends to follow. Table 10.4 shows some typical metrics adopted by departments as they implement Lean.

Another management principle that can be incorporated into this system is explaining why each metric is important. For example, in a lab where they measured the "percentage of tests resulted before 7 a.m.," the metrics sheet explained, "This is a key measure that physicians use to judge lab effectiveness. Physicians get dissatisfied if results are not on the patient chart when they do morning rounding, and this can delay patient care decisions or discharges." Even if employees are experienced, they often do not understand the true impact of certain measures on their patients or internal customers.

One hospital lab implemented all of the Lean approaches to metrics, except that every metric was focused on different types of turnaround time. After a few weeks, an employee asked if management was saying that quality was not important. They were afraid that some coworkers, having competitive personalities and wanting their measures to look good, would cut corners on quality. The managers of the lab responded by emphasizing that safety and quality were certainly priorities. Employees would not be (and had not been) blamed or made to feel bad when turnaround times were worse than their goals. In addition, though, the lab looked for quality measures that could be quantified and began tracking those as well.

Table 10.4 Typical Metrics for Measuring Lean Improvements

Metric Area	Pharmacy Example	Laboratory Example
Safety	Number of adverse drug events	Number of unsafe or near-miss behaviors seen
Quality	Number of reworked prescriptions Number of med cabinet stockouts in units Nurse satisfaction surveys	Percentage of time "critical values" are called Number of lost/missing specimen cases Number of mislabeled specimens
Delivery	Response time for "first-dose" orders	Turnaround time average for key tests Percentage of morning draw test results on patient charts by 7 a.m.
Cost	Inventory levels in pharmacy	Cost per test Overtime hours per week
Morale	Employee satisfaction surveys	Quarterly employee satisfaction surveys Number of suggestions submitted each month

Metrics Should Be Visible, Visual, and Statistically Meaningful

Metrics and chart boards should be located right inside the department, where they can be seen as people are doing their work. Since employees might not take the time for a detailed look at the charts and metrics each day, visual management elements can be used so everyone can gauge department performance at a quick glance.

In many pre-Lean environments, department results are posted in the form of tables of numbers. The tables typically show comparisons between two data points, as in performance versus last month or last year. These simple comparisons can be misleading, particularly when compared to more visual ways of displaying multiple data points. If in the average emergency room, the "left without being seen" metric was down from 3% to 2% this month, for example, there are still many unanswered questions:

- What does that tell us about the process?
- Did we really improve, or was that a fluctuation in the data?
- Will the number be the same in the next month, meaning we have a predictable process?

Some departments have existing scorecards with densely packed tables of numbers. One perioperative services department that had not yet implemented Lean had 50 different metrics, each measured for the last 12 months, all squeezed into a single page. While there were more data available, the presentation was overwhelming. Lean metrics (those that are displayed visually for the employees) are often a critical few key indicators of the overall health of the department. We

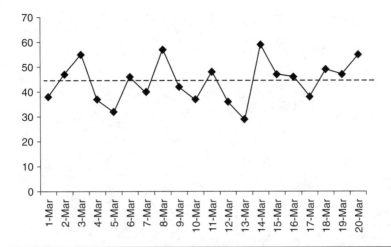

Figure 10.2 Example of a trend chart in which data points appear to be fluctuating randomly around an average (the dashed line).

might track more measures, for financial reporting purposes or to meet the requirements of upper management, but we do not have to post everything that we track.

Lean metrics are made visual through the use of trend charts and color coding. Trend charts show patterns so we can see if a metric is just fluctuating (as shown in Figure 10.2) or shifting in a statistically significant way (as shown in Figure 10.3).[16] Being able to view trends is an improvement over simple comparisons to goals (our turnaround time is better than our 30-minute goal) or comparisons to the past (our turnaround time is 3 minutes better than yesterday).

These trend charts can use a formal statistical process control (SPC), or control chart methodology, that allows managers and teams to avoid overreacting to every fluctuation in the metrics. SPC gives us tools to know when those ups and downs are just "noise" and when we have a

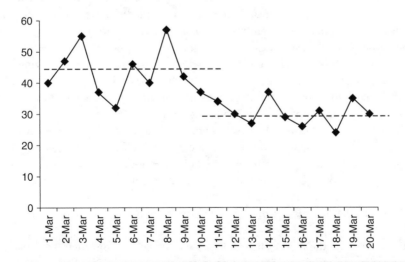

Figure 10.3 Example of a trend chart in which the data show a statistical shift from a higher average to a new lower average (the dashed lines).

Figure 10.4 A clinical laboratory posts its turnaround time metrics and volume levels each shift. The display board is in the department, so all employees can see, and team meetings are held in front of the display.

significant change to which we should react, or a "signal." With SPC, we take process data, such as daily turnaround times for a particular test, and determine if the process is "in control" statistically. If a process is in control, it means we can reliably predict how that process will perform tomorrow. When we make a significant process change, seeing a process shift, as in Figure 10.3, helps us confirm if we made a statistically significant change or not.

SPC charts also help us avoid situations for which we think we are improving based on an Excel linear trend line. Having one bad data point at the start and one good data point at the end can create an upward linear trend, making it look like we are improving when the process is actually stable and in statistical control, as shown in Figure 10.2.

Some departments have established color coding to indicate if a particular metric is better, slightly worse, or much worse (green, yellow, red color coding, respectively) than a goal or customer requirement. We must take care that the goals are not arbitrary, and that employees are not blamed or pressured for being consistently in a yellow or red zone since that is a reflection on process capability, not the people. These metrics are posted in a high-visibility location, as pictured in Figure 10.4. In this example, a laboratory has posted three sets of daily metrics, one for each shift.

If employees walk by the metrics board or can see the board from their workspaces, they can use the color coding as an indication of how the process is performing. Seeing a lot of green is a visual indicator that we are meeting customer and patient needs. It is not, however, a reason to stop looking for *kaizen* opportunities.

Daily Stand-up Team Meetings

Another way to engage employees is the use of daily update and communication meetings. These meetings are structured using a standardized work approach in terms of the agenda used for each day on each shift. Meetings should be held in a stand-up format, often around the board where metrics, process audits, or suggestions are posted. This helps to keep the meeting short, to keep the team close to the workplace, and to focus on the results of efforts and improvements.

The meetings need to remain focused and be kept at 5 or 10 minutes, avoiding the tendency for meetings to lengthen over time. In a meeting of this length, it is not possible to discuss every issue or to do complex problem solving. The intent is quick communication, prioritized around immediate needs. As problems or suggestions are brought up, they can be captured on a whiteboard (or in our suggestion management system, discussed further in this chapter) for more detailed discussion as time allows later in the day. If we have six or seven people for a team meeting, we might only need two or three specific people for investigating a particular root cause, so the full group meeting needs to be kept short to avoid wasting people's time.

Sample Team Meeting Agenda

Safety reminder of the day; review safety issues or risks
Immediate problems to be aware of (instruments down or people called in sick)
Review of yesterday's metrics and trends
New employee suggestions or ideas; updates on previous ideas
Share any positive feedback

Harvard Vanguard Medical Associates (HVMA) is among the organizations using this daily huddle approach. For example, their Kenmore Clinic in Boston has a 10-minute huddle each day in the orthopedics clinic; the huddle includes physicians, physician assistants, nurses, and medical assistants. They follow a standardized format, discussing recent problems in a very nonhierarchical team environment. Problems and ideas for improvement are posted and tracked on a whiteboard where the huddles are held, with clinicians and staff members at all levels taking the lead on different improvements. To help build collaboration across departments, the huddles initially included a representative from the radiology clinic that was located down the hall. This facilitated open and honest discussion about patient flow and other possible issues throughout the value stream. Based on that initial success, the standardized huddle process has been spread across multiple clinics in the Boston area.

One pitfall to avoid was highlighted by a manager, who said his hospital had gotten away from having regular team meetings. The corporate staff was punishing managers, via productivity standards for team meetings, and managers became reluctant to pull frontline staff for this reason. This highlights another example of how, unfortunately, the best local Lean efforts can be undermined by a lack of alignment with corporate or senior leadership attitude, policies, or metrics.

Kaizen *and Suggestion Management*

The acronym TPS has traditionally stood for the Toyota Production System. In recent years, Toyota executives have started calling TPS the Thinking Production System to emphasize the important role of employees' creativity and thinking in continuous improvement.[17] Toyota needs its employees to be engaged and thinking, rather than "checking their brains at the door."

> Toyota highlights the importance of employee engagement, stating, "Every Toyota team member is empowered with the ability to improve their work environment. This includes everything from quality and safety to the environment and productivity. Improvements and suggestions by team members are the cornerstone of Toyota's success."[18]

We have already briefly introduced how *kaizen* is a key Lean strategy. *Kaizen* allows us to build on our standardized work. *Kaizen* is meant to be a daily process by which many small improvements are implemented in an ongoing basis. *Kaizen* should not be a bureaucratic process by which ideas are generated or approved only by managers or senior leaders. It should be a process that engages employees in fast improvement cycles, allowing them to take ownership of improving their processes instead of just lobbing complaints at their leaders. Employees should be encouraged to bring suggestions directly to their coworkers or supervisors in a face-to-face manner as often as possible.

Wherever an improvement idea comes from, it should be treated as a PDCA experiment. Not every new idea will work in practice, so a trial must take place in a limited area (one unit or one room, rather than the whole hospital) and over a limited timeframe. During and after the trial period, all participants need to evaluate if the change really improves the system or if there were side effects caused in adjacent areas. If the change is deemed positive, it can be accepted as the new process. If not, the team can go back to old methods or continue looking for a new one.

Since the scientific method and the Lean change process allow for a hypothesis ("This change will improve the system") to be proven incorrect, leaders must create an environment in which rapid experimentation is encouraged. Rather than pondering the problem forever and trying to come up with the perfect solution the first time, it is better to try something, in a limited way, to see if it works. Part of the approach is that employees must not be shamed for making a suggestion that does not work as expected. It is something that provides learning. As the PDCA cycle suggests, the team can try a different idea, starting with rethinking the problem statement and going through the rest of the improvement cycle. On the other hand, this environment of rapid experimentation should not be considered an excuse to try ideas that are not well thought out just for the sake of trying something new.

General agreement on this approach often leads to specific questions about how we actually implement *kaizen*:

- How do we manage suggestions?
- How do we evaluate ideas?
- How do we keep continuous improvement from being uncontrolled or chaotic?

- How do we get input from everybody and keep everybody informed without being too bureaucratic?
- What if people change things they should not have changed?

Problems with Suggestion Boxes

Organizations often use suggestion boxes as the primary means of employee involvement. While well intended, these boxes often impede the flow of ideas, leading to frustration and cynicism among employees.

Suggestions tend to accumulate in boxes, with long periods of time elapsing before they are actually read as a batch. At one hospital laboratory, managers had misplaced the key to the box and did not know the last time it was opened. The team jokingly asked if the hospital had been afraid that their ideas would be stolen by a competing hospital. After asking facilities personnel to cut off the padlock, the managers decided the box could remain unlocked until a better method was put in place.

Traditional suggestion systems often feature a monthly (or less-frequent) suggestion review meeting, at which managers or a designated team read and evaluate the merits of each suggestion. This is often done without any direct interaction with the person who submitted the suggestion. If the team is reviewing anonymous suggestions, there is no opportunity to give feedback or to dig deeper into the idea.

One advantage of real interaction over suggestion boxes is that some suggestions are not practical. An example might be: "We should hire five more people for the night shift." With a suggestion box and review meetings, all we can do is say no, especially when the suggestion is anonymous. When an employee brings us an idea verbally, we can thank him or her and explain why that particular solution might not be practical, due to budget or technology constraints, for example. The discussion can then turn to finding a solution that would work. Toyota's high percentage of suggestion approval is a sign that they work toward finding something that can be implemented; that sometimes takes effort, but it is for the good of the organization and shows respect for people by being engaged with them instead of just saying no.

The Role of Supervisors in Kaizen

Supervisors and managers should be appreciative of employees coming forward with a complaint or a problem. Exposing and embracing problems instead of covering them up or avoiding them is a positive step forward. When a complaint is brought to their attention, such as "We are too busy between 8 and 10 a.m.," supervisors should challenge the employees to come up with a solution or a suggestion. A simple, yet effective, question is, "What should we do to address that?" The question should be asked in an open, honest tone rather than in an accusatory tone that suggests there is no solution to be found. Asking employees what they think might catch some people by surprise, given common pre-Lean environments. Some supervisors find it threatening not to be the ones coming up with answers all of the time. Supervisors and managers are not necessarily to be excluded from the problem-solving process, but they are not the ones who must come up with all of the answers. The frontline employees doing the actual work are more likely to have effective, practical solutions.

In some cases, employees do not have the authority required to solve the problems themselves. For example, if a laboratory employee brings a complaint or a problem forward, saying nurses in the emergency department are not properly labeling specimens, that is a problem outside the employee's control. In situations such as these, leaders must step forward to take action on behalf of and in support of their employees. Leaders should play the dual role of encouraging and empowering employees by challenging them to develop their own solutions and stepping in to help when needed, particularly with value stream problems that cross department boundaries.

The surest way to stop the flow of employee ideas is to respond negatively to them. How many times is our initial reaction to an idea or suggestion one of the following?

- "That's a dumb idea."
- "That won't work."
- "We can't do that."
- "We tried that before."

Supervisors have to go out of their way to be positive when suggestions or ideas are presented. Even if the idea seems like a "dumb" one, supervisors should respond by asking questions. Ask the employee to step back and state the problem. Do anything other than saying no. Since employees are not required to give suggestions, in a formal sense, supervisors must treat suggestions like a gift.[19] This also ties back to assuming that people are trying to do a good job. When presented with a seemingly inappropriate suggestion, a manager should try to understand why the employee thinks it is a valuable suggestion and then use it as a developmental opportunity.

Imai wrote that there are three stages that an organization goes through in learning how to have a *kaizen* culture. This progression is important because we want to push people to be more effective problem solvers while not discouraging their participation. In the first stage, supervisors must make every attempt to help them with even the most basic of ideas. Once people are interested in *kaizen*, the second stage allows us to educate employees about how to provide better suggestions, such as emphasizing better root cause analysis and not jumping to solutions. Only in the third stage, after gaining interest and educating people, should managers be "concerned with the economic impact of the suggestion."[20]

Finding a Better Method for Managing Kaizen

Having standardized work for managing suggestions can help create the proper balance between bureaucracy and completely uncontrolled changes. Many departments have implemented a method in which ideas are brought to supervisors or coworkers face to face, ideally in the daily stand-up meeting.

One version of a standardized *kaizen* card, or idea card, is shown in Figure 10.5. Rather than just listing what should be done, the form prompts the employee to define the problem and think about what the measurable impact would be for the patients or the department. The cards are meant to follow the A3 thought process, as mentioned in Chapter 7.

One hospital lab, at the start of its initial Lean project phase, generated 151 employee suggestions in the first eight weeks, most of which were acted on almost immediately. Over time, this lab generated an average of one formally documented suggestion per person per year. By comparison, one of the best automotive parts suppliers, Autoliv, went from 0.5 implemented ideas per person per year to 63 per person in 2009.[21]

After a suggestion is made, action should be taken as soon as possible. While having a bias for action is good, we need to temper against the temptation to rush into fixes without checking to see if things really improved (skipping the check step of PDCA) or without properly communicating the change to others (skipping the act step). If we move too quickly, we might lose the opportunity

Front of Card		Back of Card	
Problem		Implementation Steps	
Suggestion			
Date Originated	By:		
Expected Benefits			
		Results Verified? YES/NO	
Input Needed From		New Method Standardized? YES/NO	
		Completed Date	

Figure 10.5 A sample *kaizen* idea card as developed and used by one hospital.

to get input from others or to check to see if we are fixing the right problem (skipping the plan step). While in the case of minor, local, and isolated changes, we might be able to "just do it," in many other cases we are better off "just PDCA-ing it."

The *kaizen* card prompts the employee (often along with his or her supervisor) to write a problem statement. Often, when we give a suggestion, we jump to an answer (such as "We need a new centrifuge"). By forcing a statement of the problem, we must focus and define what is wrong. Instead of jumping to an answer, we are not locking ourselves into a single solution to evaluate. The supervisor can ask questions about what is wrong with the current centrifuge. Maybe there are other options instead of signing a purchase order (the Toyota ideal of "creativity before capital").[22] The goal of the discussion between employee and supervisor is to find something that can be implemented, even if it is not the original idea.

The *kaizen* card also prompts the employee to write a proposed countermeasure, to explain it in terms of outcomes. We need to list not only the idea but also how we expect the idea to improve safety, quality, time, or cost. These might be rough estimates or even just qualitative understanding of the benefits, but it gets employees thinking about results, not just what they want to implement.

Instead of jumping to just one solution, Lean thinkers will ask employees what alternatives they considered. John Shook, an early American employee at Toyota, told a story about how managers at Toyota never just said yes to an idea. They always asked why the employee thought that was the best solution, in the name of probing and finding better solutions, not to second-guess the employee.[23] The manager can ask questions like the following:

- What makes that the best countermeasure?
- What alternatives did you consider?
- Are we solving the root cause of the problem?

Jim Adams, senior director of laboratory operations at Children's Medical Center in Dallas, Texas, implemented a suggestion system in which employees were encouraged to verbally bring suggestions to the new team stand-up meetings held at the beginning of each shift. In the meeting, the team reviewed the previous day's metrics on turnaround time. After just a few weeks of reviewing data that measured service quality for the patients and the physicians, Adams noticed a clear trend, saying, "The suggestions made a sudden shift to ideas that were focused on how to improve care and quality for our patients instead of being inwardly focused on what the employees wanted or needed. It was an amazing change, as Lean helped improve our customer and patient orientation."[24]

The *kaizen* card and the method also prompt employees to obtain input from coworkers or leaders. Some ideas can be implemented quickly with just some input from coworkers (such as the organization of a workbench top). Other ideas might have an impact on clinical results or patient care, so managers or pathologists might need to be consulted. A team might formally list and post the types of suggestions that can be done with feedback from coworkers and which types of changes require manager or medical oversight.

Many, including Toyota, have experimented with giving financial rewards or incentives for employee suggestions. Toyota pays employees in some locations modest incentive payments for implementing (not just making) suggestions.[25] Many would argue that we should rely on people's intrinsic motivation as *kaizen* is supposed to make your own work easier, so that is the incentive. In healthcare, we have a strong intrinsic motivation to make improvements that benefit patients.

Leaders need to be careful that the financial reward does not become the goal in and of itself. Depending on the culture of the organization, employees might get no financial reward, a reward for submitted suggestions, or some percentage share of cost savings. There is no blanket answer to the question of whether we should pay people for suggestions. There are benefits and drawbacks to each approach, so the answer is best left to your own judgment based on the existing culture in your organization.

One of the gurus of *kaizen*, Masaaki Imai, compared the traditional Western view of suggestions with a "Japanese" view (which we could read as meaning the Lean view), "The Japanese-style suggestion system emphasizes morale-boosting benefits and positive employee participation over the economic and financial incentives that are stressed in a Western-style system." Not every small improvement has a specific return on investment (ROI), and ROI is not the only important reason why we would do *kaizen*.[26]

Figure 10.6   A visual idea board as used in a hospital laboratory.

Visual Tracking of Suggestions

In a Lean environment, suggestions are posted visually on a board for all to see.[27] As ideas are being considered, employees and leaders can review the board to see what ideas are in progress, as illustrated in Figure 10.6. With that visual method, employees who see concerns or want to have input into a suggestion can do so. Managing the process visually avoids situations where either a selected few employees or the managers are the only ones who have input. This also helps avoid charges of favoritism that often come from less-transparent systems.

The visual tracking board also allows the team to see what is being implemented. As ideas are piloted and accepted (or rejected), progress is tracked visually as the cards are moved to columns further to the right. The four columns are typically labeled:

- Idea
- To do
- Doing
- Done

The team can see if ideas are being submitted but not being acted on. Hospital leaders, in their rounding, can also see this and follow up with department managers to better respect their employees' suggestions by taking action or encouraging employees to take action. As people walk by, they often stop and read the cards, adding their thoughts to the idea or taking that idea (or a variation) to their part of the workplace.

After our planned trial period for the change, the suggestion submitter and the team can evaluate the results of the experiment (moving into the check phase of PDCA). If the piloted process had positive results, we can work to formalize that as the new standardized work method.

Communicating Kaizen Changes

Organizations often struggle with communicating process changes to employees, especially in a 24/7 workplace like a hospital. A Lean organization will create standardized work for how to update the standardized work documents and how to communicate that change to employees. Informal methods that often do not work well include posting signs, using change logbooks, or updating the standardized work document without telling anybody. Signs can be ignored, and change logbooks can go unread. Even if employees are supposed to initial changes in the logbook, supervisors often do not formally track who has read and initialed those changes.

Whether an improvement has gone through a formal *kaizen* tracking process or was a small "just did it" change, the department and its employees can benefit from taking time to document what they have accomplished or even what they have tried.

The *kaizen* form has places to record what communication has taken place and if the relevant standardized work has been updated. The exact communication channels used for standardized work changes may vary, depending on the culture at your hospital, but the daily team meeting is a good way of communicating that a change has occurred. Formal standardized work documents should be updated, with changes highlighted. If any training resources are required for the change, managers should make them available.

Another approach that has worked well in hospitals can be called a celebration wall (some sites call it a *kaizen* wall of fame). For any improvement made in the department, no matter how big or how small, employees or supervisors create a quick one-page summary that is displayed for all to see. Posting successes (and even some well-intended "failures" that did not pass the PDCA cycle) gives recognition to employees for their efforts, helps share ideas across work areas, and creates a permanent record of your *kaizen* activities. An example of the use of this form is shown in Figure 10.7.

The goal is for this to be a simple process, with improvements documented in just a few minutes—simple and quick, not time consuming and detailed. The completed forms can be posted on a wall, near where team meetings are held or in another common, high-visibility location.

Conclusion

Since employee development is at the core of Lean, we have to let employees experiment with ideas if we expect them to learn and grow. Problems or mistakes should be treated as something to be learned from (and prevented) rather than covered up. By managing differently, we can start a virtuous cycle in which employees feel good about making improvements that improve patient care and improve their own work environment. As this enthusiasm grows, employees will want to make more improvements. Employee engagement and *kaizen* are the keys to improving quality and safety, reducing costs, and improving employee morale.

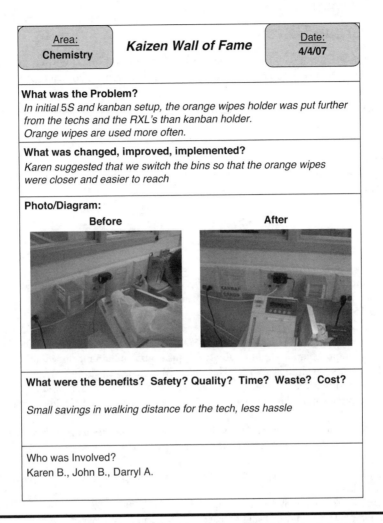

Figure 10.7 An example of a *kaizen* wall-of-fame sheet filled out by laboratory employees at a hospital.

Lean Lessons

■ Lean is not just about asking our employees to change; managers need to change their methods as well.

■ Managers must inspire their employees to take initiative to improve the system, while keeping them aligned with the big picture.

■ Standardized work applies to managers and how we manage; auditing the standardized work is a form of standardized work.

■ Employees should know how their processes are performing, but we should not pressure them to improve results by working harder.

■ Daily, visual metrics are more effective than monthly averages.

■ Suggestions should be managed in a way that avoids chaos, yet is not bureaucratic.

Points for Group Discussion

- Why might our supervisors and managers be afraid of empowering their employees?
- Is our organization very top down or command and control? If so, what problems are caused by this?
- How does a new frontline supervisor or manager get trained in our organization today?
- Why do we need to audit the audits?
- What are some reasons why our employees might not make more suggestions for improvement?
- Is our current culture more of a helpful coaching leadership style or a corrective and punitive style?

Notes

1. Convis, Gary, "Role of Management in a Lean Manufacturing Environment," Society of Automotive Engineers, http://www.sae.org/manufacturing/lean/column/leanjul01.htm (accessed April 10, 2011).
2. Jones, Dan, "The Beginner's Guide to Lean," Lean Enterprise Institute, http://www.lean.org/common/display/?o=15 (accessed April 3, 2011).
3. Vasilash, Gary S., "David Mann and Leading Lean," *Field Guide for Automotive Management,* http://findarticles.com/p/articles/mi_m0KJI/is_9_118/ai_n26997935/ (accessed April 10, 2011).
4. Toussaint, John, presentation, Lean Healthcare Transformation Summit, June 9, 2010.
5. Shook, John, "Lessons from Toyota for Healthcare Management?," Lean Enterprise Academy, http://www.leanuk.org/pages/event_summit_2007_speaker_shook.htm (accessed April 3, 2011).
6. Shook, John, presentation, First Global Lean Healthcare Summit, June 25, 2007.
7. Ibid.
8. Toussaint, John, and Roger Gerard, *On the Mend: Revolutionizing Healthcare to Save Lives and Transform the Industry* (Cambridge, MA: Lean Enterprise Institute, 2010), 76.
9. Ibid, 78.
10. Taninecz, George, "Strategy Deployment," ThedaCare Center for Healthcare Value, 4. (Appleton, WI: white paper, 2011).
11. Liker, Jeffrey K., *The Toyota Way* (New York: McGraw-Hill, 2004), 37.
12. Shea, Connor, "Do You Have a Daily Management System, or Just Parts?" *Daily Kaizen Blog,* May 23, 2010, http://dailykaizen.org/2010/05/23/do-you-have-a-daily-management-system-or-just-parts-by-connor-shea/ (accessed April 3, 2011).
13. Toussaint and Gerard, *On the Mend,* 172.
14. Joiner, Brian, *Fourth Generation Management: The New Business Consciousness* (New York: McGraw-Hill, 1994), 9.
15. Donnelly, Laura, "Patients Forced to Wait Hours in Ambulances Parked Outside A&E Departments," *The Telegraph,* http://www.telegraph.co.uk/health/healthnews/5412191/Patients-forced-to-wait-hours-in-ambulances-parked-outside-AandE-departments.html (accessed April 3, 2011).
16. Wheeler, Donald J., *Understanding Variation: The Key to Managing Chaos* (Knoxville, TN: SPC Press, 1993), 28.
17. Public Affairs Division, "The 'Thinking' Production System: TPS as a Winning Strategy for Developing People in the Global Manufacturing Environment," October 8, 2003, http://www.toyotageorgetown.com/tps.asp (accessed April 10, 2011).
18. Tozawa, Bunji, and Norman Bodek, *How to Do Kaizen,* (Vancouver, WA: PCS Press, 2010), 299.
19. Bodek, Norman, personal interview, December 30, 2007.
20. Imai, Masaaki, *Kaizen: The Key to Japan's Competitive Success* (New York: McGraw-Hill, 1986), 113.
21. Tozawa and Bodek, *How to Do Kaizen,* 301.

22. Smalley, Art, and Isao Katō, *Toyota Kaizen Methods: Six Steps to Improvement* (New York: Productivity Press, 2010), 4.
23. Shook, presentation.
24. Adams, Jim, Personal interview. June, 2007.
25. Magee, David, *How Toyota Became #1* (New York: Portfolio, 2007), 34.
26. Imai, *Kaizen: The Key,* 112.
27. Mann, David, *Creating a Lean Culture* (New York: Productivity Press, 2005), 149.

Chapter 11

Getting Started with Lean

How Do We Start?

Starting to understand Lean concepts is just the beginning. Knowledge without action likely will not bring results for patients and other key stakeholders, so it is time to look at how to get started with Lean in your hospital.

The goal should be learning from the examples set by others rather than blindly copying Toyota or other hospitals. For any organization, be it a factory or a hospital, there is no simple programmatic approach for implementing Lean methods and transforming a culture. Every hospital has its own starting point, its own starting point culture, and its own goals.

> Richard Zarbo, MD, DMD, senior vice president of pathology and laboratory medicine at Henry Ford Health System (Michigan), has led the Lean transformation efforts at their lab since 2005. Zarbo stated, "There is no cookbook approach to Lean," as organizations and leaders must create a program that is their own. Zarbo emphasized Lean must be introduced a way that is not traditional "top-down leadership," as he openly admitted to having tried and failed with that, initially. "The tools you can read about, the results you can read about, but how Lean is applied is different [in each environment] because Lean is a living thing—it's the people," he said.[1]

As important as thinking and planning are, we also need action, experimentation, and learning. What is stopping you from getting started today? Start small with your Lean efforts and learn as you go. Find out what works (and understand why). Keep doing the things that work and share the ideas with others in your organization (and even those outside), without expecting them to copy blindly. If something does not work, ask why and learn from the experience. Hospitals that have been working with Lean the longest are the most likely to say, "We still have so much to learn!" Hospitals cannot wait until it is all figured out; we have to start taking action now.

Where Do We Start?

It is not practical to start using Lean across the whole organization, all at once. The resources and attention required to support these efforts properly with coaching and training would be too high, and our focus would be spread too thin. Instead, it is preferable to find a single area or value stream in which to start—but where?

To help identify priorities for Lean, look at your strategic drivers or ongoing problems that need solving. A hospital is less likely to succeed if it is pushing Lean on an area, as opposed to people "pulling" on resources and ideas for improvement, or if it is focused on implementing tools instead of solving problems. Questions that leaders might ask to help prioritize Lean efforts might include

- What is a patient safety problem or risk to solve?
- What are the most pressing complaints from patients?
- What major issues do physicians or other employees bring to your attention?
- What departments have been struggling with employee shortages?
- Who is proposing large capital purchases or new construction projects?

In a survey conducted for this book, 50 hospitals stated their motivations for starting Lean, as shown in Table 11.1, with multiple responses accepted for each respondent.

Initial direction might have to be set by the senior leadership team based on their understanding of the strategic needs of the hospital. If employee satisfaction levels among nurses are very low and turnover has soared, there might be no need or time for debate about where to start. This might lead to a project in one inpatient unit, with the goals of reducing waste and eliminating roadblocks and problems that frustrate nurses, leading to better patient care and reduced turnover.

Parrish Medical Center (Titusville, FL) emphasizes the following balanced high-level performance measures in its improvement work:

- Service: patient satisfaction
- People: employee satisfaction and employee initiatives
- Quality: quality goals and initiatives
- Growth: any new program market growth initiatives
- Finances: the financial condition of the hospital[2]

Another method for prioritizing needs would be to conduct a high-level Lean overview seminar for departmental directors and senior leaders. After there is a shared understanding of Lean, ask for an initial volunteer. Who is pulling on Lean efforts harder than others? Especially for a first implementation, it is best not to force Lean on a leader who is not ready to admit there are problems or does not believe Lean methods can help. Avoid the temptation, though, to think the organization can start by giving a one-hour Lean overview class, or just a workshop on 5S (sort, store, shine, standardize, and sustain), to all employees and then expect Lean improvements just to happen without coaching or support. There is a proper time for such widespread training, but this comes later in the Lean journey, after success in a few departments or value streams. Lean success requires desire, action, and discipline—things that training cannot provide.

Table 11.1 Motivations for Instituting Lean

Motivation	Percentage
Quality and rework costs	56
Patient satisfaction	50
Labor shortages	50
Overall cost pressures	42
Culture change	44
Employee satisfaction	38
Labor costs	38
Patient safety (proactive)	34
Need for growth	30
Emergency department waiting time	20
Need for revenue increases	18
Employee retention	18
Operating room utilization	16
Payer reimbursement reductions	16
Patient discharge delays	12
Patient safety (in response to incident)	12
Emergency room boarding	2
Other: lab turnaround times, space constraints, physician satisfaction	

Another approach to identifying and prioritizing Lean opportunities is to conduct short assessments of multiple departments, among those who have identified themselves as candidates for Lean. An assessment is a focused effort that might last anywhere from two days to two weeks, depending on the complexity of the department or value stream being assessed. Value stream mapping, process observation, and discussions with employees and patients can be used to identify waste, delays, rework, and other non-value-added activities in a process. Quantitative data can be collected to help determine which improvements are possible, including

- Patient safety
- Turnaround time or patient flow improvements
- Quality improvement (reductions in rework time or costs that result from errors)
- Labor cost savings (through attrition or reductions in overtime)
- Inventory savings (from reductions or consolidation of inventory and supplies)
- Revenue growth opportunities (eliminating backlogs, improving utilization, or expanding services)
- Avoiding or delaying capital expansion or construction

Areas in which hospitals first used Lean methods include

- Laboratory
- Phlebotomy
- Food services
- Home health division
- Outpatient clinics
- Outpatient surgery
- Medical records
- Pharmacy
- Materials management
- Ambulance services
- Emergency department (ED)
- Inpatient medical/surgical units
- Wound care
- Catheterization lab
- Patient scheduling
- Sterile processing departments

This wide range of responses comes from a set of just 50 hospitals (responding to the survey for this book) and shows there is no single best place to start; it depends on the needs, culture, and existing situation at the hospital. Many hospitals start with departments that seem more production oriented in nature, including the laboratory and pharmacy, where employees interact with physical products and machines or instrumentation. Support departments, like pharmacies and laboratories, have an impact on many value streams and patient pathways, so one project can initially have a broad impact on the hospital. Some hospitals choose to start with a high-volume patient care value stream, such as outpatient surgery or the ED, looking to make a very visible impact that can inspire Lean efforts in other departments.

What Do We Call It?

The word *lean* often has many negative connotations in everyday usage, as people often associate the word with not having enough people or money. Headlines about living in "lean times" are usually not positive news stories. Some healthcare organizations will brand their approach as Lean, making sure they educate employees about the Lean management system and what it really entails.

Many organizations, though, will give their overall improvement program a different primary branding, using a term such as process improvement, performance excellence, or operational excellence. Leaders and implementers certainly will talk about Lean as a methodology, but the name of the department and posters on the wall do not use the term in a formal way. Another advantage of a more general term is that something like operational excellence as an umbrella can encompass Six Sigma and other methods, along with Lean.

Other organizations create their own primary branding around the name of the organization, with examples including the ThedaCare Improvement System, the Virginia Mason Production System, the Michigan Quality System, or the Bolton Improving Care System. Using the name of the organization emphasizes that they are creating something of their own, even if it borrows from

Table 11.2 Types of *Kaizen*

Kaizen Method	Scope of Problems	Duration	Examples
Point *Kaizen*	Small	Hours or days	Using 5S principles to reorganize a nurse's station; solving an equipment downtime problem
Kaizen events	Medium	One week (often longer, including planning)	Reducing operating room changeover time, pharmacy mistake proofing; standardizing automated inventory cabinets across units
System *Kaizen*	Large	9–18 weeks	Layout and process redesign of a department, such as clinical lab, pharmacy, or ED triage process

Toyota and earlier healthcare examples. Some of these terms keep the focus on the end result, such as quality or the patient.

Types of *Kaizen*

While *kaizen* generally means "continuous improvement," there are different methods for improvement that all use that term. Table 11.2 summarizes the three types of *kaizen* improvements.

It is important to choose the proper scope of problems to be solved with each of the methods. Toyota tends primarily to use point *kaizen in its factories* because they generally have well-designed processes after decades of improvement, but it uses three types of *kaizen* to solve different types of problems. Toyota teaches that the plan-do-check-act (PDCA) thought process is the same, regardless of the scale of the problem. They use infrequent *kaizen* events to teach people how to make smaller point *kaizen* improvements on a more continuous basis in their workplace.[3] All three types of *kaizen* are required and fit together as shown in Figure 11.1, which is adapted from the *The Toyota Way Fieldbook*.[4]

The same is true in hospitals, including ThedaCare (Appleton, WI), where they shifted from initial reliance on events to a balanced approach that also allows for what they call "continuous daily improvement," or smaller improvements that use the PDCA (or PDSA, plan-do-study-adjust) model.[5] Some hospitals rely exclusively on *kaizen* events to drive change and improvement. The overall approach of a hospital can incorporate events but should also train and encourage employees and supervisors to make small improvements every day (through point *kaizen*). Some problems are large and broad enough that a system *kaizen* approach would be most effective.

Kaizen Events

It may seem confusing that the term *kaizen* means continuous improvement, yet so many organizations use weeklong quick-hit *kaizen* events to solve problems. How can a short-term, one-time event (or series of events) be continuous? *Kaikaku* is a different Japanese word that can be

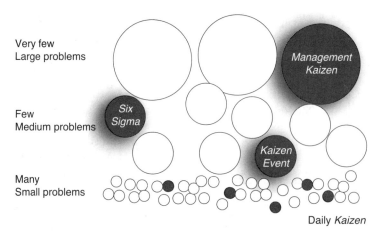

Different Types of Kaizen

Very few Large problems

Management Kaizen

Few Medium problems

Six Sigma

Kaizen Event

Many Small problems

Daily *Kaizen*

Figure 11.1 The three types of *kaizen*. Mgmt, management. (Adapted from *"The Toyota" Way Fieldbook*, Liker and Meier.)

translated as "radical, revolutionary improvement," a description that might be more accurate for this type of change.[6] *Kaizen* events are somewhat misnamed but can be an effective approach to certain types of problems. While the phrase "*kaizen* event" is popular in the manufacturing world, many hospitals use terms such as rapid process improvement workshop (RPIW) or rapid improvement event (RIE), but the concept is the same.

An event is conducted by a team formed specifically for the event and disbanded afterward. The team is often cross-functional, led by a *kaizen* leader experienced with Lean principles. Events are typically structured in this schedule, shown in Table 11.3.

Many of the improvements at ThedaCare have been a result of their RIEs. Their Friday "reportout" sessions often have six event teams presenting to senior leaders and up to 100 other people in an auditorium. The session is described as "part teaching session, part evangelical Lean revival."[7] While ThedaCare sets a goal for 50% improvement of a core metric during the event, the audience cheers loudly just the same for teams who do not reach that stretch goal. That 50% goal is meant to spur creative breakthrough thinking, as opposed to being a strict target.

Pitfalls of Kaizen *Events*

One pitfall with *kaizen* events can be the lack of focus after the intense weeklong event. If decisions and changes were driven by outside experts rather than the people doing the work on a daily basis, there is a greater risk that the old process might reappear. If team members and supervisors have not been taught or encouraged to continually improve their new process, performance might degrade. One hospital manager said, "We have a lot of 'do-over' RPIWs because the results disappear as soon as the team does. We only do RPIWs; there is very little culture building."

Even Virginia Mason Medical Center (Seattle, WA), with their impressive Lean results, reported that in 2004 they were "only holding the gains on about 40% of those changes, partially because it is easy to slip back into old ways of doing things if there is a lack of accountability and follow through."[8] One could say they applied *kaizen* to their RPIWs, as by 2011, their leaders reported that 90% of projects showed sustained results after 90 days, but only 50% held results and methods 6 or 12 months out.[9]

Table 11.3   *Kaizen* Event Structure

Day	Purpose/Goals
Monday	Conduct Lean and *kaizen* event training Observe the current process firsthand, collect data, talk with employees
Tuesday	Brainstorm, identify, and discuss opportunities for improvement Establish performance improvement goals
Wednesday	Start implementing changes to layout or process Experiment with changes, follow PDCA
Thursday	Finalize what works and standardize the new process Design management methods for sustaining change
Friday	Document results and improvements, compare to plan Present event to management, celebrate success, plan for future changes

Having a strict weeklong deadline can drive risk-averse organizations or leaders to choose problems that are easy to solve, to help ensure they can complete the event in a week. This fear could lead to events that are severely underscoped, leading to unimpressive results. In addition, an individual event without an overall "big picture" focus might only improve a single area, causing problems in other areas beyond the scope of the event.

Kaizen events do not have to be four or five days long. Some problems do not require a full week, and it is often difficult to get physicians or other clinicians to devote an entire week away from patient care. Barnes-Jewish Hospital (Missouri) has developed a shorter "6–3" event that has a smaller scope. As described by Dr. David Jaques, vice president of surgical services, "The team is prepared to determine the solution during the six hours and has at least one day in between the two work days to try and verify their solution. The last three hours is spent analyzing and finalizing the outcome of their solution."[10]

Group Health Cooperative (GHC; Seattle, WA) is a consumer-governed, non-profit healthcare system that coordinates care and coverage for its members. GHC has used Lean methods since 2004, starting with a *kaizen* event-driven model. Over time, GHC realized that deeper involvement was needed from senior leadership to change the thinking in the organization. Lee Fried, an internal Lean *sensei* said, "When we did a lot of rapid process improvement workshops, we really started changing the thinking of a lot of folks. But, it didn't reach high enough in the organization to change the fundamental processes and behaviors of some of our key leaders. We recognized that with that shift, you can really do some of the transformational change."[11] As a result, GHC has now shifted to a model that relies more on Lean-based strategic deployment principles, focused on longer-term change through direct leadership involvement.

Lean Transformation

A system *kaizen* approach, sometimes called Lean transformation, consists of a larger project, or series of projects, that solves a broader set of problems than is typically addressed in a *kaizen* event. In each project, a transformation is made from the current-state to a future-state process, using methods that can include

- Improving the physical layout and structure
- Improving the work processes to increase flow
- Error proofing and quality improvement
- Improving the scheduling process
- Standardized work
- Inventory management and control (*kanban*)
- 5S and visual management
- Engaging employees and starting a Lean management system

These transformation projects usually take 9–18 weeks, which is a greater time investment than event-driven Lean improvements. With an extended project, we can solve bigger and more important problems by implementing a wider range of Lean methods than can be achieved in just one week. Lean transformation projects focus not only on quick improvements, but also on sustained success and continuous improvement. This approach allows for giving a broader set of employees more extensive training and experience with multiple Lean tools. It also allows the extended time needed to train supervisors and other leaders to start managing in a Lean manner. This was the primary improvement model used at Children's Medical Center (Dallas, TX) and Avera McKennan (Sioux Falls, SD), as discussed in Chapter 1.

The initial project is just the starting point, as our goal is to transition from a project mentality to a new way of working, every day. Progressing through transformations in multiple departments allows the hospital to form a critical mass of Lean thinking and success, which can set the stage for incorporating Lean into all processes of the hospital. Many Lean transformation efforts are followed up with continued point *kaizen* efforts as well as formal *kaizen* events. No department or hospital becomes "fully Lean" after a Lean transformation project; problems remain, and some amount of waste will always be present since perfection is a difficult goal to reach.

Many *kaizen* event efforts start resembling the transformation or system *kaizen* approach. Virginia Mason uses multiple planning and data collection weeks to prepare for the workshop week in their RPIW methodology. Virginia Mason also builds in plans to reevaluate metrics multiple times after the project to test for sustainment. Table 11.4 shows some highlights of the event preparation that takes place.[12]

Rather than having a debate about which *kaizen* method works best, hospitals should investigate all methods, using them appropriately depending on the type of problem that needs to be solved. In some organizations, working with *kaizen* events across many departments is the best way to spread Lean broadly across the hospital, but at the risk that deep understanding and system *kaizen*-level change does not occur quickly in any one department. Other hospitals use system *kaizen* to make fundamental and sustained changes in one department or a few departments, but at the risk of not introducing the rest of the hospital to Lean concepts and methods. There are many trade-offs and therefore no easy answer about which approach is best.

Table 11.4 *Kaizen* **Event Preparation**

Timing	Activities
8 weeks before	Identify area of need
6 weeks before	Document current process, create value stream map, collect data
4 weeks before	Form team, identify metrics
2 weeks before	Finalize target metrics, complete observations of current state
1 week before	Finalize planning
Workshop week	Create changes to current state and implement, measure results
Postworkshop	Remeasure gains at 30-, 60-, and 90-day intervals

Executive Sponsorship and Leadership

Systemic hospital-wide Lean improvements will only succeed with the strong support, involvement, and leadership of top hospital leaders and influential physicians. Lean efforts will be less likely to reach their full potential if executives are not willing to tackle difficult cross-functional issues that will be identified in events or transformation projects. Another failure mode is leadership not understanding Lean principles, leading them to ask for suboptimization of departments or laying off people as a result of productivity improvements.

Jackson-Madison Laboratory at West Tennessee Healthcare first gained Lean experience in its clinical lab areas. The lab improved turnaround times, reduced head count requirements, and saved $1.2 million from reduced construction and space requirements at a new facility.

Moving to microbiology, the lab applied the same concepts and lessons learned from the first project. They improved the flow through the accessioning and plating areas from batch processing to single-piece flow. As in many labs, West Tennessee had previously only read and provided results for plated specimens during the day shift. Looking at their value stream and patient needs, the lab realized there would be benefits from reading specimens 24 hours a day, so that change was made.

Microbiology also found an opportunity to make a major improvement that, while costing the lab more, would benefit the hospital as a whole. Leadership embraced the Lean principles of not suboptimizing that one department at the expense of the whole. The lab identified an opportunity to adopt a slightly more expensive, but faster, test for methicillin-resistant *Staphylococcus aureus* (MRSA). The new test could detect an estimated 28 cases a year of MRSA before they became full blown. Since it costs an average of $35,000 to treat each active MRSA infection, this saved the hospital an estimated $983,000. Without top leadership support, the lab might have been prevented from making the decision that was best for the whole hospital.[13]

Since process changes challenge people, leading to discomfort for many, top executives need to be consistent in their support for local leadership and the Lean process. Executives need to be effective at articulating the answer to the "Why Lean?" question. Understanding the need for change is critical, and executives must play a major role in communicating that to the rest of the organization.

Some people make excuses that their employees or leaders do not buy in to Lean, meaning employees slow or subtly sabotage the efforts or outright refuse to participate. A Lean Enterprise Institute survey about Lean obstacles illustrated the amount of finger-pointing that happens when organizations struggle with Lean. Three of the top four obstacles were exercises in blaming, including "middle management resistance" (36%), "employee resistance" (28%), and "supervisor resistance" (23%).[14] When problems arise, the best approach is to ask why. If you start looking at root causes for why employees might not be on board with Lean, they might include fear, anxiety, or a lack of understanding, all of which can be addressed by executive leadership. It is not enough for executives to say they are behind Lean. Executives have to be out in front, leading the charge, communicating and taking visible action.[15] As executives, you have to keep articulating your Lean vision and continually explain why Lean is an important strategy for your hospital. Leaders need to aim for true commitment from employees, a choice they make, rather than forced compliance.

Even better than support and understanding is direct involvement from leaders. It is often eye opening for senior leaders to spend time at the *gemba* observing the process themselves. This should not be a quick walk-through; a *gemba* walk should be a prolonged observation of a single area or a walk through an entire end-to-end value stream. Observing the process firsthand will highlight waste and problems that people struggle with daily. Who seems frustrated? Who is racing around because of time pressures? Where can you see batching and disorganization? Where do inventory levels not match the daily consumption of supplies? Observing and listening to your employees will bring a fuller view of the need for Lean than scorecards or financial measures alone.

Executives also have to identify fears that employees might have about Lean. If Lean is not seen as good for the employees, they will be less than enthusiastic. One common fear is that Lean and the resulting efficiency improvements will be used to reduce head count. Executives must be visible and vocal in their commitment that Lean will not be used to drive layoffs; otherwise, rumors and fears will spread, undermining Lean. Even if senior leaders have no intent of laying off employees, the lack of a public statement can cause rumors to spread and morale to drop. At Silver Cross Hospital (Joliet, IL), David Schlappy, vice president, quality and medical staff service, makes this pledge, saying, "We're not going to lay off anybody, nobody loses their job because of process improvement initiatives. I am committed to that personally, that if we were going to go forward with Lean, I would put my personal reputation on the line that we weren't going to do that." A pledge like this is usually one of the keys to Lean success in a health system. A number of leading hospitals, including Avera McKennan and ThedaCare, have similar no layoff commitments.[16]

Starting from the Middle

It is possible for Lean to start in a single department when driven by local leadership. In the case of Riverside Medical Center (Kankakee, IL), Stephanie Mitchell, administrative director of laboratory services, initiated the Lean efforts. She made the case to her senior leadership team to get help

Table 11.5   Initiators of Lean Efforts

Role	Percentage
CEO, CFO, or CIO	32.6
CMO or CNO	10.9
VP, administrative	28.3
VP, clinical/medical	19.6
Director, administrative	37.0
Director, clinical/medical	30.4
Manager or supervisor	15.2
Physician or nurse	4.3

for the first project and directly oversaw the effort. While leaders were willing to hire a consultant, they were not yet completely sold on the idea. Chief executive officer (CEO) Phil Kambic said while he believed in the "sound management practices of Lean" and was willing to let the lab try, he was "skeptical" it would be successful based on experiences with other improvement methodologies.

After initial success in the lab, where turnaround times were reduced dramatically and internal customers (like the ED) were happy with the improved performance, the executive team became excited to be out in front leading the effort for the whole hospital. Even though Kambic and chief financial officer (CFO) Bill Douglas oversaw the Lean efforts in the lab, through participation in regular steering committee meetings, their interest in Lean training for the entire senior leadership team grew after the first project. They also sponsored continued Lean education throughout the hospital and worked to spread the methodology to other departments, such as pharmacy and inpatient care settings. After the initial skepticism, Kambic is now sold on incorporating Lean into the core strategy of the hospital: "Lean is the approach that makes the most sense. It's not benchmarking, where it's hard to find apples-to-apples comparisons. Lean is focused on improving our own processes, right now, with our people and their creativity."

In the survey conducted for this book, 46 respondents who have Lean hospital initiatives were asked who initiated Lean efforts for the hospital, as shown in Table 11.5 (multiple responses were allowed). Results show that director-level leaders are just as likely as, or more likely than, C-level executives to initiate Lean efforts.

Establishing a Model Line and a Road Map

Some hospitals have started with Lean by teaching and using a single tool, such as 5S, across all departments. An effort like this risks spreading your coaches or trainers too thin. This approach also increases the risk that the hospital is not solving the primary problems for the patients or employees. Sure, using 5S alone will eliminate some waste, but nurses might get frustrated if they are asked to spend time organizing their station when the poor patient flow through the ED has everyone at a breaking point. Lean will get a reputation as the latest "flavor of the month" (and that might be how long Lean lasts) if more significant results are not achieved through initial efforts.

Rather than trying to implement a Lean method (or set of methods) throughout the entire hospital, an effective approach is to establish a model line around one department (such as the pharmacy or a laboratory) or one particular patient pathway (such as patient flow starting at arrival to the ED). Creating a limited model line scope reduces the time required to implement a full set of Lean methods and management systems. Implementing Lean in a department of 100 people is far less intimidating than trying to spread the same ideas across 5,000 employees all at once.

The model line can be selected based on prioritizing a number of factors, including the needs assessment (which problems need solving?), current state assessment (what waste can be eliminated?), and readiness assessment (do the managers, staff, and physicians agree change is needed and possible?).

The senior leadership team may start with a plan or road map for implementing Lean beyond the initial department. Hospitals often plan their first two or three projects, based on the current view of goals and priorities. For example, in the first year of the Lean journey at a hospital, it might plan to complete two projects, for example, in the lab and in radiology, since each transformation project takes approximately 3 or 4 months.

Chartering a Project

When an initial project department or value stream has been selected, it is important for the project to be properly defined and scoped. One has to find the balance between a scope that is too large (which will take longer and might increase complexity) and one that is too small (which might not have a significant impact).

A formal charter document can be created by department leadership and the Lean project team to ensure that goals and objectives are aligned. To further emphasize that the project is about improving performance more than just implementing Lean methods, the team should determine what metrics it plans to improve. A baseline set of metrics should be gathered so the team can measure improvement during and after the project. Goals for improvement should be established for each metric based on customer needs and the potential for waste reduction that was identified during the assessment.

A formal problem statement, as with any Lean problem solving, is important so that the goals are understood, along with understanding why the project or improvements are critical to the hospital. The charter should include a statement about how the project aligns with the strategic plan of the hospital. The document should also show the expected timeline and key milestones for the project.

Dedicating Internal Resources: The Lean Team

A lament that is often heard is: "We don't have time for improvement." Employees are often struggling just to get through the day due to the waste, rework, and workarounds. Having the time to do some root cause problem solving seems like a luxury. It is often thought to be easier to keep putting fires out than it is to take the time to put preventive measures in place.

If we were to ask people to implement Lean on top of their daily duties, the initial effort might be strong; however, the temptation is always there to let Lean become a lower priority than getting the daily work done. Managers are tempted to pull employees off Lean work when other employees are sick, causing Lean efforts to lose momentum or stop altogether. It is a classic catch 22—needing to improve, but not having enough time to work on improvement.

One approach that works well in hospitals is to dedicate a full-time process improvement team to kick-start Lean efforts. When leaders free up personnel, the improvement team can be trained, analyzing the current process and taking time to work on designing new and improved processes. Organizations must identify Lean team members and leaders who are change agents, those who can work well with others and those who can influence their coworkers.

Clay York, laboratory manager at Children's Medical Center (Dallas, TX) reflects on their Lean success, as highlighted in Chapter 1, saying, "We saved $419,000 annually in labor cost, without layoffs, as a result of our initial Lean implementation project. These savings would not have been possible without the continual flow and implementation of ideas and suggestions from the people who do the real work. Freeing up their time to actually write up and follow through with their plans is absolutely necessary to achieve these types of results."

Stephanie Mitchell, laboratory services director at Riverside Medical Center (Kankakee, IL) adds, "For Lean to be successful, you need dedicated staff and dedicated time to accomplish the goals of a project or improvement. They can't give the attention needed while still doing their regular job. So, we had four staff members dedicated to Lean for about 12 weeks as we redesigned our lab and we still occasionally schedule days for staff to process improvement and redesign. It takes time to work on improvement, but in the end the return on the investment was well worth it."

To create the dedicated team, hospital leaders must ensure employees are not pulled back into daily work; they must have 100% of their time dedicated to Lean. People can be freed up by spending on agency or PRN (as needed) staff or overtime to cover the absence of the team from the department. This is a short-term investment that allows the team to drive improvements that will reduce waste, reducing the need for as many employees in the future.

The process improvement team should be cross-functional and diverse. Successful teams typically consist of four to six employees who are mainly drawn from inside the home department for the project. Having a long-time employee on the team with a new employee creates an effective combination of perspectives. Having an employee who has worked in other hospitals is helpful for bringing an understanding of the ways different hospitals operate.

It is also helpful to have a team member or two from outside the home department. These internal outsiders bring fresh eyes to the process. For example, a nurse from an inpatient unit might be selected for a pharmacy project team. The nurse brings the perspective of an internal customer, someone who interacts with the pharmacy. The nurse would have an understanding of process defects and problems that cause waste and rework for the inpatient units. Building a team of insiders and outsiders can help bridge communication gaps between hospital departments, leading to joint problem solving and a reduction in finger-pointing. The nurse can ask honest questions about the process, asking why as often as possible. When internal team members have to explain their processes to an outsider, it helps surface waste better than when everybody on the team has the same background and understanding of the old methods and processes.

An internal outsider might intentionally be a member of a future Lean department. For example, a radiology technician might be made available for the initial lab project team. This provides an outside perspective for the lab team and gives the radiology technician experience with Lean. Lean hospitals often plan team staffing resources "one ahead and one behind," carrying over a person from the previous department in addition to pulling ahead one from the next.

At one hospital, an ED nurse was placed on the Lean team for the laboratory. During initial team-building meetings, the nurse introduced herself as from the ED and immediately apologized. Most of her interactions with anyone from the lab had been angry phone calls, made in an attempt to find the status of test results. She explained that she was not normally like that, but the pressure of the ED led people to yell and be short with others. The nurse had a strong motivation to help improve the lab, as both she and her coworkers in the ED would benefit from her work when she eventually returned to her normal job.

Regardless of the exact makeup, the Lean team requires a project leader and coach, either an outside consultant or an internal Lean leader from a process improvement department. The coach should not be expected to come up with all of the answers or be expected to "make you Lean" without any effort of your own. In fact, many coaches will, after training the team in Lean concepts, insist on not giving answers. Instead, the coach, or *sensei*, will guide the team by asking questions and having the team develop its own solutions. Having a Lean process developed by the people who work in the department leads to greater buy-in compared to a case where the answers come from an outside expert. Even if the outside expert has the right answers, there will be less ownership (or none) over the Lean changes and the improved process.

The Importance of Change Management

Implementing change, including Lean, is difficult. It consumes a great deal of energy and requires persistence, dedication, and a formal change management plan. It is commonly said that 80–90% of the Lean implementation challenge is related to people and the acceptance of change. The remaining 10–20% of the challenge is the implementation of technical tools and methods.

Key performance measures may go down slightly when new processes are put into place or changes are made, as shown in Figure 11.2, whether measured in terms of labor productivity or customer service measures (such as waiting time for an ED or turnaround time for a laboratory). If training on new processes or communication is poor or haphazard, organizations run the risk of introducing chaos and further hurting performance.

That dip in the measure will be smaller and of a shorter duration, however, if there is effective change management in place. Employees, especially Lean team members, need to understand that system improvements that might seem undeniably better from a logical standpoint will still cause

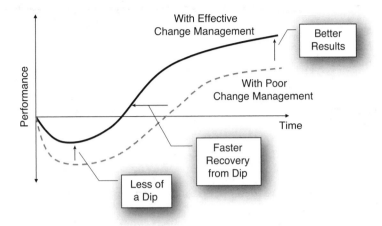

Figure 11.2 Example change curves, showing how performance may change over time, with or without effective change management practices.

a sense of loss or grief among employees. Changing and dismantling old processes can sting, particularly among those who had put those old processes in place. After all, today's wasteful process often used to be somebody's great idea.

During a Lean implementation, the hospital department and employees typically go through a cycle of denial, fear, and stress before gaining belief that the improvements will actually happen and will improve their working environment. Employee satisfaction scores may decline before they recover and improve beyond the baseline number.

Teams need to be prepared that their coworkers may go through such a cycle. This cycle can be dampened through constant communication and feedback. There are cases when nothing but time and experience with a new process will build support, acceptance, and enthusiasm for Lean and new systems. Employees and coworkers may give strong, sometimes emotional, feedback that the old system and layout worked fine, that they do not feel the need to make changes. Leaders need to support their team and remain involved throughout the project.

A Snapshot of Hospital Success: Avera McKennan Hospital

Avera McKennan Hospital and University Health Center (Sioux Falls, SD) is a 510-bed facility that is part of Avera Health. The hospital started its journey in 2004 in its laboratory, as many hospital labs in that period were early adopters of Lean methods. In the first year, testing turnaround times were reduced by 46%, 1,000 square feet of space was freed, and productivity was improved by more than 10%. Lean has become a sustained part of their culture and management system, under the leadership of Leo Serrano, the director of laboratory services.

Moving ahead to 2011, the laboratory has maintained or continued to reduce its turnaround times while increasing its testing volume by 40% with a lower staffing level than they had before Lean. "Collect-to-result" times now average 34 minutes for chemistry tests and just 17 minutes for complete blood counts (CBCs). Variation has been reduced, as 98% of CBC results are received within 20 minutes. Quality is now measured at a rate of 59 defects per million opportunities (a 99.9958% success rate, or a 5.4 sigma level for those versed in six sigma terms). With all of this improvement, Serrano said, "Our employee satisfaction is at its highest in 6 years that I have been here. The staff attributes a great part of this to Lean."[17]

Avera McKennan has applied Lean in many departments, including

Laboratory and histology
Pharmacy
Emergency department
Operative services
Case cart builds
Housekeeping
Behavioral health
Women's center
Inpatient units, including medical, surgical, nursing, and telemetry
Clinic operations
Business office and health information management

Beyond the lab, Avera McKennan improved its inpatient discharge process to reduce the delay between the patient leaving the room and that room becoming available for the next patient. This improves room utilization and prevents delays for admitted patients who might otherwise cause congestion in the ED or in postoperative recovery areas.

This improved patient flow, along with other process improvements, has led to lower construction costs. The ED expansion was cut from a planned 24 rooms to just twenty, resulting in a savings of $1.25 million in construction costs. The rooms and the department layout were designed to be more effective for the physicians, nurses, and other employees, saving space without negatively impacting patient care. The rooms are arranged in a U-shaped configuration, with department personnel working in the middle. This improves communication, teamwork, and visibility while reducing walking distances. Patients can enter and depart from the hallway outside the "U," being spared the typical ED noises and sights. Each room, other than trauma, is completely standardized, which improves patient flow because patients no longer wait for specialized rooms. The team created specialty carts, such as a cast cart, that can be wheeled into rooms as needed for a specific patient. Patient satisfaction increased from the 60th percentile to the 90th and the average length of stay was reduced to just over 2 hours, well below national (4:07) and state (2:59) averages.

Applying Lean to clinic operations has led to improved patient satisfaction and better financial performance for the physicians and the hospital. The sequence of gathering patient information was changed to eliminate a common patient annoyance—having to repeat the same information to multiple caregivers. This, along with other improvements that ensured tools and supplies were easily available in each exam room, led to a 34% reduction in patient visit durations, without rushing them through their appointments. Exam blocks were reduced from 20 minutes to 15 minutes, allowing for up to four additional patients each day (and increased revenue).

The hospital also redesigned core components of inpatient care, through their "first cycle of care" program, in work directly initiated by the chief nursing officer. With the executive sponsorship came an opportunity for frontline staff to identify things they wanted to improve. Staff complained that they were overwhelmed and they could not get all of their work, including charting, done. Detailed process observation identified that it took too long for all patients to be seen in the morning, with initial patient assessments often stretching out until after 9 a.m. Patients received medications within 30 minutes of the planned time only 40% of the time.

Specific processes were streamlined to reduce waste and free up time, but that represented mere incremental improvement. The team reinvented the morning rounds as a two-stage cycle, using the first hour of the day for assessment (with real-time documentation done in the rooms) and then using the second hour for medication administration. Time with the patients has doubled, and medications are now delivered in a timely manner 94% of the time. When surveyed, 92% of staff members agreed the workload was now manageable, as overtime had been reduced by 63%. Maybe more important to the staff, they are able to take needed breaks instead of being constantly on the go. "The breakthrough was that nursing began to look at Lean as a way to solve some of their other problems," said Kathy Maass, director of process excellence and the nurses initiated other improvement projects, such as more timely discharges, working in partnership with the process excellence department.

Avera McKennan showed that productivity improvement and cost savings could be accomplished in ways other than layoffs or head count reductions. The hospital made a promise to employees that they would not be laid off as a result of Lean or other improvements. CEO Fred Slunecka said, "We basically promise the employees we will do everything we can to protect their careers, but not their specific jobs, if they in turn do every thing possible to keep the organization economically secure." Jobs and roles might change, but individuals are transitioned into new roles or could be assigned to spend time working on further improvements.

One example of a new role can be the internal Process Excellence department. Staff members from departments that have worked with Lean transformation projects can become part of a group of internal consultants who run the longer improvement projects of the hospital, filling the role initially played by external consultants. There are four full-time internal consultants, led by their director. Avera's consultants do not run weeklong "*kaizen* events" as many hospitals do. They facilitate longer 10- to 16-week transformation projects, making more radical changes than could be accomplished in a week.

The consultants follow up the projects with ongoing coaching for departmental leaders, who own the new process and continue to improve it as part of the new management approach. Projects help jump-start change, but sustainability requires ongoing effort and new leadership styles. "It's a continuous improvement process. It's a way of life, a way of doing business," Maass said. Part of this follow-up includes the nurse manager shadowing one nurse a day, acting as a coach and helping identify problems. "We are managing the process rather than the outcomes," said Maass.[18] For example, the team identified an opportunity to create standardized work to ensure that central lines and intravenous lines are changed properly, as needed.

The transformation projects are selected by a steering committee that takes the hospital's strategic plan and objectives into account, but projects can also be initiated out of the employee suggestion program, Bright Ideas. These longer projects are important, as Slunecka said, "I believe that doing just *kaizen* events is like applying so many Band-Aids. A weeklong event is extremely helpful in improving a process that has been completely redesigned using a lean design process. But the full redesign must be completed first. Health care design is too complex to accomplish in a week and it takes far longer than that to change a workplace culture."[19]

Avera McKennan's experience also shows that Lean is not about cutting heads. In the ED project, the analysis of current processes showed that the work could not effectively be accomplished with current staffing. So, in that case, the hospital actually added to the head count to improve patient throughput. Slunecka summarized the goal of optimizing the entire system rather than just suboptimizing labor costs by saying, "Every project has saved money more than the cost of the project—not all show labor savings."

A key to Avera McKennan's success has been the recognition that Lean is about people. The hospital created custom training material that was used for all 4,000 hospital employees. Slunecka said employees—the human factor—are the key. Employees are engaged in the process, submitting improvement ideas, and persevering through the difficulties of implementing change. The hospital now assigns an Employee Assistance Program representative to implementation projects to help employees cope with the stress caused by change.

Other results from Lean at Avera McKennan include

- A saving of 600 hours of surgical nurse time annually by eliminating end-of-shift inventory.
- Assessment time in ambulatory surgery reduced from 45 minutes to 25, reducing nurse walking distance by 90%.
- Mammography waiting room time reduced from 40 minutes to 12.
- Babies in the neonatal intensive care unit (NICU) are no longer awakened to give medications, as teams changed to a process to better consider their natural sleep cycles.
- A new women's center and outpatient surgery center were designed and built using Lean principles.
- The size of standard surgical instrument sets was reduced, saving purchasing costs, reducing reprocessing work, and improving ergonomics for staff.[20]

The hospital has made a commitment to its employees, along with its commitment to quality and productivity. Most hospitals complain about a shortage of key clinical and medical personnel. Slunecka sees the situation differently, being aware of all of the waste and inefficiency that are built into a hospital's processes. "There is no shortage of healthcare professionals—only the shortage of a capable management system," said Slunecka. It is executive champions like Slunecka who will convince other hospital leaders that the problem is not with the employees. Lean success will not come from asking people to work harder or try harder. It comes from changing the mindsets of the people and the way we lead and manage. "Now that Lean is over seven years old at Avera McKennan, people are starting to think process," Maass said. "Lean now pervades our thinking. When problems exist, employees recognize that if we can improve the process, we can improve the outcome." Avera McKennan is one hospital that is a long way down that Lean path of improving outcomes for patients and creating a better workplace for physicians and staff.

Conclusion

There is no single road map or cookbook for a hospital to follow in its pursuit of Lean. Certain key elements are necessary, including problems to be solved, executive leadership, and the willingness of frontline employees and managers to make improvements to their own processes. Starting with the transformation of a model line area can help demonstrate the potential of Lean to the rest of the organization. Focusing on the management system and sustaining improvements is important for making sure that Lean is not just the new flavor of the month, but instead is part of the vision and strategy for the future at the hospital.

Lean Lessons

- Hospitals should focus their Lean efforts based on need and the readiness of area leaders to drive change.
- There are different styles of *kaizen* that may be appropriate depending on the problem that needs to be solved.
- Executive leadership and involvement are critical for Lean success.
- Lean success requires action, hard work, and discipline.
- Lean cannot be done everywhere all at once; start with a model line area that can set an example for others.
- Having a dedicated cross-functional process improvement team is vital to success.
- Training cannot be ignored, yet training is not a cure-all.
- While a few quick fixes are positive steps, do not lose sight of the bigger picture and a more strategic plan.

Points for Group Discussion

- What problems really need solving? Where should we start?
- Why is a pledge of no layoffs due to Lean so important?
- How can we transition our Lean efforts from a project mentality to a way of working every day?
- Who make the best Lean team members?
- How do we get our senior leaders engaged and involved with Lean if they are not already?
- How would we design our department or hospital differently, given the chance with our understanding of Lean principles?

Notes

1. Lusky, Karen, "Laying Lean on the Line, One Change at a Time," *CAP Today*, July 2009, http://www.cap.org/apps/cap.portal?_nfpb=true&cntvwrPtlt_actionOverride=%2Fportlets%2FcontentVie wer%2Fshow&_windowLabel=cntvwrPtlt&cntvwrPtlt%7BactionForm.contentReference%7D=cap_ today%2F0709%2F0709h_laying_lean.html&_state=maximized&_pageLabel=cntvwr (accessed April 3, 2011).
2. Ruhlman, Jeannie, and Cheryl Siegman, "Boosting Engagement While Cutting Costs," *Gallup Management Journal*, June 18, 2009, http://gmj.gallup.com/content/120884/boosting-engagement-cutting-costs.aspx (accessed April 6, 2011).
3. Meier, David, presentation, Lean Enterprise Institute workshop, October 6, 2009.
4. Liker, Jeffrey K., and David Meier, *The Toyota Way Fieldbook* (New York: McGraw-Hill, 2006), 310.
5. Toussaint, John, and Roger Gerard, *On the Mend: Revolutionizing Healthcare to Save Lives and Transform the Industry* (Cambridge, MA: Lean Enterprise Institute, 2010), 67.
6. Marchwinski, Chet, and John Shook, *Lean Lexicon* (Brookline, MA: Lean Enterprise Institute, 2003), 34.

7. Toussaint and Gerard, *On the Mend,* 66.
8. St. Martin, Christina, "Seeking Perfection in Health Care: Applying the Toyota Production System to Medicine," *Performance and Practices of Successful Medical Groups: 2006 Report Based on 2005 Data, Medical Group Management Association,* 20.
9. Patterson, Sarah, presentation, Institute for Healthcare Improvement National Forum, December 7, 2011.
10. Graban, Mark, "LeanBlog Podcast #76—Dr. David Jaques, Lean in Surgical Services," LeanBlog Podcast, October 14, 2009, http://leanblog.org/76 (accessed April 4, 2011).
11. Graban, Mark, "LeanBlog Podcast #23—Group Health Cooperative Lean Panel," LeanBlog Podcast, April 29, 2007, http://www.leanblog.org/23 (accessed April 10, 2011).
12. Nelson-Peterson, Dana L., and Carol J. Leppa, "Creating an Environment for Caring Using Lean Principles of the Virginia Mason Production System," *Journal of Nursing Administration,* 2007, 37: 289.
13. ValuMetrix Services, *West Tennessee Healthcare Case Study,* http://www.valumetrixservices.com/sites/default/files/client_results_pdf/CS_WestTennessee_Jackson%20Madison_Lab_OC4020.pdf (accessed July 1, 2011).
14. Lean Enterprise Institute, "New Survey: Middle Managers Are Biggest Obstacle to Lean Enterprise," July 18, 2007, http://www.lean.org/WhoWeAre/NewsArticleDocuments/Web_Lean_survey.pdf (accessed April 10, 2011).
15. Flinchbaugh, Jamie, *The Hitchhiker's Guide to Lean* (Dearborn, MI: Society of Manufacturing Engineers, 2006), 39.
16. Graban, Mark, "How Lean Management Helped Hospitals Avoid Layoffs," FierceHealthcare.com, October 1, 2010, http://www.fiercehealthcare.com/story/how-lean-management-helped-hospitals-avoid-layoffs/2010–10–01 (accessed April 4, 2011).
17. Serrano, Leo, personal correspondence, February 2011.
18. Maass, Kathy, telephone interview, February 2011.
19. Slunecka, Fred, personal correspondence, December 8, 2009.
20. Avera McKennan, "Leading the Way with LEAN," internal newsletter, http://www.avera.org/pdf/mckennan/Leading%20the%20Way%20with%20LEAN%20update.pdf (accessed April 3, 2011).

Chapter 12

A Vision for a Lean Hospital

Introduction

So far, we have seen where Lean comes from: Henry Ford, W. Edwards Deming, and Toyota, among others. The core concepts, philosophies, tools, and leadership styles have been defined and introduced. We have shared real examples of hospitals that have already used these methods to make improvements that matter for the patients, employees, physicians, and the hospital. The questions that are sure to follow are "How do I get there?" and "What will I look like when I'm done?"

First, there is no "done" or "there" as a final destination with Lean. There is always a problem to solve, waste to eliminate, and new forms of value-adding work to create. After more than 50 years of developing and using Lean methods, Toyota still has waste and problems to solve. They are, however, significantly better than their competitors in many ways, and they continue to improve. There is no perfectly Lean organization, so the term *Lean hospital* might really be shorthand for "a hospital that is using Lean methods in a systematic way to improve and manage."

When Is a Hospital Lean?

Using the original definition of Lean from *The Machine that Changed the World*, is there a hospital anywhere that operates with half of everything, compared to other hospitals? A Lean hospital in those terms would have, among other measures:

- Half the errors
- Half the infections
- Half the patient harm
- Half the waiting time
- Half the length of stay
- Half the head count (or more likely, half the employee turnover)
- Half the cost
- Half the space
- Half the complaints from patients and physicians

Hospitals might not improve to a Toyota-like point of being literally twice as good as their competitors (that gap has been closed by their competitors over time, anyway). That said, we should set the bar high for our hospital. History has shown that Lean concepts allow break-through thinking, leading to dramatically better performance, rather than modest incremental gains, such as the 95% reduction in central-line associated bloodstream infections at Allegheny General Hospitals.[1] ThedaCare and Gundersen Lutheran (WI) have each demonstrated 25% to 30% lower costs for inpatients and cardiac surgery patients.[2,3] Even if we had half the defects or half the patient injuries as another hospital, is that good enough? No, but we have to strive for perfection, even though absolute perfection might seem difficult or impossible.

We might even reach outside the boundaries of the hospitals, looking to improve the larger healthcare system. Lean hospitals might work to reduce emergency department visits by half by better coordinating the entire continuum of care in their communities. Group Health (WA) has reduced emergency visits of its members by 29% through its patient-centered medical home approach, based on Lean principles.[4] Lean hospitals can also work to prevent readmissions, as did UPMC St. Margaret Hospital (PA), which reduced readmission rates for chronic obstructive pulmonary disease (COPD) by 48%.[5] The impact of payer systems and financial incentives for this is left for your own discussion.

Hospitals are getting results with Lean. The challenge now is to spread those ideas so every hospital can improve. We should learn from the leaders and the example they are setting, adapting their methods to our own hospital. We can also share ideas and collaborate with other hospitals that are learning as they go. An example of this is the Healthcare Value Network, a joint effort of the Lean Enterprise Institute and the ThedaCare Center for Healthcare Value; dozens of organizations from across North America share and learn from each other in a collaborative environment. The Pittsburgh Regional Health Initiative, initially led by Paul O'Neill, is an example of a regional effort; it is hoped it will be duplicated in other regions, states, or countries.

What Would a Lean Hospital Look Like?

Having a chance to tour or walk through a hospital that has embraced Lean, you might look for visible Lean methods in use. Visible indicators might include 5S and visual controls, marking and labeling where items are supposed to be stored. You might also see standardized work or *kanban* cards posted and in use. Suggestions, performance measures, or A3 reports might be displayed on walls. The physical structure and layout might be compact, logical, and neatly organized.

Much of what makes a Lean hospital, however, cannot be directly observed during a tour. Can we directly observe the thought processes and mindsets of the organization? Can we see how people solve problems? Given enough time, we might be able to directly observe supervisors inter-acting with their employees, but we usually do not get that chance on a tour. Toyota has been very open in letting other manufacturers, even direct competitors, tour their factories. Other companies have typically copied the tools and the visible methods, often coming away not understanding the true nature of the Toyota Production System.[6]

What Would a Patient Experience in a Lean Hospital?

A good exercise might be to think through what the perfect patient care experience would look like and how it would feel. For example, for an outpatient surgery patient, what would be an experience of perfect service and perfect care? This might seem similar to the creation of an ideal state version of a future state value stream map. We can challenge ourselves on how things should work to set goals for our Lean improvements.

The patient would be able to promptly get an appointment or procedure scheduled, with the hospital doing everything it can to minimize delay by increasing capacity and throughput with low-cost process improvements. The hospital provides a clear estimate of total expected cost for the payer and out-of-pocket costs for the patient (if applicable), relying on transparent standard prices for routine procedures.

The patient's Lean experience begins before arrival, which can include presurgical steps such as scheduling and making sure everything is communicated properly (such as the need to arrive for labs or presurgical fasting) to avoid miscommunications, rework, or delays. Think through the patient experience from the time the patient drives up to the hospital. Is everything clearly labeled for where to park and where to come for registration? Is the patient able to get registered without repeating the same information to multiple people? Is the patient able to avoid excessive delays before the procedure starts?

From a clinical and surgical standpoint, does the hospital ensure that all proper preparation and quality steps are followed before the procedure, including confirmation of the patient identity, marking of the site, and the time-out of the universal protocol? How is the process error proofed to protect the patient from harm? Are all of the participants (nurses, physicians, anesthesiologists, etc.) aware of their role, interactions, and standardized work? Is there a team environment in which everyone is focused on the patient instead of hierarchy and titles? Are clinicians following evidence-based practices that are best for the patient?

Beyond the surgery itself, what service is provided to any family or loved ones who are waiting? Are they kept informed of the patient's status to ease their worrying? Is the patient able to get through the postoperative recovery area and discharged without any avoidable delays beyond the required recovery time? Has clear and unambiguous communication been made about the patient's postoperative responsibilities to help in recovery and to prevent infection? Does the patient receive a billing statement that is 100% accurate and easy to comprehend (again, if applicable)?

Whatever vision you create for perfect care, be sure to include both the clinical care and the service aspects of the patient's experience. Starting with fresh eyes and thinking toward perfection will drive better improvements than looking for incremental improvements over today's practices and waste.

What Would It Be Like to Work in a Lean Hospital?

Working in a Lean hospital should be a positive experience for employees, leaders, and physicians. After seeing many cases of morale and employee engagement improvement with Lean, employees should not want to leave a Lean hospital to work someplace else. In some cases, work life has become so fundamentally different (and better) that employees who have left to go to a traditional hospital or clinic have come running back, no longer able to (or wanting to) operate in a non-Lean environment and culture.

Many of the key points have already been covered, but employees in a Lean environment should expect, among other things,

■ To be listened to by supervisors, to have their ideas solicited, to have the freedom to make improvements for the betterment of the system, and to be treated with respect

- To develop the discipline to work within a system, but also to maintain the creativity required for *kaizen*
- To not be overburdened with more work than can be done in a high-quality manner or to be standing around with nothing to do
- To be challenged to grow, personally and professionally, always striving to learn and improve personal technical, leadership, and problem-solving skills
- To feel a sense of pride for contributing to a high-performance organization, for understanding their personal roles and how their work has an impact on patients, coworkers, the hospital's bottom line, and the community

Again, Lean is not a system that is soft on people or an environment where everyone is nice to each other, avoiding conflict. The Lean culture of "respect for people" also demands a sense of responsibility, as true respect challenges employees, and each other, to get better for the sake of the patients and the organization.

Managers and leaders could expect an environment in which the direction and goals from senior leadership are clear and actionable. Managers at all levels would have a voice in shaping the strategy of the hospital, also working with their employees to develop improvement plans to meet these true north goals. Managers could expect that staff members will be open about problems, waste, and near misses, creating an open blame-free environment for improvement.

How Would We Describe a Lean Hospital?

To create a vision, we can define in aggregate how to describe a prototype Lean hospital. One good starting point might be for a hospital to follow the general 14 principles of *The Toyota Way*. A Lean hospital might also be characterized by the following traits: strategy and management system, patients, employees, waste and *kaizen*, and technology and infrastructure.

Strategy and Management System

A Lean hospital has efforts and goals that are tightly integrated with hospital strategy and vision, moving beyond the isolated use of tools to the engagement of all employees and leaders in the building of a Lean culture. The Lean strategy and the hospital strategy are one and the same, being communicated widely and consistently throughout the organization.

A Lean hospital realizes that success comes not only from technology and clinical excellence, but also through employee engagement and operational excellence. Lean hospitals help stakeholders understand that spending money on new technology and new space is not the only way to demonstrate a commitment to serving the community.

A Lean hospital has a leadership method and model that is taught to supervisors and managers and is practiced by all leaders. Lean behaviors, such as going to the *gemba*, auditing the process, collaborating on improvement efforts, and being a servant leader, are used as criteria for employee selection, performance reviews, and advancement.

A Lean hospital creates collaborative relationships for all partners and stakeholders, including physicians, vendors, and payers. Patient safety practices and quality data are shared openly with other hospitals and the community, rather than using those methods as a source of competitive advantage.

A Lean hospital has a small, centralized group that maintains consistent Lean practices and training. This group coaches leaders and staff to drive improvements and to own their processes, rather than doing it for them. This central team, along with senior leadership, continually mentors and develops managers in Lean behaviors and management philosophies.

A Lean hospital has specific leaders who are responsible for the overall flow, management, and improvement of key patient care value streams.

A Lean hospital determines proper staffing levels based on patient volumes, actual workloads, and the time required to do work in a safe, high-quality way. Best attempts are made to match staffing to volume in different time periods. Reliance on benchmarking or budget constraints as a primary staffing driver decreases.

Patients

A Lean hospital is passionately and meticulously focused on the patients, families, and guests, aiming for perfect, harm-free care, while respecting patients and their time. The patient comes first in all activities, decisions, and priorities. Leadership helps create that expectation with all stakeholders.

A Lean hospital involves patients, as the ultimate customers, and their loved ones in process improvement efforts. New designs and processes are tested to make sure they meet patient needs.

A Lean hospital provides excellent service in addition to the best clinical care. The patient is surrounded by a warm, caring environment in which staff and clinicians have the time to fully attend to their physical and emotional needs.

A Lean hospital sets goals of zero preventable errors that cause patient harm, as any other goal is unacceptable. The staff works tirelessly toward that goal through standardized work, root cause problem solving, and error proofing, rather than relying on individuals to be careful or relying on inspection. When preventable errors occur, patients and payers are not charged for the work required as a result.

Employees

A Lean hospital recognizes that employees are the true source of value for patients and the hospital, rather than being viewed strictly as a cost to be reduced. Top leadership makes a consistent commitment to all employees that Lean improvements will not lead to layoffs.

A Lean hospital helps employees understand that not all activity is value added. Rather than defining waste as being "our job," everybody works to eliminate it so more time can be focused on the patients.

A Lean hospital fully engages every employee in improving the employee's and the team's work, supporting the innate desire to provide perfect care to patients. Leaders help employees understand how their work fits in to the value stream and work collaboratively with them in *kaizen*. Employees are not sent home every time census drops, as that is seen as an opportunity for *kaizen*.

A Lean hospital does not overburden employees with more work than can be done in a high-quality manner or pressure people to work harder or be more careful as a means to quality, safety, or efficiency.

Waste and Kaizen

A Lean hospital recognizes that there is waste in every process, focusing on continuous improvement and root cause problem solving instead of workarounds and firefighting. Individuals (employees or leaders) are not blamed for the waste or problems.

A Lean hospital proactively fixes problems and reduces waste, rather than being strictly reactive. Employees are encouraged to expose waste and make improvements to the system, instead of hiding problems and making things look good.

A Lean hospital breaks down departmental silos to focus on improving care and preventing delays for patients, allowing employees to feel pride in their work, by being able to cooperate across value streams instead of suboptimizing their own area.

A Lean hospital values the standardization of work methods in the name of improving safety, quality, and productivity, rather than allowing people to develop their own different methods for doing the same work or precluding one patient to not get the best-identified method of care.

A Lean hospital is never satisfied with being better than average, being in a top percentile, or with winning awards; it always strives to get better. Perfection is a difficult goal to reach, but it is the only acceptable goal to a Lean hospital.

Technology and Infrastructure

A Lean hospital is physically designed to minimize waste for patients and for all who work inside its walls. It is designed with direct input from staff to support efficient workflows and value streams, rather than forcing departments and employees to adjust their work to the space. A Lean hospital focuses more on what is functional and effective for the patients and staff rather than glossing over bad processes with marble entryways and lobby fountains. Lean hospitals use collaborative and iterative design and build practices like integrated project delivery.

A Lean hospital has process technology, automation, and information systems that make work easier or less error prone. The hospital does not install automation or new systems for the sake of having new systems. Employees and physicians are deeply involved in the selection of technologies that meet their needs. A Lean hospital takes the time to properly train all stakeholders in new technologies, ensuring they can be used most effectively rather than blaming individuals for not using the systems.

In 2001, the industry started to say, "We want to see a Toyota in healthcare."[7] At that point, there was no clear leader in terms of a hospital that had dramatically different processes or results from the others. Even if some clear leaders in Lean healthcare are becoming widely known, Lean success stories can be found at hundreds of hospitals around the world. It is more likely that, over time, a top tier of hospitals will emerge, hospitals with results that are much better than the industry as a whole. Lean advocates would assume that many in this top tier will be the ones who are most effectively using Lean principles. This top tier will continue to learn from each other, improving continually. The hospitals outside that top tier will likely fall further and further behind—some will likely be forced to close. We all have the opportunity to aim high, working hard every day to reduce waste, respect our people, and provide better and better care for our patients, through Lean methods.

Points for Group Discussion

- What core measures can we improve by half in our organization?
- How might people react to a goal of "zero" or "perfection"?
- How are some of these patient-centered goals complicated by the payer system and financial incentives in our country?
- What is your own long-reaching vision for a Lean hospital?

Notes

1. The Commonwealth Fund, "Case Study: Perfecting Patient Care at Allegheny General Hospital and the Pittsburgh Regional Healthcare Initiative," September 30, 2008, http://www.commonwealthfund. org/Content/Innovations/Case-Studies/2008/Sep/Case-Study--Perfecting-Patient-Care-at-Allegheny-General-Hospital-and-the-Pittsburgh-Regional-Health.aspx (accessed July 1, 2011).

2. Toussaint, John, "Writing the New Playbook for U.S. Health Care: Lessons from Wisconsin," *Health Affairs*, September 2009, 28, no. 5: 1343–50.

3. Boulton, Guy, "Integrated Systems Hold Down Costs while Keeping Up Quality," *Milwaukee Journal-Sentinel*, September 12, 2009, http://www.jsonline.com/business/59087997.html (accessed April 4, 2011).

4. Reid, Robert J., Katie Coleman, E. A. Johnson, et al., "The Group Health Medical Home at Year Two: Cost Savings, Higher Patient Satisfaction, and Less Burnout for Providers," *Health Affairs*, May 2010, 29, no. 5: 835–43.

5. California Health Advocates, "Creative Interventions Reduce Hospital Readmissions for Medicare Beneficiaries," October 7, 2010, http://www.cahealthadvocates.org/news/basics/2010/creative.html (accessed April 4, 2011).

6. Taylor, Alex, "How Toyota Defies Gravity," *Fortune*, December 8, 1997, http://money.cnn.com/magazines/fortune/fortune_archive/1997/12/08/234926/index.htm (accessed December 22, 2007).

7. Appleby, Julie, "Care Providers Slam Health System," *USA Today*, May 9, 2001, p. A01.

Glossary Terms

A3 report: A standard Toyota method for planning and problem solving, taking its name from the use of a single sheet of the A3 paper size, which is approximately 11 × 17 inches.

***Andon* cord:** A method for signaling that a problem has occurred, alerting supervisors that assistance is needed. Often a physical cord hanging down from a production line. If the problem cannot be solved immediately, the process or work activity is stopped to ensure *jidoka*, or quality at the source. More generally, any method for empowered employees to stop the work temporarily to ensure quality.

***Baka yoke*:** Japanese phrase that translates as "fool proofing" or "dummy proofing," not preferred in Lean usage. *See poka yoke.*

Batching: Doing work or moving material in quantities greater than one, such as running batches of tests or producing batches of medications. In a batch of cookies, we make more than one at a time, given the size of cookie sheets and the oven. Batching usually connotes waste but may be necessary given constraints in the system.

Boarding: Keeping patients waiting in an emergency department, often in a hallway, after being seen because there is a problem preventing them from being admitted and physically moved to an inpatient room.

Bottleneck: The stage in a process or value stream that is the constraining step for overall flow.

Current state: Version of a value stream map that shows how things work today.

Defects, waste of: A type of waste where something was not done right the first time. Can apply to products in a process (a defective blood specimen) or to the process itself (a treatment order is not sent by a physician's office, delaying treatment). Defects often lead to rework.

Diversion: The practice of a hospital asking ambulances to take patients to other hospitals, unless the patient would be put in jeopardy by the delay, because of overcrowding in the emergency department.

Downstream: The next step or department in a value stream. For example, after a patient is ready to be admitted from the emergency department, the inpatient unit to which he or she is going is the downstream department. The opposite of *upstream.*

Errors: Describes the result of something that has gone wrong, even if all participants in the system had the best intentions and were performing properly. Types of errors include skill-based errors, for which an unintended action took place; lapses, a mental error; and slips, or physical errors.

Error proofing: The practice of designing or modifying systems, processes, or equipment to prevent errors from occurring or making it harder for errors to occur. Also includes practices that make errors more apparent or make systems more robust to tolerate errors.

FIFO: First in, first out. Describes the flow of materials or people in a system; the item that has been in inventory the longest is used first, or the patient who has been waiting the longest is seen first.

Fishbone (*Ishikawa*) diagram: A visual diagram that shows multiple contributing causes for an event. The bones of the fish typically represent categories such as people, methods, machines, materials, or environment.

Five whys: The method of continuing to ask why to reach a root cause (or root causes) for an error or problem.

Flow: The absence of waiting in a value stream. *See also* one-piece flow.

FMEA: Failure modes and effects analysis. A method for brainstorming and analyzing potential defects or errors in a system for the sake of prioritizing improvement activities.

Future state: Version of a value stream map that shows how things can, should, or will work in the future.

Gemba: Japanese word that means "the actual place" or "the place where the work is done."

Genchi genbutsu: Japanese phrase that means "go and see."

Heijunka: Japanese word that means "level loading," either demand for a service or the workload for people in a system. A level-loaded system would have the same patient volumes or workloads in every time increment.

Hoshin Kanri: *See* strategy deployment.

Ideal state: Version of a future-state value stream map that shows how things should work, given ideal circumstances and processes.

Inspection: Looking for defects or quality problems after the fact, inspecting products one at a time or in batches. Error proofing is more effective for ensuring 100% quality.

Jidoka: Japanese word meaning "quality at the source."

Kaizen: Japanese word meaning "continuous improvement" or "small changes for the good."

Kaikaku: A Japanese word meaning "radical or transformational change."

Kaizen event: A formally defined event, typically one week long, with a team that is formed to analyze the current process and to make improvements in a process or value stream, with the team being disbanded after the event.

Kanban: A Japanese word, now adopted in English, that is translated as "signal" or "card"; a method for managing and controlling the movement and ordering of materials in a system.

Lean: A quality and process improvement methodology, based on the Toyota Production System, that emphasizes customer needs, improving quality, and reducing time delays and costs, all through continuous improvement and employee involvement.

Level loading: *See heijunka.*

Metrics: Performance measures that are tracked or charted to gauge the effectiveness of a department or process.

Motion, waste of: Type of waste related to employee motion, particularly walking.

Nemawashi: A Japanese term that means "laying the groundwork," often used in the context of sharing and discussing A3 documents.

Non-value-added: A term that describes an activity that fails one or more of the three conditions for being value-added.

One-piece flow: A Lean ideal by which patients or products are treated, worked on, or moved one at a time. Also *single-piece flow*. One-piece flow is a direction or goal, more than an absolute mandate.

Overprocessing, waste of: Doing more work than is necessary for good patient care or for customer needs. For example, spinning tubes of blood longer than necessary in a centrifuge does not lead to better test results; the unnecessary time is overprocessing.

Overproduction, waste of: Doing work earlier than is needed by the customer or creating items or materials that are not needed. An example might include drawing tubes of blood that might not be needed for testing.

PDCA (PDSA): Plan-do-check-act (or plan-do-study-adjust). A continuous improvement cycle, similar to the scientific method. Originally credited as the Shewhart cycle, after an influential quality improvement statistician. It became more widely known as the Deming cycle, after W. Edwards Deming.

Phlebotomist: A hospital employee who draws and collects patient blood specimens.

Piecework: A system of paying employees based on their production of a manufactured product or per unit of service performed. Frequently used in the garment industry (dating to the sixteenth century AD) and in healthcare (dating to the eighteenth century BC). Piecework is meant to provide incentives to employees, but also creates incentives for overproduction.

Point *kaizen*: An improvement that is small, impacting just one person or one part of the process, taking a short period of time to complete.

***Poka yoke*:** Japanese phrase that means "error proofing" or "mistake proofing."

Policy deployment: *See* strategy deployment.

Practical state: Version of a future state value stream map that shows how things can realistically work after some process improvements. The process will be better than the current state, but not as good as it could be in the ideal state.

Product: Term that generally refers to the one being acted on in a process or value stream. Can be a patient or a physical product, such as a medication or patient specimen.

Production Preparation Process (3P): A space and process design methodology, often run as a three-day event, that is characterized by staff involvement, a focus on flow, and iterative designs that are tested in physical mockups.

Pull: Moving patients, products, or supplies only when they are needed, based on a signal from a downstream department or process. The opposite of *push*, which triggers movement whether the downstream is ready or not.

Quick changeover: *See* setup reduction.

Rework: Work and activity done to correct a defect or replace defective work. Example: A pharmacy order incorrectly missed a patient allergy, so the order was reworked to call for the right medication.

RIE: Rapid Improvement Event (*see Kaizen* event).

Root cause: A fundamental cause for a problem, error, or defect in a system. Called a root cause because you often have to look beyond the surface of a problem to find it. Related to the five whys approach.

RPIW: Rapid process improvement workshop. *See kaizen* event.

Safety stock: Inventory of supplies or materials held specifically to protect against expected vendor delays or against usage that is higher than normal.

Setup reduction: A methodology for reducing the amount of time required to change over a resource, such as equipment or a room, from one use or patient or another.

Single-piece flow: *See* one-piece flow.

Six Sigma: A quality improvement methodology that is driven by statistical analysis and other tools, led by experts called Green Belts and Black Belts. A Six Sigma quality level refers to a process with just 3.4 defects per million opportunities.

SMED: Single-minute exchange of dies, another term for setup reduction or quick changeover.

Spaghetti diagram: A pictorial representation of movement of an employee or product through a physical area, drawing its name from the way a plate of cooked spaghetti might look. Also spaghetti chart.

Standardized work: A Lean method that documents the current one best way to safely complete an activity with the proper outcome and the highest quality. Also refers to the management method for ensuring that standardized work is followed and improved on.

Stock out: Having zero on-hand inventory available for an item, tool, or supply.

Strategy deployment: System *kaizen*. A longer-term (often 12–16 weeks) improvement project or series of projects, with goals to improve a broader area than a point *kaizen* or *kaizen* event. Also known as Lean transformation.

***Takt*:** The pace of customer demand or workload, expressed in time units. *Takt* equals the available working time in a period divided by the number of units of work to be completed. Example: If a clinic has 240 minutes to give a projected 100 flu shots, the *takt* time is 2.4 minutes.

Talent, waste of: Type of waste referring to not fully utilizing the talents and potential contributions of employees.

Total quality management: A quality management system based on statistical methods and variation reduction, popular in the 1980s and 1990s.

Transportation, waste of: Type of waste related to the movement of a product in the value stream.

Turnaround time: The elapsed time between an order being written until a result or other product (such as a medication) is ready. May also be measured from the time the order is received or from the time a specimen is received in a laboratory.

Two-bin system: A type of *kanban* system in which an item is kept in two equal-size bins. An empty bin acts as the signal for a replacement bin's worth of items to be purchased or moved.

Upstream: The preceding step or department in the value stream. The opposite of *downstream*.

Value-added: Activity that meets all three rules: (1) the customer must be willing to pay for the activity, (2) the activity must transform the product or service in some way, and (3) the activity must be done correctly the first time.

Value stream: The entire end-to-end process for patient care or the flow of a product, typically crossing multiple hospital departments.

Value stream map: A diagram that shows a value stream, including the process steps, waiting times, and communication or information flows. Also illustrates time elements and value-added or non-value-added designations for activities.

Violations: Intentional actions that go against accepted practices, as opposed to errors, that may occur even if everybody was following the correct method.

Waiting, waste of: A type of waste for which there is no activity for the observed employees, patients, or products in a system.

Waste: Activity that does not add value for the customer or patient. Synonymous with non-value-added.

Workaround: A reaction to a problem that is focused on minimizing the short-term impact without doing anything to prevent the same problem from occurring in the future. For example, if a medication is missing, a workaround would be the nurse walking to other cabinets to find a dose for the patient. This action does nothing to prevent the medication from being missing the next time.

Index